The People vs. The Courts

Judicial Review and Direct Democracy
in the American Legal System

The People vs. The Courts

Judicial Review and Direct Democracy in the American Legal System

Mathew Manweller

Academica Press, LLC
Bethesda

Library of Congress Cataloging-in-Publication Data

Manweller, Mathew.
 The people vs. the courts : judicial review and direct democracy in the American legal system/ Mathew Manweller.
    p. cm.
 Includes bibliographical references and index.
 ISBN 1-930901-97-6
 1. Judicial review—United States. 2. Referendum—United States. 3. Political questions and judicial power—United States. I. Title: People versus the courts. II. Title.

 KF4575.M36 2005
 347.73'12—dc22

                          2005012638

British Cataloguing data are available

Editorial Inquiries:
Academica Press, LLC
7831 Woodmont Avenue, #381
Bethesda, MD 20814
Website: www.academicapress.com
(650) 329-0685 phone and fax

Acknowledgements

I would like to thank three professors from the University of Oregon who helped this project move from vision to reality. Dr. Julie Novkov served as my principal advisor during the research phase of this project. I am indebted to her for the continual feedback and suggestions she provided. This book would not have been possible without her help. I would like to thank Dr. John Orbell for giving me the confidence to pursue intellectual interests regardless of whether they conform to current academic fads. And I would like to thank Dr. Patty Gwartney for her methodological training and guidance.

Several chapters in this book were originally delivered as papers at meetings of the Pacific Northwest Political Science Association and the Western Political Science Association and I must thank the participants in those panels that offered critical feedback, especially Dr. Todd Donovan. Of course, all errors and omissions are my own.

And finally, I am grateful to the unwavering support of my parents and my wife, Oralynn.

TABLE OF CONTENTS

LIST OF TABLES AND FIGURES

Chapter One

Introduction

Rob Natelson is a veteran of Montana politics. Twice a candidate for the governor's office in 1996 and 2000, he is also a founding member of *Montanans for a Better Government,* a political grass-roots organization that promotes limited government. Natelson is also an experienced direct democracy activist. In 1986, he led a successful referendum effort to repeal an unpopular tax increase passed by the Montana Legislature. In 1998, concerned with what he felt were more unwarranted tax increases by the Montana Legislature, Natelson drafted and passed Constitutional Initiative 75 (CI-75). CI-75 fundamentally changed the way the Montana government levied taxes in the state. The amendment required that most tax increases passed by the legislature would subsequently have to be submitted to a public referendum before they went into effect. The goal was to democratize the taxation process.

Being a veteran of Montana politics and especially the Montana system of direct democracy, Natelson understood that drafting and passing a state constitutional initiative that would withstand judicial scrutiny was a complicated process. Fortunately, he was well suited for the task. As a professor at the University of Montana's School of Law, he is knowledgeable about the complexities of constitutional law, and having experience with Montana's system of direct democracy, he understood that such an undertaking would require extensive historical and legal research. Therefore, before drafting his bill, Professor Natelson researched and examined every Montana Supreme Court decision regarding the initiative process dating back to 1889. In addition, he researched the details of the 1972 Montana Constitutional Convention at which

Montana adopted its current constitution. Not just relying on his own expertise, he also sent his measure to the Montana Legislature's legal team. The legislative council noted the bill had some potential legal problems and suggested some clarifying language. Natelson adopted the suggestions verbatim.

In addition to legal scrutiny, Natelson also attempted to emulate the legislative lawmaking process.[1] He solicited public input in a series of open hearings around the state. Based on the feedback at these hearings, and that of other legal experts, he eventually went through 17 drafts of the amendment before submitting it to the voters. On Election Day Professor Natelson was rewarded for his detailed work with a slim 51% victory at the polls. The victory, however, was fleeting.

As is becoming increasingly common with citizen sponsored initiatives, CI-75 was immediately challenged in court.[2] Fearing a loss in tax revenue, a coalition of teacher, school board, education, and government employee associations and unions filed suit to enjoin the enforcement of CI-75. Despite the legal challenge, Professor Natelson was relatively confident that his bill would be upheld. First, because it was a constitutional initiative rather than a statutory initiative, the only way the measure could be struck down was if the Montana Supreme Court ruled that it violated some procedural requirement. Having read every case concerning the procedural requirements of the Montana initiative process, and having got the approval of the Montana Legislative Council, he was again confident the bill would be upheld. However, to his shock, and to the shock of many other Montana activists, the Montana Supreme Court invalidated the entire constitutional amendment. Joe Balyeat, the Chairman of *Montanans for a Better Government,* was so frustrated with the Court's decisions he declared Montana is "held hostage by seven black-robed terrorists."[3] However, it was the reason the Montana Court struck down the amendment that caused such astonishment. In one of the most peculiar rulings in Montana history, the Montana Court invalidated a Montana constitutional amendment because it violated.....Oregon law. Ignoring all of their state's own precedent, the Montana

Court borrowed a ruling from a recent Oregon Supreme Court decision to invalidate CI-75.

There is more to the story of CI-75's ultimate destruction than first glance might reveal. In order to understand how the Montana Court could use Oregon precedent to invalidate a legally passed constitutional amendment, one first has to go back a decade and shift their attention to the state of Oregon.

On November 3, 1992 Paul Farago and Ted Piccolo accomplished a rare event in Oregon politics. They challenged their own state legislature and beat them. Farago and Piccolo, both frustrated with what they felt was an unresponsive and overspending legislature, founded Oregon Term Limits. The goal of their organization was to establish term limits for their state's local and federal representatives. The culmination of their efforts resulted in Measure 3 which limited individuals to serving no more than six years in the Oregon House and eight years in the Oregon Senate. The measure also limited persons to serving no more than six years in the United States House of Representatives and no more than 12 years in the United States Senate.

Election night was a resounding victory. Measure 3 passed with 70% of the vote and was the first Oregon initiative to ever receive more than 1 million votes. By the end of the night, both activists felt they had reformed Oregon's political system. Victory at the polls had been overwhelming. It looked like it was time to ride off into the sunset and enjoy the fruits of their success. But jump forward 10 years to 2002 and their victory lay in shambles. By 2002, not one of Measure 3's provisions was still part of Oregon law.

What went wrong? Did the people of Oregon change their minds about term limits? Polling data suggests they did not. Did the Oregon Legislature end run the people and repeal Measure 3? That didn't happen either. In the case of Measure 3, the Goliath that slew the grassroots David was the federal and state courts. By 2002, a series of federal and state legal decisions eliminated every provision that was enacted by Measure 3.

The story of how the courts turned Measure 3 from success to failure sheds light on the complicated and extremely political nature of direct democracy, constitutional law, and America's federalist judicial system. When initiatives are invalidated by courts, the conventional wisdom is typically to blame those who drafted the initiative. After all, grass roots direct democracy activists are not trained legislators. Most are not lawyers. Few have access to the institutional benefits of a legislature such as legal council, hearings, and legislative staff. The common assumption is that if an initiative is struck down by the courts, it was because the initiative was poorly drafted. But the story of Measure 3 offers an alternative explanation; a story that suggest that the courts have high jacked the democratic process by imposing their values over those of the voters.

The first setback for Measure 3 came in 1995 with the United States Supreme Court ruling in *Thornton v US Term Limits*. *Thornton* ruled that all state laws term limiting federal representatives were an unconstitutional expansion of the Qualification Causes found in Article I, Section 3 of the US Constitution. The impact of the *Thornton* decision for Farago and Piccolo was that the entire second half of Measure 3 was invalid. Measure 3 was drafted in two sections. The first half term limited state representatives. The second half term limited federal representatives. After *Thornton*, only the first half of the measure remained in force.

For seven additional years, the state level term limits of Measure 3 remained in effect. However, unknown to Farago and Piccolo, a completely unrelated legal battle was brewing that would eventually sink the other half of Measure 3. In 1996, Oregon Legislator Kevin Mannix was trying to pass through the Oregon Legislature a "victim's bill of rights" that would alter the criminal justice system in Oregon. His bill would have, among other things, allowed for 11 to 1 juries to convict criminals, require that criminals serve their entire sentence, and allow victims to be present at plea bargains. Unfortunately for Representative Mannix, he could not get his bill through the Oregon Legislature. So, like Farago and Piccolo, he decided to go over the head of the Oregon Legislature and appeal directly to the voters. In 1996, he qualified for the ballot and eventually passed Measure 40 which made all of his "victim's bill of rights" provisions part of Oregon law.

Mannix's victory was also short lived. Measure 40 was immediately challenged by several Oregon citizens claiming that a variety of procedural requirements for amending the Oregon Constitution had been violated. The Oregon Supreme Court agreed with the plaintiffs and in 1998 issued its *Armatta v Kitzhaber* ruling which invalidated Measure 40 in its entirety. Normally, such a development would not have raised many eyebrows. By 1998, the Oregon courts had become progressively more hostile to laws passed by direct democracy. What made the *Armatta* decision noteworthy is that the Oregon Supreme Court ignored the Oregon Constitution and fundamentally re-wrote the provisions relating to how citizens could amend their constitution. The Oregon court ruled that Measure 40 violated the "separate vote" rule embedded in Article 27 of the Oregon Constitution. Article 27 states that two separate changes to the Oregon Constitution must be voted upon separately. However, Article 27 specifically exempts constitutional amendments passed via the initiative process from this requirement. In fact, Article 27 specifically states, "This article shall not be construed to impair the right of the people to amend this Constitution by vote upon an initiative petition thereof." The Justices who wrote the *Armatta* decision simply ignored the final clause of Article 27. Despite an explicit prohibition to use Article 27 to invalidate citizen sponsored initiatives and amendments, the Oregon Court did exactly that. The ruling held that all initiatives altering more than one part of the state constitution would, subsequently, be held invalid.

The impact of the new and judicially manufactured "separate vote" rule on Oregon's direct democracy system was enormous. According to the new rule, any initiative that changed more than two separate sentences in the state constitution would be unconstitutional. As a result of the new rule, direct democracy activists all over Oregon began to narrow the scope of their initiatives. However, no one anticipated how the separate vote rule would be used to kill the last remaining part of Measure 3.

In a completely unforeseen development, opponents of term limits used the *Armatta* decision to ex post facto invalidate the last standing provisions of Measure 3. Opponents of term limits, specifically two state representatives facing removal from office if the limits were upheld, argued that even though the "separate vote" rule did not exist in 1992, Measure 3 should still be invalidated because it changed two separate sections of the Oregon Constitution. Defenders of Measure 3 countered that the drafters of Measure 3 should not be held to a standard that *did not exist* at the time they drafted the bill. However, in a stunning move, the Oregon Court, in *Lehman v Bradbury* (2002), invalidated the rest of Measure 3 eliminating state level term limits. The Court argued that the drafting of Measure 3 in 1992 violated the procedural rules established in 1998. The end result is that a bill that was constitutional for 10 years was eventually nullified because the Oregon Supreme Court created new procedural rules for the initiative system in 1998 and then held initiatives that were passed before 1998 accountable to the previously *non-existent* rules.[4]

How then does a story about Oregon term limit and criminal procedure initiatives impact a Montana tax reformer? When the challenge to Natelson's CI-75 came before the Montana Supreme Court, the Court ignored all of its own common law, and adopted Oregon's common law, specifically the *Armatta* separate vote standard, to facilitate the repeal of CI-75. In the course of the Montana *Marshall v Cooney* (1999) ruling which invalidated CI-75, the Court rejected all of its existing precedent concerning the procedure for passing citizen sponsored amendments. After rejecting all of its own precedent, the Court established a completely new standard, offering only Oregon's *Armatta* decision as justification for the radical change.

The long and complex history that intertwines the lives and work of Paul Farago, Ted Piccolo, Kevin Mannix, and Rob Natelson highlights a growing issue in American politics. America is a culture that values democratic principles. From its history of Puritan town hall meetings, to its fundamental belief that the "common man" has the facilities to govern himself, calls for a more democratic society have permeated America's political history. Yet, at the same time, America is a nation that values civil rights, fundamental constitutional principles, and a rule of law that trumps majority rule. Just as Americans have a strong affinity for democracy, they also have a healthy dose of elitism. Nowhere do these competing preferences produce more tensions than at the intersection of direct democracy and constitutional law.

Democracy and Law: A Paradox of Values

Democracy in its purest sense is an absolutely majoritarian system. The rule of law, in contrast, protects the interests and rights of the one over the interests of the many. Therefore, when democratically passed laws are challenged in American courtrooms, the classic tension between majority rule and minority rights is played out. This book seeks to examine this tension through the emerging practice of direct democracy and the ever increasing use of court decisions to invalidate the results of direct democracy. The paradox of American political values is confronted every time a judge, with the stroke of a pen, overturns the will of millions of voters. The examples of Oregon term limits and Montana tax reform only scratches the surface of an ongoing problem in American politics. The increasing use of direct democracy throughout the United States to fashion legislation and reform is running head first into activist courts.

In the past decade, activists utilizing direct democracy have attempted to institute term limits, campaign finance reform, doctor assisted suicide, the legalization of medical marijuana, reform of the criminal justice system, abortion regulation, control of illegal immigration, alter primary voting systems, and pension reform. Each of the activists supporting these movements has stories similar to those of Farago, Piccolo, Mannix, and Natelson. Almost universally, these attempts, although successful at the ballot box, have been defeated by insulated courts. Clearly, American politics is at a crossroads. While on one hand there is increasing rhetoric about individual political empowerment, democratization, and common political slogans all revolving around the notion of "taking our country back," the reality is that powerful courts raise the spectrum of an increasingly elitist political system. Whereas direct democracy increases the possibility of grass roots empowerment, judicial invalidation of successful movements splashes the cold water of disillusionment upon such activism.

Professor Ken Miller has studied the rates of judicial challenge and nullification of ballot measures. His research examines the states of California,

Colorado, and Oregon over the four decade time period between 1960 and 1998. His empirical data suggests that initiatives approved at the ballot box are challenged about 55 percent of the time. Of those initiatives that end up in court, over 50 percent are either partially or completely nullified by the courts. Table 1 highlights how often initiatives are challenged in court and Table 2 indicates how often those challenges result in a partial or complete invalidation.

Table 1: Rates of Initiative Challenge

Decade	Initiatives Challenged in Court[5]	Percent Challenged
1960s	3 of 6	50%
1970s	10 of 20	50%
1980s	21 of 41	51%
1990s	35 of 60	58%
Totals	69 of 127	54%

Source: Miller (1999)

Table 2: Rates of Initiative Invalidation

Decade	Initiatives Challenged	Invalidated in Part	Invalidated in Full	Percent Invalidated
1960s	3	0	3	100%
1970s	10	5	0	50%
1980s	21	6	4	48%
1990s	35	8	7	58%
Totals[6]	69	19	14	54%

Source: Miller (1999)

These rates of judicial nullification for ballot measures are significantly higher than the rates of judicial nullification for legislative acts. According to Landes and Posner (1975), the Supreme Court nullifies, on average, only one Congressional statute per two year term. In all, the court rejected only 97 statutes between 1789-1972. The highest judicial veto rate came between 1963-1972 where 25 statutes were rejected. Craig Emmert (1987) reports similar findings for state supreme courts. He records that, typically, each state supreme court only nullifies about two state laws per year.

The data from Tables 1 and 2 show that the conflict between direct democracy and judicial review has been percolating for the past three decades.

However, it is in the past decade that the raw number of nullifications has begun to increase significantly. Although the data suggests courts have become more hostile towards citizen sponsored legislation, it does not shed light on why courts have recently adopted such an attitude. The experiences of Natelson, Farago, Piccolo, and Mannix suggest that courts are arbitrarily and erratically exercising their countermajoritarian sword to pursue personal preferences regardless of the rule of law. But, examining the behavior of judges only illuminates one side of the story. Some of the citizens who utilize the tools of direct democracy also bear some responsibility for the increasingly hostile relationship between themselves and the courts. In the past three decades, citizen sponsored initiatives have been used to prevent racial desegregation in schools, restrict the rights of homosexuals, deny immigrant children access to education and health care, and promote one industry at the expense of others. In each case, the courts stepped in to prevent such initiatives from taking effect. Under such circumstances, most Americans support the use of courts to protect minorities from oppressive majorities. In a system of direct democracy which has no committee hearings, gubernatorial vetoes, filibusters, or any other type of "minority veto," the courts stand as the only barrier between the will of 51% of the voters and the rights of powerless minorities.

Given the fact that judges often ignore their own constitutions, and that direct democracy activists often ignore the constitutional rights of minority groups, it is clear that both parties bear some responsibility for the deteriorating relationship between judges and citizen activists. In order to fully understand the battle between the people and the courts, a variety of questions about direct democracy must be addressed. For example, who are the people who choose to utilize direct democracy? Are they mainstream political activists or are they fringe elements of radical political movements? Why do some direct democracy campaigns succeed while others fail? One must also understand the role the courts play in the inter-institutional battle between direct democracy and judicial review. For example, have the courts always been hostile to direct democracy? If not, why has the hostility increased in the past decade? If courts have become more hostile towards direct democracy, do direct democracy activists deserve such hostility? If direct democracy activists are utilizing the initiative process to restrict civil rights, maybe activist courts play an important role in insulating minority groups from dangerous and oppressive majorities. And finally, what is the political impact of the ongoing battle between direct democracy activists and courts? What does the future hold? Will one side eventually "win"? Will there be harmful fallout that results from such an inter-institutional battle?

Answering these questions is the guiding purpose of this book. The subsequent chapters will look at the evolution of direct democracy's interaction with America's court systems. The research elucidates a complex institutional environment that encompasses a myriad of strategic actors, complex "rules of the game," and shifting power endowments. The combination of which results in an ongoing competition between the courts and the people who engage in direct democracy.

Organization of the Book

When examining why initiatives face higher rates of judicial nullification than legislative statutes, it is important to understand that not all initiative activists adopt the same strategies, or have the same goals. Some drafters are willing to scale back their policy goals in order to increase the likelihood the initiative will withstand judicial scrutiny. Others are not. Some activists are pursuing immediate policy goals. Others are pursuing long term strategies to alter their political and social environment. Therefore, after a brief history of direct democracy in America in Chapter 2, a typology of initiative elites is presented. Chapter 3 outlines the different type of activists that participate in the process and identifies the different strategies they adopt. In turn, this typology provides insight into why some elites adopt seemingly self-destructive strategies while other elites adopt strategies more sensitive to existing legal doctrines.

Conventional wisdom suggests that ballot measures are more likely to be invalidated by the courts because initiative drafters are amateurs lacking the legislative experience to craft quality legislation. Although it is accepted that a small subset of initiative activists are clearly amateurs, in Chapter 4 the assertion that amateurism predominantly explains the divergent rates of nullification between initiative and legislative statutes is rejected. It is shown that initiative elites are often experienced political actors with the ability to learn from past mistakes, draw upon the experience of others in their field, and react to the behaviors of other institutional actors in order to prevent future nullifications. Not only do initiative proponents benefit from institutional learning, but they also engage in actions to protect the autonomy of their institution while at the same time taking actions to limit the autonomy of "competitor" institutions such as the executive and judicial branches.

In rejecting amateurism as the single explanatory variable for nullification rates, several alternative hypotheses are offered. There is no single cause for higher rates of ballot measure nullification. Like most complicated political processes, no silver bullet explains everything. The initiative process involves hundreds of independent actors, multiple institutions, and evolving political environments. Although studying individual-level explanations for judicial nullifications can be enlightening, the institutional context in which these individual behaviors occur is extensive. The larger interplay both between institutions and individuals proceeding within institutional constraints needs to be examined to fully understand why initiatives fail. Therefore, the causes of judicial invalidation can be subdivided into two categories—behavioral and institutional—and that each category has a number of supporting explanatory variables.

In Chapter 5, it is argued that high rates of initiative invalidation occur for institutional reasons. Primarily, initiative drafters suffer from a lack of institutional guidance from the courts. Institutions in a multi-institutional context send signals to each other indicating which types of behaviors will be accepted and which types of behaviors will be challenged. Because initiative drafters typically deal with issues that are relatively new to the political arena, very few signals exist showing how other institutions will react. The lack of signaling creates an information deficit that can hamper the ability of initiative elites to draft constitutional legislation. Furthermore, courts often send vague or even contradictory signals making it very difficult for direct democracy activists to interpret. And finally, recent history shows that courts are now more willing to ignore long established precedent, or even their own constitutions, to fashion new and arbitrary legal doctrines designed to thwart direct democracy activists.

Another institutional hurdle initiative drafters face is the "principal-agency" dilemma. Because initiative drafters are institutionally dependent upon other institutions to execute their measures (i.e. judicial and executive branches), they are subject to the discretion of other "hostile" political institutions. For example, initiative elites often depend on attorneys general to defend their initiatives in court, even when the attorney general may have been the most outspoken critic of the measure during the campaign. Or, initiative drafters may be attempting to alter the behavior of justices—the very justices ruling on the constitutionality of their measure. As a result, initiative elites wishing to see their measure implemented require the cooperation of other institutional actors; often, institutional actors whose interests are in conflict with the policy changes of the initiative.[7]

Moving beyond the courts, the initiative process also has "rules of the game" that are specific to that institution. For example, initiatives cannot be amended after the first signature has been collected. This constraint prevents drafters from making last-minute changes that would ensure the constitutionality of the measure in an ever-changing legal environment. Because the initiative process has its own set of institutional procedures, initiative drafters face a unique set of institutional pitfalls.

The second set of hypotheses focuses on the behavioral causes of judicial nullification. Initiative elites sometimes engage in behavior that leads to judicial invalidation, and these reasons are not *directly* related to the institutional rules and procedures of the initiative process. For example, most initiative campaigns involve the creation of coalitions. And, like most political coalitions, individuals bring to the group different values and intensities of opinion. Initiative coalitions suffer from a tension between those who seek ideologically pure legislation and those who seek to make practical compromises to ensure the measure is constitutional. These tensions typically cause fractures in coalitions that either lead to the disabling of the group, or the splintering of the group into two separate but ideologically consistent groups. Through a process of self-selection, most of the ideological zealots end up in one group, and the practical politicos who seek compromise end up in another. Obviously, despite the clear dichotomy presented here, the institutional design of the initiative system encourages coalition building and is therefore *indirectly* related to judicial nullification. The symbiotic relationship of institutional design and behavioral decisions is examined in Chapter 6.

Chapter 6 focuses on the strategic errors ideological purists make. Purist groups tend to suffer from the Iron Law of Oligarchy, which pushes the core leadership of an initiative campaign farther from the values of the group they supposedly represent. As they become more isolated, the core leadership tends to ignore the moderating influences of peer review and ends up drafting legislation that is only acceptable to the most ideologically extreme in their group. Ideologically extreme measures face significantly high rates of nullification. Responding in frustration to the courts, these activists turn towards symbolic measures that are designed to accomplish goals other than actually implementing legislation in the short run. They begin to focus their efforts on sending political messages, depleting the resources of opposition interest groups, or challenging existing legal precedents. Initiatives do not need to be constitutional to accomplish these goals. As a result, fewer resources are expended on ensuring the constitutionality of the measure.

Chapter 7 examines how direct democracy activists are reacting to activist courts. As one might suspect, direct democracy activists are not limiting their actions to simply griping about court decisions. Instead, they are taking the battle to the courts. In the past decade, direct democracy activists started utilizing their resources to attack the independence of state courts. These activists are challenging the autonomy of state courts by participating in judicial elections.

Chapter 7 offers a glimpse into future relations between judges and direct democracy activists.

Broader Questions

In addition to offering empirical insight into the relationship between courts and direct democracy, the text also provides some polemical and practical insight into the ways that courts must deal with initiative nullification. Recent public opinion polls suggest that among America's several political institutions, the federal courts have the greatest level of public support (Gallup, 2000). In political science terms, the courts enjoy a high level of political legitimacy. Despite this, members of the court have always understood that the legitimacy they enjoy can abate given highly salient, unpopular decisions. In fact, despite the fact that judicial review was "declared" in *Marbury vs. Madison*, at least at the federal level,[8] the court rarely used its power of judicial review until the late 1800s. Once judicial review was more firmly established, the courts continued to be hesitant to use it. As an example, the Supreme Court of the 1950s chose to nudge, rather than shove, America down the path of desegregation. In the recent *Bush vs. Gore* decision, many political commentators questioned if the legitimacy of the Court would be hurt given the Court's apparent willingness to involve itself in "political matters." In *Bush vs. Gore*, the decision clearly expressed the court's discomfort with being involved in such a high-level political conflict. However, state and federal courts are forced into "political matters" every time they approve or reject a popularly elected initiative. Every time a court strikes down a ballot measure it is rejecting a bill that was drafted by the people and approved by the people. Such an environment forces the courts to expose their countermajoritarian tendencies on a regular basis. At some point, continual initiative nullifications may begin to erode the courts' public support and legitimacy. And the courts, more than any other branch, need political legitimacy to survive. The courts do not have armies or police forces. The courts do not have control over tax dollars. The only power the courts have to enforce their decisions is public legitimacy. However, if courts are continually called upon to strike down popularly elected ballot measures, their legitimacy may erode along with their public support. Of course, it is only speculation whether a loss of political legitimacy will translate into individual or state actors actually ignoring judicial rulings.

Continual judicial review of ballot measures also threatens support for democratic institutions. In overturning a lower court's decision to invalidate California's Proposition 209, the federal appellate court noted that "a system which permits one judge to block with the stroke of a pen what 4,736,180 state residents voted to enact as a law, tests the integrity of our constitutional democracy." Furthermore, legal observer Mads Qvortrup warns, "judicial review of initiatives--especially popular ones--risk engendering the perception that the citizens have been subverted, and is likely to result in an even higher level of political discomfort" (1999). In an era of increased political alienation (Teixeira, 1992), it may be difficult to energize democratic tendencies via the initiative process if one person can overturn the will of an entire polity. Recently, Dan Smith's (2001) research indicated that citizens who live in states with a healthy initiative process exhibit greater "civic abilities." He measures civic abilities as both political knowledge and an understanding of political processes. Southwell and Paasco (2001) offer research that indicates voter turnout is higher in states that use the initiative process. These two studies suggest that a healthy initiative process goes a long way towards erasing some of the political alienation that occurred after the scandals of the 1970s. However, these increases in civic tendencies may be squashed if the courts are called upon to continually reject the work of a civically engaged populace.

Other commentators have noted that continual judicial review of ballot measures may lead to a politicization of the courts. Uelmen (1997) calls the initiative process "the angriest crocodile in the bathtub." He highlights several instances in which supposedly insulated state Supreme Court justices have been removed from the courts based on their decisions with respect to overturning a popularly elected ballot measure. Ex-California State Supreme Court Justice Joseph Grodin agrees. He admits that the threat of popular reprisal has a tendency to influence judicial decisions. He writes, "It is one thing for the court to tell a legislature that the statute it has adopted is unconstitutional; to tell that to the people of the state where they indicated their direct support for the measure through the ballot is another." It is also true that in all but two of the states which possess the initiative process, there is some form of popular judicial retention process. When Justice Lanphier overturned Nebraska's popular term limits law, opponents of the decision organized a campaign to challenge him in the next election. For the first time in his career he was forced to attend fundraisers and engage in a political campaign, which he ultimately lost.

Given the three primary problems associated with consistent judicial review of state ballot measures—loss of political legitimacy, loss of support for democratic institutions, and increased politicization of the courts—we need to understand why the competitive relationship between the courts and the initiative institution has not established the same level of nullification that the courts have established with other institutions (federal and state legislatures). If the reason initiatives suffer higher rates of invalidation can be ascertained, structural changes can be suggested that might ease tension between the initiative process and the courts. Simply put, the cause of the problem must be determined before a solution can be prescribed. Furthermore, beginning with the Ludlow Amendment in the 1930s, steady calls have promoted an initiative process at the national level (Cronin, 1988). If such a proposal is ever adopted on the national level, it would be better to work out the problems at the state level before such a national process is put into place.

Collecting the Data

In order to study the relationship between courts and direct democracy, one needs data that illustrates the behavior of both direct democracy activists and judges. To collect data on direct democracy activists, 45 in-depth interviews were conducted. To collect data on judicial behavior, every decision that ruled on the legality of an initiative between 1990 and 2000 in the states of Washington, Oregon, California and Colorado were examined. In all, there were 40 cases that either invalidated or upheld an initiative. Appendix A identifies each of these cases.

Because the number of court cases dealing with the ballot measure nullification is relatively low, it was possible to examine every case. Therefore, no methodological selection issues arose. However, the number of activists engaged in direct democracy is comparatively larger. Therefore, it was necessary to select a subset of initiative elites to interview. The unit of analysis comprises initiative elites, not the initiatives they drafted. "Initiative elites" can be initiative writers, high-level advocates, and organizational leaders. "High-level advocates" refers to individuals who had or have the ability to add or remove clauses to the final draft of an initiative. For example, many initiative elites do not draft their initiatives, but instead hire lawyers or other activists to perform this function. However, they still have significant influence over the initiative's content and what pre- and post-election campaign strategies are pursued.

Elites who participated in legislative referenda or recalls are not in the data set. Nor are any legal decisions that dealt with referenda or recalls in the data set. Legislative referenda are a completely different political phenomenon than initiatives and have a significantly higher success rate. The success rate is a function of the fact that most legislative referenda deal with mundane constitutional housekeeping legislation. They are rarely salient with the public and almost never attract political or financial opposition. Concurrently, referenda are almost never challenged in court. The same is true for recalls.

Initiative elites are the appropriate unit of analysis for two reasons. 1) The research examines the strategic behavior of human actors, not the initiatives they write. 2) Humans act and react. Initiatives do not.

Ken Miller's (2000) data set identifies every initiative that passed in California, Colorado, Oregon, and Washington from the years 1960 to 1998. Miller's data set was used to identify DDC activists who had passed at least one initiative between 1990 and 1998. The data set was expanded in two ways. The regional focus was widened to include activists in Idaho and Montana who had also passed at least one statewide initiative. The time frame was shifted to include activists who were active between 1990 and 2000. Interviews were limited to individuals who were actively involved in the initiative process between the years 1990 and 2000. However, in some cases, elites who actively participated in the 1990s had also drafted measures in the 1980s, and some in the 1970s. This did not disqualify them from my research population. The time scope was limited for a variety of reasons. Individuals who participated in the system prior to 1990 were very difficult to locate. Some of them were deceased, and in the rare cases where I could locate them, their memory of events was minimal. In total, 71 subjects were identified for the research population. From this population, 45 in-depth interviews were conducted.

Records from the Secretary of State's office were used to identify the chief petitioner(s) for each ballot measure. In most cases the chief petitioner was the person or persons most responsible for the initiative's content, and the person from whom an interview was sought. However, in a few cases, the chief petitioner was an honorary or symbolic figure. In those cases, interviews with the chief petitioner determined who was actually responsible for the content of the measure, and the appropriate replacement in the research population was made.

As Miller already notes in his original study, the regional focus of the data set is appropriate for several reasons. California, Oregon, Colorado, Idaho, Montana, and Washington demonstrate variation across legal cultures, initiative procedures, and state population. At the same time, the study includes states that use the initiative process extensively and states that rarely employ the process.

My sampling procedure was not randomized. Some individuals were purposefully selected based on the inordinate amount of influence they wielded.[9] For instance, a credible sample of initiative elites in Oregon, Washington, and Montana includes such individuals as Bill Sizemore, Tim Eyman, and Rob Natelson.[10] Because it was essential to include specific individuals in the sample, far more effort was exerted to contact and schedule interviews with certain subjects.[11]

Using semi-structured interview questions as suggested by Merton (1954, 1990), in-depth interviews provided most of the data for this research project. In some cases, interview data was supplemented. Some individuals offered access to internal and/or personal email correspondence and legal documents. Other groups allowed observation of their internal meetings. In some cases access to ongoing internal listservs of initiative groups was provided.

To ensure that the responses received during interviews were as accurate and honest as possible *all respondents were guaranteed complete confidentiality.* The confidentiality covered all interview responses, internal documents and emails, and any internal sessions attended. As a result, any quotes, anecdotes, or descriptions of process in this book will only identify the speaker by an interview number.

---

[1] One of the common criticisms of the initiative process is that committees do not debate and refine a measure as is done in the legislative lawmaking process. See Mark Tushnet, (1996) *Fear of Voting: Differential Standards of Judicial Review of Direct Legislation*, 1996 Annual Survey of American Law, pp. 373-392. Professor Natelson sought to overcome this shortcoming by creating a pseudo-legislative process.

[2] The measure was challenged by a coalition of groups that would be hurt by lower tax revenues—public employee unions, school districts, and local city governments.

[3] See Michael Moore. (2000). "Duel for the Top Seat" *The Missoulian* accessed at http://www.missoulian.com/specials/supremes/duel.html.

[4] Montana initiative drafters experienced a similar event in 1999. See *Marshall v. Cooney*, 975 P 2nd 325. In Oregon, the *ex post facto* concerns became so great, the legislature feared every initiative ever passed in Oregon would be suspect. They considered calling a special session of the Legislature to protect measures passed in the early 1980s. See "Special Session Unneeded," *The Register-Guard*, August 26, 2001. 3B.

[5] Data are only for California, Oregon and Colorado. However, these states historically use the initiative process more than any others.

[6] At the time this datum was published, nine cases were still pending—all from the 1990s.

[7] As will be discussed further in subsequent chapters, this situation is different than typical legislative lawmaking, which also needs the cooperation of independent institutions. Lawmaking by legislature must pass through the executive "filter" before it becomes law. Therefore, governors opposed to legislative laws will simply veto them. No such opportunity exists for the executive branch when dealing with initiatives. Therefore, the only way a governor may obstruct an initiative (other than campaigning) is to use the discretionary powers of the Attorney General.

---

[8] Alan Tarr (1998) highlights periods in American history during which state courts were more willing than federal courts to use their powers of judicial review, most notably during the post-Civil War era.

[9] Once I committed more resources to ensure the inclusion of some individuals for the research population, my sample was no longer a randomized sample, but a "purposive sample," or what is sometimes called a parallel sample (Warwick and Lininger,1975). Warwick and Lininger explain that a parallel sample is needed when a specific individual must be included in the sample or when the research population is so small that randomization is irrelevant.

[10] All three men are extremely influential activists in their respective sates.

[11] In an effort to find some subjects, interviewees were asked to help locate other initiative elites. This approach may raise the concern that the data set reflects a "circle of friends" or a "snowball" sample. This is not the case. The research population was determined before asking respondents for contact information. In addition, potential respondents were not selected from suggestions of other respondents.

Chapter Two

The History and Procedures of the Initiative Process

The History of Direct Democracy

Direct democracy refers to the initiative, referendum and recall processes present in most states' constitutions.[1] The process offers citizens the ability to propose and pass statutes and constitutional amendments (initiatives), reject legislation passed or suggested by the legislature (referenda), and recall elected officials (recall). Citizens and interest groups use initiatives proactively to write laws or constitutional amendments when they feel the legislature has been remiss. Referenda are used retroactively. If a citizen or interest group objects to a law passed by the legislature, they can use a referendum to repeal the law. Or sometimes, legislatures wish to avoid bearing the political costs of passing unpopular legislation and will instead submit the bill to the people in the form of a referendum. Recalls are rare events when the public removes an elected official from office.

Forms of direct democracy have been around as long as democracy itself. Ever since Socrates and the Greeks introduced the world to democracy over 2000 years ago, political bodies have debated the question of how much popular participation in government is appropriate.[2] Direct democracy has a vibrant history in the United States as well.[3] It was common for early New England towns to call town hall meetings where all citizens (i.e. adult white males) could propose and pass legislation (Cronin, 1988). In America's revolutionary era, Massachusetts became the first state to adopt its constitution by statewide referendum.

In general, however, America's political framers were unenthusiastic about direct democracy. Even a brief examination of the *Federalist Papers* and the Constitutional debates highlights a strong aversion to direct democracy. James Madison's *Federalist # 10* is the most often cited example. He claims, "The instability, injustice and confusion introduced into the public councils, have, in truth, been mortal diseases under which popular governments have everywhere perished." Madison was not alone in his fear about direct democracies. Alexander Hamilton was a well-established elitist and his negative opinions about democracy are well documented in *Federalist # 71* and *# 49*. Fisher Ames, a Massachusetts delegate, sums up the Framers' general opinion about direct democracy. "I would not have the first wish, the momentary impulse of the publik [*sic*] mind, become law. For it is not always the sense of the people, with whom, I admit, that all power resides." Or, put more bluntly by Charles Beard, "Everything about the tone of the Convention suggests that they would have looked upon such schemes [initiatives] with a feeling akin to horror" (quoted in Faigman 1996, p. 105).

Opinions about direct democracy began to change in the United States during the late 1800s. At the time there was widespread discontent with the legislative process. Large segments of the population felt that legislatures had been co-opted by powerful and wealthy business elites and special interests (Piott, 2003). Legislatures were seen as recalcitrant to the wishes of the common citizen. After some high profile trials of elected officials, citizens also began to view state legislatures as corrupt. In response, many groups began to call for the initiative, referendum, and recall as a way to clean up local politics. In the United States, the Socialist Party was the first to call for the initiative and referendum process. Being a relatively small group and considered on the fringe of American politics, their calls were largely ignored. However, in 1893, the push towards direct democracy received a jolt when J. W. Sullivan published *Direct Legislation by the Citizenship Through the Initiative and Referendum*. Sullivan was a journalist and political activist who, in 1888, took leave from his position at the *New York Times* to travel in Switzerland so that he could observe first hand how direct democracy functioned. While there, he observed how the Swiss used the initiative and referendum process and wrote several descriptive articles for different periodicals back home. In 1892, he published his first book, *Direct Legislation*. After returning home, Sullivan started editing and publishing the *Direct Legislation Record*, a periodical designed to educate and promote direct democracy. At the same time, his book was becoming widely read among many activists in the People's Party (Populists). Several Populist magazines listed Sullivan's books as recommended reading.

After initial lukewarm support, the Populist Party put a call for an initiative and referendum process in their official platform and re-energized the debate over direct democracy (Piott, 2003). However, the Populist push for direct democracy was not successful either. In general, the Populists were calling for a national initiative and referendum process. At the national level, there was too much opposition.

But the calls for a national initiative and referendum process spilled over into state politics. Although William McKinley won a landslide presidential victory over William Jennings Bryan in 1896, Populist candidates fared far better in statewide elections. In 1896, Andrew Lee, representing a "fusionists" coalition of Populists, Democrats, and free-silver Republicans won the South Dakota governorship by 317 votes. The victory eventually resulted in South Dakota becoming the first state to add the initiative and referendum process to their Constitution.

Utah and Oregon quickly followed in 1900 and 1902, respectively.[4] Oregon's movement towards direct democracy mirrored that of South Dakota. Populist political activist William U'Ren was able to capitalize on Oregon voters' resentment towards a corrupt and business dominated legislature. U'Ren was elected to the Oregon House and subsequently formed the Non-Partisan Direct Legislation League. While a representative, U'Ren was able to control a block of 13 Populist legislators. Although not a majority, it was enough votes to logroll support for his direct democracy policies. In 1899, both houses of the Oregon

Legislature adopted initiative and referendum amendments and the voters ratified those amendments in 1902.

Despite the successes in South Dakota, Utah, and Oregon, the Populist Party was not able to carry the initiative and referendum revolution much further. The Populists movement never resulted in a permanent or majority political party. After sweeping to power in South Dakota in 1896, they were just as quickly removed from office in the subsequent election. Fortunately for advocates of the initiative process, the Progressive movement took up the cause after the Populists began to fade from political view. The Progressives were less radical than the Populists. Progressives did not have an inherent faith in rule by the "common man," but, like the Populists, they were concerned about legislative corruption. Progressives began to adopt the attitude that "the cure for the ills of democracy is more democracy." Because of the push by the Progressives, by 1918 twenty-four states had adopted some form of the initiative and referendum process (Cronin, 1988).[5] The timing of the Populist and Progressive parties explains why most initiative states are in the West. These political movements were more successful in agrarian areas—primarily the midwestern and western states. As a result of their political success, they were able to garner enough seats in their respective state legislatures to act as swing vote coalitions. Capitalizing on rifts between Republicans and Democrats, or pro-silver and pro-gold standard coalitions, Populist representatives were able to act as "king makers." However, before crowning a king, they demanded support for initiative and referendum proposals.

From the very beginning, the Populists and the Progressives held differing views about the initiative process and the actual functioning of the initiative process. In some cases the initiative process worked exactly as its advocates claimed it would. Citizens of various states did wrest the power from their state legislatures to select US senators (Ellis, 2002). Other Progressive reforms, especially labor and procedural reforms, were enacted through the initiative ballot (Tolbert, 2000). At the same time, from its earliest inception, the initiative process has run into problems. One of Oregon's first initiatives was a rent-seeking[6] measure designed to capitalize on a privately owned road (Ellis,

2002). And, Richard Ellis points out that from the very beginning, initiatives could be hostile to minority rights. Despite the oft-repeated myth that women's suffrage was won through the initiative process, the reality is that most early initiatives that sought to grant voting rights to women were defeated. More often than public votes, it was the legislatures who gave women the right to vote (Ellis, 2002).

Once the initiative process was adopted, it was relatively popular for several decades. The years between 1910 and 1930 averaged over 200 initiatives nationwide each decade. Beginning in 1940, however, the numbers began to drop. In the 1960s, there were only 95 initiatives nationwide.[7] Most scholars agree that the modern era of the initiative process began in 1978. That year, two Californians named Howard Jarvis and Paul Gann successfully passed Proposition 13. Their successful tax rollback initiative sparked a series of copycat initiatives across the West. But more significantly, the measure served as a catalyst. Other activists came to realize the potential effectiveness of the initiative process. Other states close to California, such as Oregon and Colorado, also began to experience an increase in initiative use. As seen in Figure 1, the frequency of initiatives qualifying for the ballot (but not necessarily passing) has grown steadily since the late 1970s. As the use of initiatives to implement public policy has become more common, social scientists, elected officials, and political pundits have expressed a variety of concerns (Ellis, 2002, Linde 1994, Broder, 2000). Some have argued the initiative process strips elected officials of agenda setting power, fails to protect minority rights, can be co-opted by special interest money, and breaks down the barrier between the populace and the government so fundamental to republican government. In response to these concerns, in 1998, the courts began to take a more activist role in reviewing initiatives. In *Armatta v. Kitzhaber* (1998) the Oregon Supreme Court established the "separate vote" rule which gave courts much more discretion to invalidate measures. Other states later adopted the *Armatta* standard and used it as a signal to initiative drafters that the courts would examine ballot measures more strictly in the future. Despite the courts' attempts to limit direct democracy, the initiative process remains a vibrant part of political life.   Given that it is unlikely to be removed from state constitutions, it is imperative that we begin to understand the process and understand the people involved in the process.

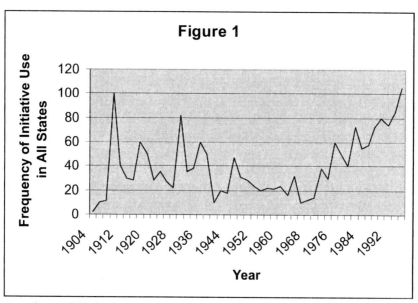

Source: Initiative and Referendum Institute (2000)

What Others Have Said

Prior scholarly literature reveals very little empirical research about judicial review of statewide ballot measures. The existing research focuses primarily on the frequency of judicial review of ballot measures, and certain normative and theoretical implications associated with high judicial review levels. However, no previous systematic research reveals how initiative elites react, in a strategic manner, to courts' actions, and why judicial nullification of state ballot measures remains so high.

Most research examining the relationship between the courts and the initiative process focuses on normative questions. A large body of this literature focuses on whether courts should subject initiatives to a higher standard of review than legislative acts. Many judicial theorists argue that because the initiative process lacks the numerous "checks" inherent in the legislative process, initiative statutes should face stricter scrutiny in the judicial arena (Eule 1990; Bell 1978; Dority, 1994). These arguments usually include all or some combination of the following. Because the initiative process lacks potential gubernatorial vetoes, legislative logrolling, minority faction compromises or committee information gathering processes, the courts have a responsibility to act as the only counter-majoritarian check (Vitiello and Glendon, 1998). Specifically, some theorists suggest the greatest danger the initiative process poses is the restriction of minority civil rights (Bell 1978; Linde, 1994). Bell and Linde argue that the initiative process is often used to restrict the rights of homosexuals and racial minorities. These arguments have resulted in theoretical debates suggesting the courts should use the Guarantee Clause[8] to nullify more state ballot measures (Chemerinsky, 1994).

Other researchers and legal scholars focus on establishing consistent standards of judicial review for ballot measures (Stern and Holman, 1998; Tushnet, 1997; Salik, 1996). Many initiative elites and initiative scholars complain about the inconsistent manner in which the courts invalidate measures within the same state. The matter is compounded by the fact that federal district and appeals courts sometimes use different standards than state courts. Some courts examine initiatives with strict scrutiny, looking for any possible constitutional tension. Other courts give initiatives more deference because they come directly from the people. In some cases, courts strictly enforce the single subject rule,[9] while other courts do not. As a result, legal scholars occasionally call for a uniform set of standards to guide the courts (Nagle, 1997). As will become evident and important later, empirical research shows that state and federal courts behave differently with respect to state ballot measure judicial nullification (Stern and Holman, 1998).

Finally, some research examines the rate of judicial nullification (Miller, 2000; Price, 1997). These studies suggest very high rates exist and result in political consequences. On a normative level, they argue that the continual nullification of popularly elected initiatives threatens both the courts' independence and their legitimacy. They fear that if initiative elites become upset when the courts invalidate their ballot measures, drafters will react by challenging judicial candidates and the courts will be drawn into partisan electoral battles.

Indirectly, a small amount of research focuses on the questions this book examines. Some researchers suggest possible reasons why courts invalidate initiatives so frequently. One source of friction between the initiative process and the courts results from the fine line between constitutional revision and constitutional amendment. Many state Constitutions allow for the initiative process to amend the Constitution but not to revise it (Tolbert, Lowenstein and Donovan, 1998; Collins and Oesterle, 1994).[10] Whenever a question about the difference arises, it falls to the courts to decide whether a ballot measure stepped past the line of amendment and crossed into the arena of revision. This very vague standard is subject to multiple interpretations not only among different courts but also among various initiative elites.[11] Others point out that ballot measures often contain politically fringe content (Cronin, 1988). Often, political advocates utilize the initiative process because state legislatures avoid politically extreme proposals. By using off year elections, where turnout is low and more politically extreme, initiative backers can sometimes pass initiatives that do not have the support of the general populace. However, the fringe nature of ballot measures does not lie entirely on one end of the political spectrum. Researchers show that both ultraconservative and ultraliberal interest groups use the initiative process equally (Tolbert, 2001).

Tolbert, Lowenstein, and Donovan suggest another reason for state ballot initiatives' high judicial nullification rate. Initiatives are challengeable under two auspices. A ballot measure can be reviewed on both procedural and content grounds. However, legislative bills are rarely challenged under procedural questions (Nagle, 1997). In contrast, a ballot measure can be reviewed on the basis of how many articles of the Constitution it alters, how the title of the bill was drafted, and how petition signatures were gathered.

Still other researchers suggest initiatives are often challenged because court battles are less expensive than election campaigns (Campbell, 2001). Conducting a statewide initiative campaign can be very expensive, reaching into the tens of millions of dollars.[12] Rather than fighting a ballot measure via a several months-long media campaign, opponents of a ballot measure can simply wait until after the election and file a court challenge.

Finally, the amateur nature of the initiative industry may cause the high judicial nullification rate (Collins and Oesterle, 1994). The initiative process is often referred to as citizen lawmaking, meaning the authors of ballot measures are often everyday citizens who lack the experience of drafting technical legislation. The fact that initiatives are poorly written opens many doors for the courts to find justification for nullification. State legislatures, in contrast, maintain a sense of institutional memory. When the courts overturn bills, legislatures learn not to repeat the same mistakes.[13] However, the decentralized nature of both the initiative process and the courts do not facilitate institutional cohesiveness to the same degree. These two "diffused institutions" rarely have the same "players" engage in iterated encounters, and therefore do not develop an "evolution of cooperation" (Axelrod, 1980).

The research presented in this book shows that the aforementioned arguments only provide a partial explanation as to why courts veto initiatives so frequently. A combination of behavioral and institutional forces that affect ballot measure drafting causes initiative proponents to fail. The previous research on ballot measure judicial nullification misses the complex nature of how initiative coalitions are created and how they eventually dissolve. It is critical that researchers understand how initiative coalitions collapse and then re-form into more homogeneous, and often more politically radical, coalitions. In addition, previous research fails to explain how the courts contribute to initiative invalidation. Beyond the obvious fact that courts invalidate measures, no research has examined how the courts tend to protect their own institutional autonomy at the expense of initiatives, or how they fail to signal initiative elites as to what is constitutionally sustainable legislation.

Initiative Procedures—The Rules of the Game

Direct democracy offers citizens the ability to write, propose, and pass statutes and constitutional amendments (initiatives), reject legislation passed by the legislature (referendum), reject laws suggested by the legislature (referendum), and to recall elected officials (recall). Throughout this book, all of these processes are collectively referred to as the initiative process.[14] However, each of the above listed legislative actions has its own terminology and procedures.

There are two types of initiatives—direct initiatives and indirect initiatives. A direct initiative involves a state citizen placing a proposed statute or constitutional amendment directly on the ballot to be voted upon by the people. An indirect initiative occurs when a citizen first submits a proposed statute to the state legislature (Waters, 2001). If the legislature passes the statute, the law is enacted and the process is completed. If, however, the legislature fails to pass the statute it is then referred to the ballot for public vote. If the electorate passes the indirect initiative it becomes law over the objections of the legislature.

A direct initiative that enacts a statute and a direct initiative that enacts a constitutional amendment are different. Statutes only carry the weight of statutory law. Statutes can be easily amended by the legislature with a simple majority vote. Therefore, direct initiatives that enact statutes tend to be less permanent and more easily thwarted by the legislature. Second, statutes are subject to state constitutional review based on the content of the initiative. Constitutional amendments, however, carry the weight of organic law. Therefore, once enacted, they are de facto constitutional and beyond judicial review. Furthermore, constitutional amendments are not amendable by a simple majority vote in the legislature. However, despite the fact that constitutional amendments are automatically constitutional on content grounds, they are still subject to judicial review on procedural grounds. For example, if an initiative amends more than one part of the Constitution or contains multiple subjects, it can be declared unconstitutional.

There are two types of referendum—popular referendum and legislative referendum. A popular referendum occurs when an individual seeks to nullify a bill passed by a legislature. If the state legislature passes a bill and the governor signs a bill, it becomes law. However, through a popular referendum the public can vote to reject that enacted law. A legislative referendum, however, involves a state legislature deferring to the will of the people. This occurs when the legislature approves a bill but submits it to the people for approval or rejection before officially enacting the law (Waters, 2001).

A recall occurs when the public removes from office a previously elected and currently serving official.

The initiative process involves several steps. No two states have the exact same system, but they all share similar procedures. The initiative process begins when a citizen drafts an initiative and submits it to the appropriate state official. In most states the appropriate official is the Secretary of State. However, in some states, initiatives are submitted to the Attorney General or a state board specifically set up to review initiatives. A complete listing of all state regulations concerning the initiative process, as compiled by the Initiative and Referendum Institute, appears in Appendix A.

In many states, individuals who draft initiatives may submit their bills to a Legislative Council. The Legislative Council is a branch of the state legislature and usually reviews legislative bills for compatibility with the existing body of law and for constitutionality. In some states, Colorado for instance, it is mandatory to submit all initiatives to the Legislative Council.

Once the initiative has been submitted to the state it is forwarded to the Attorney General's office or some other review board for analysis. The Attorney General is responsible for setting a title and drafting a summary for the initiative. These two steps are extremely important politically. The title of an initiative alone can determine the likelihood of electoral success. If the Attorney General drafts a title that highlights negative aspects of an initiative or fails to highlight popular aspects of the bill, support for the initiative will fall. In the same respect, how the Attorney General summarizes the content of the initiative will also affect how voters interpret the initiative. As a result, many experienced and professional initiative drafters will file multiple versions, with slight changes, of the same initiative (Interview # 23, #46, # 91). This way, the Attorney General is required to draft multiple titles and multiple summaries. The initiative drafter can then pursue the initiative which received the most favorable title and ballot summary. It is at this stage that an increasing number of legal challenges occur. Interested groups often file suit with the Attorney General's office, the Secretary of State's office, or legal review boards if they feel the title and summary do not accurately reflect the content of the initiative.

In some states, the Attorney General will ask for a fiscal review of an initiative so that information may accompany the ballot summary. In other states, the Supreme Court or the Attorney General may review an initiative for constitutionality prior to its appearing on the ballot. This practice is referred to as prior review. It is a relatively rare process, only occurring in Florida, Utah, and Montana (Initiative and Referendum Institute, 2002).

Once the appropriate state official has officially certified an initiative, the signature collection process begins. Again, each state has different rules. Some states allow a very short time period for signatures to be collected.[15] California allows 150 days. Colorado allows six months; Montana allows a year.[16] More important, each state requires a different number of signatures to be collected. The number necessary is usually based on a percentage of how many votes were cast in the last general election for a specific position. For instance, Oregon requires that initiative drafters collect signatures equal to six percent of the votes cast for the governor in the last general election. Some states base their signature requirements on percentage of votes cast for the Secretary of State. However, no state requires less than three percent and no state requires more than 15 percent.[17] As a general rule, states require more signatures for a constitutional amendment than a direct statute (Waters, 2001).[18]

After enough signatures have been collected, they are submitted to the Secretary of State, or the appropriate body for that particular state, to be verified for accuracy. Rarely does the state verify every signature. In most cases states engage in statistical sampling.[19]   The state examines a certain percentage of signatures and verifies that the signatory is actually a registered voter and that the signature on the petition matches the signature on their voter registration card. In some cases, if one signature does not match or one person is not a registered voter then the entire petition page (which usually holds about 20 signatures) is checked. If, after review, enough signatures have been gathered the initiative is placed on the ballot.

Besides procedural hurdles, initiatives also have requirements about subject matter. In some states like Nebraska and Oklahoma, the same subject cannot appear on a ballot more than once in three years. Other states simply bar initiatives from dealing with some specific subjects. In Montana, for example, initiatives cannot deal with appropriations. In California, an initiative can only amend the Constitution but not revise it. In Massachusetts, initiatives cannot deal with the subject of religion.

More importantly, many states require that initiatives only deal with a single subject. Currently, 18 states have this requirement (Campbell, 2001). The purpose of these requirements is to prevent legislative logrolling. Many experts in the initiative field feel that without the single subject rule initiative, drafters could hide sinister legislation behind popular legislation (Eule, 1990).   For instance, an initiative drafter could write an initiative that offers large tax cuts in one section and restricts minority rights in the second section. Unfortunately, the problem with the single subject rule is that, in the words of Florida Justice Lewis, what constitutes a single subject is "in the eye of the beholder." Often, initiative drafters don't know if their initiative encompasses a single subject or not. State courts have tried to establish criteria for single subject restrictions, but the criteria are usually as vague as the single subject rules themselves (Lowenstien, 1999).[20]

Closely tied to the concept of the single subject rule is the separate vote rule. It's possible for an initiative to encompass a single subject but alter multiple sections of the Constitution. For example, a tax restructuring initiative would meet the single subject requirement by only dealing with one subject—taxes. However, because there are so many interconnected tax statutes, the initiative may alter multiple parts of the Constitution. In some states (Oregon, Washington and Montana, for example), initiatives can neither violate the single subject rule nor alter more than one section of the Constitution.

And finally, initiatives cannot be amended once the signature collection process has begun. If an initiative drafter alters any part of an initiative, he or she must restart the signature collection process (Miller, 2001).

If an initiative is adopted by the voters, the process is still not over. Although no state allows a governor to veto an adopted initiative, almost every state allows the legislature to repeal or amend statutory initiatives after they have been approved.[21] To repeal or amend an initiative, states vary from requiring a simple majority vote to a supermajority vote.[22] No state allows a constitutional amendment to be amended or repealed by legislature without resubmitting that change back to the people.

If an initiative survives all of these procedural and subject matter hurdles there is still the possibility of post-election judicial challenges. As chapter 1 indicated, this is a very common occurrence. Constitutional amendments can be challenged on both procedural grounds (single subject rule, separate vote rule) and content grounds (violation of federal constitutional issues). Statutory initiatives are subject to challenge on both state and federal constitutional grounds, as well as some procedural rules (single subject rule, but not separate vote rule). This book focuses on why these post election challenges occur so often, and why they are so often successful.

Conclusion

An examination reveals the initiative process to be complicated, time consuming, and expensive. The initiative process has a variety of procedural hurdles, legal restrictions, and expensive signature gathering requirements. This fact raises some interesting questions and provides some insights into why someone would choose to utilize the initiative process. If the process is so expensive and complicated, why would a political activist choose to use the initiative process when a simpler legislative process already exists? The simple answer is that the legislative process is closed to many political activists. Those activists who find the legislative option closed to them are forced to venture into the initiative process. Legislatures are not hospitable to legislation that challenges the security of legislators or raises politically salient but controversial issues. It is these types of issues that often make up the content of initiatives. The next chapter examines why initiative elites are forced to become initiative activists rather than simply political activists.

---

[1] According to the *Initiative and Referendum Institute*, 24 states have the initiative process. Of those 24, 18 allow an initiative to amend the constitution.

[2] Under the leadership of Cleisthenes in the fifth century B.C., the Greeks developed one of the first systems of direct democracy. Each year, citizens could identify an incompetent politician on a piece of baked clay called an 'ostroca'. If the identified politician received enough ostroca, they were officially ostracized from the polis (Farah & Karls, 1999).

[3] The Plymouth Colony started with a government based on direct democracy. When the population grew too large, they moved to a representative form of government. However, once a year, the entire colony's voting population was allowed to invalidate legislatively passed laws they did not like.

[4] Although not the first to put the initiative process in their constitution, Oregon was the first to actually pass an initiative in 1904.

[5] As of today, 27 states have some form of the initiative process.

[6] "Rent-seeking" is a public choice term used to describe behavior in which individuals or groups use the power of government to create a market failure that results in economic gains for a few at the expense of the general public.

[7] The scholarly literature on the initiative process offers little explanation why this is so. Most of the attention is focused on reasons for the process' revival in the late 1970s.

[8] The Guarantee Clause (Article IV, Section 4 U.S Constitution) requires all states have a "republican form of government." Some have argued that the initiative process is not a republican form of government.

[9] The single subject rule exists in many initiative states and requires each initiative to deal with only one subject. The separate vote rule limits each initiative to changing only one section of the constitution.

[10] Easily measurable criteria to determine if an initiative is one or the other does not exist. The California Supreme Court tried to define a revision as an act which enacted "comprehensive changes" or served "far reaching changes in the nature of our basic governmental plan." However, both "definitions" are more synonyms than definitions.

[11] For example, California's Supreme Court upheld Proposition 13 as a state constitutional amendment even though it completely altered how the government financed itself.

Yet the same court struck down Proposition 115 as a revision of the state constitution because it required the courts to adopt the federal courts' interpretation of civil rights laws. See *Amador Valley Joint Union High School District v. State Brd of Equalization (1978) (149 Cal. Rptr. 239) and Raven v. Deukmejian (1990) (276 Cal Rptr. 326)*

[12] In the Oregon 2000 election, advocates spent over $5 million on Measures 92/98 which sought to limit the ability of unions to use dues for political purposes.

[13] See the entire body of Commerce Clause/Civil Rights legislation from the years 1895 (*United States v. E.C. Knight Co.*) to 2000 (*United States v. Morrison*). At times, the Court nullified Congressional acts on the basis that legislators did not conduct sufficient "findings" to prove an event affected interstate commerce. Congress responded by holding extensive hearings to prevent such grounds for future judicial review.

[14] However, my study of initiative nullification does not look at recalls.

[15] Massachusetts allows the shortest time with only 64 days.

[16] Arizona allows the longest time with 20 months.

[17] Massachusetts only requires 3% of votes cast for governor but Wyoming requires 15% of votes cast in the most recent general election.

[18] If the state allows constitutional amendment by initiative. Sixteen states do not allow their constitutions to be amended in this process.

[19] States will examine a small number of signatures to determine the percentage of acceptable signatures. The state will then accept that percentage of all the signatures submitted.

[20] For example, Oregon courts have required that initiative subjects have a "unifying principle." California has used a "reasonably germane" standard.

[21] California does not allow the Legislature to amend initiatives.

[22] Arizona (3/4), Arkansas (2/3), Michigan (3/4), North Dakota (2/3) and Washington (2/3) require supermajorities.

Chapter Three

Who Participates in the Initiative Process?

Sometimes researchers need more than a simple definition or label to completely describe a concept or a group of actors. As a result, political scientists have found it useful to create classification systems, or typologies. Previous research categorizes representatives (Fenno, 1978) and presidents (Cronin, 1980; Barber, 1976) to better understand their "mindset." For example, it is useful for political scientists to categorize representatives as "trustees," "delegates," or "politicos." Other typologies have been created for studying presidents. Barber (1976) classified presidents based on personality and Skowronek (1998) has used regime differences. By creating typologies, we hope to gain insight into the actions of political actors.

The same rationale is appropriate for initiative elites. Initiative elites are not all "cut from the same cloth." Each one brings to the process a unique set of goals, experiences, institutional mindsets, and political histories. These differences influence the way initiative drafters engage the initiative system. Just as we can predict the way a member of Congress will vote based on whether he sees himself as delegate or trustee, we gain insight into the motivations of initiative elites by classifying them based on similar characteristics.

The purpose of Chapter 3 is to create a typology of initiative elites, or what might be termed, "The Players." Based on the 45 interviews conducted, the typology identifies six "players" in the initiative game. They are: the zealot, the amateur, the professional, the politician, the lawyer, and the victim. Based on the interview data, a composite for each player is developed below. Table 3 identifies the numerical distribution of the different types of players.

Table 3: Types of Initiative Elites

Player Type	Primary Classifications¥	Multiple Classifications†
Zealot	8 (18%)	12 (20%)
Amateur	6 (13%)	11 (19%)
Lawyer	7 (16%)	10 (17%)
Professional	13 (29%)	13 (22%)
Politician	7 (16%)	8 (15%)
Victim	4 (8%)	4 (7%)
Totals	45 (100%)	58 (100%)

¥ This column represents totals when each subject could only be classified once, based on their dominant characteristic. Therefore, the total in this column is equal to the number of interviews conducted (45).

† This column represents totals when subjects could be classified in multiple categories (no subject was classified in more than two categories). Therefore, the total in this column exceeds the numbers of interviews conducted (58).

Since no typology can be perfect, elites in the typology can have characteristics from multiple categories. As Table 4 will illustrate, the most common multiple classification is the "lawyer—politician" and the "professional—zealot." As I explain below, some pairings are mutually exclusive and never occur, such as the "professional—amateur" or the "zealot—victim."

Table 4: Elites with Multiple Classifications

Player Type	Number
Professional-Zealot	5
Lawyer-Politician	3
Amateur-Zealot	3
Politician-Zealot	1
Amateur-Victim	1

Table 4 illustrates the number of subjects that have the characteristics of more than one classification. Professional-zealots were the most common combination. Also notable is that zealots make up some part of nine of the 13 combination classifications, illustrating that zealot-like behavior is a common characteristic of all initiative "players."

The typology is based on two dominant criteria: the participant's primary motivation for drafting or supporting an initiative and why he or she chose to use the initiative process at all. In the first case, one might assume that the primary motivation for drafting an initiative is always the same—to pass legislation. But this was not the case. As Gerber (1998) has suggested, initiative proponents sometimes have goals other than passing legislation. For instance, although all initiative elites would like to experience legislative success in the long run, they varied on how much they were willing to compromise their principles to achieve that success. Zealots, for instance, would not compromise their policy values at all to ensure political and judicial victory. Given the choice between scaling back a policy preference or increasing the likelihood of judicial nullification, a zealot would choose the latter. Lawyers and politicians were more willing to scale back goals, and compromise their values to protect their initiative from judicial nullification. In some cases, elites were willing to take incremental steps to achieve their ultimate policy preference. Professionals, who have the resources to be repeat players, often adopted this strategy. Victims, however, feeling they only had one shot at making a difference to "protect" society from the same events they had experienced, took an "all or nothing" approach. Therefore, by examining participants in the initiative process based on how willing they were to subjugate their values and how willing they were to limit the scope of their legislation in exchange for actual success, helped define the classification of the initiative elite.

The second criterion focused on why they were opting to use the initiative system at all. The initiative process is complicated, expensive and offers multiple opportunities for failure (Tolbert, Lowenstein and Donovan, 1998). Therefore, understanding why elites would decide to enter a convoluted system provides insight into their strategies. To be clear, all initiative elites use the initiative system because the more traditional legislative system does not offer access— either they cannot get elected or they cannot get the legislature to consider their policy ideas. However, the legislative arena is closed to initiative activists for a variety of different reasons. Professionals, for instance, tend to have strong libertarian ideologies. It is difficult to challenge government power from within traditional government institutions. For example, legislators rarely want to impose upon themselves such policies as term limits or campaign finance limitations. Zealots, however, have ideas so far outside the mainstream that powerful interest groups can prevent their ideas from ever making it out of committee. Politicians have access to the legislative arena, but become frustrated over the ability of committees and governors to influence, change, and block their legislation. Lawyers tend to be involved in politics, but only at the fringe. Initiatives allow them to become involved without having to run for office. Amateurs see the initiative process as offering immediate and easy access to politics. Victims tend to view the initiative process as an institution of last resort. Only after being rebuffed by what they view as unresponsive legislatures do they venture into the realm of direct democracy.

Focusing on these two criteria, it was possible to classify all the initiative elites who were interviewed. However, the individual characteristics of elites are changeable over time. It is possible for elites to move from category to category as their skills, experiences and attitudes change. Amateurs sometimes out of frustration become zealots. Or, some develop political skills and become professionals. Zealots also have a tendency to become professionals. As repeat players they develop organizations and learn from past technical mistakes. Lawyers sometimes go on to become politicians and politicians sometimes leave office and return to practice law. Either way, they bring their past experiences with them. Because victims are typically single-shot players they are the least likely to transform.

Interview subjects were classified based on their characteristics at the time of the interview. If the interview data indicated the subject was a professional or a zealot *at the time of the interview*, he/she was recorded as a professional or zealot. However, in some cases professionals or zealots may have first entered the initiative arena as amateurs. They may have told stories representative of how amateurs behave and develop their strategy. Therefore, when developing composites of amateurs (or other classifications), such anecdotes were used to paint a picture of how amateurs work, even if that interview subject may not have ultimately ended up classified as an amateur.

The Zealot

The zealot is someone who is very passionate about his or her initiative's topic. Zealots are unwilling to compromise, even if compromise leads to a scaled back level of success. Zealots see compromise as capitulation. They would rather be "right" and lose, than compromise and win. Given this mindset, the zealot is not interested in incremental victories.

For the zealot, passionate views go beyond hyperbolic political speech. The zealot is sometimes willing to go to jail or face public embarrassment for the cause. Several initiative zealots spent time in jail as a result of their advocacy. One zealot chained himself to a nuclear power plant. Another spent 42 days in jail in order to gain publicity for a judicial reform initiative. In one of the more interesting cases, an initiative drafter brought petition sheets to his daughter's wedding. He noted, "What better wedding gift could I give to my daughter than a corruption-free political system (Interview # 85)?" Zealots come from all segments of the political spectrum. Religious zealots are common. However, so are Libertarian zealots. And just as common are liberal zealots, focusing on environmental issues or campaign finance reform.

Initiative elites who participate in abortion battles are commonly zealots. Ballot measures that are overly restrictive with respect to abortion rights are typically defeated at the polls or overturned in the courts.[1] More moderate pro-life activists, who use the initiative process as their vehicle for policy, have introduced into their initiatives "exception" clauses. Most common of these exceptions is to waive the abortion restrictions if the health of the mother is in danger. However, the zealot sees such language as compromise and capitulation. Consider the excerpts from internal email documents of a western pro-life organization. At the time these two emails were written, the organization was involved in a debate with other pro-life activists as to what the specific language of their initiative should be.

> I know that some states have "consent" and "regulations" laws. That's a shame, because they frame the issue wrong. The Declaration of Independence, America's "birth certificate" and statement of its raison d'etre, says that all men [human beings] have an "unalienable" right to life. The "consent" and "regulations" approaches ignore the absolute "right to life" saying instead that some people may kill others if the victims' grandparents "consent" to the killing or if the death chamber is clean and the killers are licensed.

The email below went to the entire board of the same organization. The issue was, again, whether to support moderating language for an abortion restricting initiative.

> Dang it! This is like the well-intentioned arguments *that give away the principle* [emphasis added]. You know, the efforts that argue "let's reverse *Roe v. Wade*," "lets make someone consent to the killing," "lets [*sic*] license the killers," etc. NO, NO, NO!!! A "privilege" is something that is given to someone BEYOND HIS OR HER RIGHT. A "benefit" is also something done—as a gift—for someone. But implantation is the nature, god-given DESTINY—the natural RIGHT—of an embryo.

Zealots are commonly motivated by religious fervor (Luker, 1984). Initiative zealots proved to be no different. An interview with an Oregon initiative drafter revealed that he felt the best way to prevent abortion was to pass an initiative that would instill "God" as the highest sovereign power in the Oregon Constitution. Understandably, he met with little success. When asked about the possibility of an incremental or more moderate approach, he commented,

> I am not willing to compromise. I get nothing out of it. In fact, I feel nothing but regret for supporting Measure 8.[2] Abortion is like slavery. The abolitionists refused to compromise. They were defeated many times but eventually they won. I model myself after William Wilberforce (Interview # 94).[3]

Zealots motivated by religious concerns often find themselves boxed into a policy preference that is not amendable. In their view, to compromise on issues such as homosexual rights, abortion or doctor-assisted suicide is to fall short of what the Bible calls for. As one initiative drafter put it, "you do not bargain with God (Interview # 91)."

It is also common to find zealots who are, in addition to being initiative drafters, members of the Libertarian Party. However, the libertarian zealot is typically more focused on initiatives that limit the power and scope of government. Their favorite initiatives are tax-limitation initiatives, term limit initiatives and the occasional marijuana legalization initiative.

The libertarian zealot has much in common with the religious zealot. The religious zealot pursues initiatives that have little chance of passing, but they persevere on the notion of "principle." Libertarian zealots also pursue initiatives that have little chance of passing. Some examples include: an initiative giving citizens the right to bring grand jury charges through a petition, thus limiting the power of the district attorney; an initiative limiting the number of words that can appear in the Colorado Revised Statutes; and an initiative legalizing the sale and distribution of marijuana. Like the religious zealot, the libertarian zealot rarely expects his initiative to pass, but also rarely cares. It is common to find libertarians engaged in the initiative process in order to make a political statement, or send a political message to state representatives, rather than to actually change public policy in the short run.

Zealots do not only come from the conservative side of the political spectrum. Liberal initiative advocates also have their zealots. Liberal zealots typically pursue issues such as campaign finance reform, environmental regulations, or labor rights issues. As an example, proposed Oregon Measure 85 seeks to grant state authorities the power to make binding the United Nations Universal Declaration of Human Rights to corporations. The initiative would require adherence to the UN document's principles in order to conduct civic or commercial business in Oregon. Non-compliance would result in corporate charter revocation. Despite the body of Supreme Court case law that suggests this legislation is unconstitutional,[4] the Oregon Human Rights Initiative expended resources and time to pursue this initiative. While at first glance it may not seem rational to pursue an initiative that has no chance of being upheld, only after understanding the zealot-like nature of the organization does this strategy make sense. While sitting in on a public meeting with the drafters of this bill, an audience member asked them if the initiative could survive court challenge if it were to be passed by the voters. One of the drafters responded,

> We'll get juice if we just make the ballot. If we lose [in court] we don't have these rights. If we don't have these rights then someone has to tell us why. One way or another, it will start a national conversation. And if we do lose, we'll re-file the next day (Interview #98).

It is clear from the dialogue above that the leaders of Oregon Human Rights Initiative are more interested in sending a message and creating debate than actually implementing policy.

Being a zealot does not mean one is politically unsophisticated. Many zealots are well-financed, savvy politicians. Because zealots rarely give up, zealots are oftentimes "repeat players."[5] As such, they have learned the initiative "game" better than most. They also tend to have tight networks of fellow zealots to support them. These networks have the ability to raise money, get signatures, and lead political events.

Zealots, despite having a hyper-focused political outlook, sometimes have a high level of political knowledge and sophistication. It is common to encounter zealots that can cite state and national case law off the top of their heads. They understand complicated constitutional and legal concepts such as originalism,[6] strict scrutiny,[7] and the difference between organic and statutory law.[8] And, they typically have a strong understanding of the historical forces that shape their political issue. In fact, it is because they are so passionate about their issues that they are also so knowledgeable. However, their knowledge of politics and history do not translate into court victories. Court victories require that initiatives adhere to current law. Zealots typically use the initiative system to challenge current law. As a result, zealots understand the legal and historical forces surrounding their issue, but are so adamant about normative aspects of the issue, that they fail to translate their knowledge into political success. Given their commitment and understanding of initiative procedures, zealots have some success qualifying measures for the ballot, and sometimes, even passing the legislation. However, because of their resistance to change the content of their measures to insulate them from constitutional challenge, rarely will a zealot see his ballot success translate into permanent policy success. Few zealots were able to navigate the initiative process successfully and withstand judicial challenge. The zealot with the most notable success was Doug Bruce of Colorado who passed the Taxpayers Bill of Rights (TABOR) in 1988. The measure required a public vote on all legislatively passed tax increases.[9]

The Amateur

The amateur is not politically experienced and rarely politically savvy. Amateurs are typically first time entrants into the political arena. Most amateurs have other full time jobs. Of the amateurs interviewed, there was a doctor, two teachers, an accountant, a high-tech CEO, and a union advocate. Amateurs are typically drawn into the process because they are angry with a specific policy issue or develop a "crusade mentality." They turn to the initiative system after being frustrated by a lack of access to traditional institutional outlets, or as an alternative to going through the lengthy process of lobbying the legislature or running for the legislature themselves. Unlike zealots, amateurs do not have a grasp of the initiative process' rules. Therefore, their intensity does not translate into a fervent study of legal doctrines or bureaucratic idiosyncrasies of the initiative process.

The initiative process provides to amateurs immediate access to the political system. It is often the rush to action that causes amateurs to miss the important details necessary to succeed in the initiative process.

Amateurs have little or no understanding of the legal issues surrounding the initiative process. This includes concerns such as signature gathering requirements, single subject and separate vote requirements, the differences between statutory and constitutional initiatives, and most importantly, an understanding of post election procedures concerning ballot challenges. In addition, they rarely have an understanding of the politics surrounding the initiative process. They typically fail to discuss their initiative with interested political groups and are caught unaware when they are confronted with intense political opposition.

As an example, a pair of initiative drafters seeking to reform the Oregon campaign finance system successfully passed a reform initiative that limited contributions. It was struck down immediately by the Oregon Supreme Court as violating the Oregon Constitution. Questioned as to why they didn't write the bill as a constitutional amendment rather than a statutory initiative, they responded, "We just didn't really think of that. It was one of our first initiatives and we weren't clear about the differences. But we sure changed it the next time (Interview # 85)." In a separate campaign finance initiative, the drafter was unable to appeal his district court loss to the circuit court because he did not sign on as an official intervener in the case. When asked why he did not qualify himself as an intervener, he simply confessed, "I was very ignorant. I didn't know how the system worked. I should have talked to a lawyer first (Interview # 87)."

Amateurs rarely have an understanding of the legal issues surrounding their initiative. They typically write their initiatives without giving thought to any existing national or state constitutional legal precedents. Furthermore, they almost never consider how their initiative will affect other parts of the state constitution or existing body of law. Many times, an amateur will write an initiative that is short and appears very simple but on closer examination, actually affects hundreds of existing statutes.

An excellent illustration of amateurism comes from an initiative drafter seeking to legalize the sale of marijuana. Consider the following interview segment (Interview # 97):

> Author: Are you worried federal law will preempt your initiative if it passes?
> Drafter: No. Oregon is a brave state.
> Author: Have you looked at the federal case law to make sure your initiative is compatible?
> Drafter: Oh. Wow. Is that something I should do?
> Author: Have you read *United States v. Cannabis Cultivators Club?*[10]
> Drafter: No, but I guess I should. Do you think it's going to give us problems?

Amateurs often think that initiatives are automatically constitutional because they pass as constitutional amendments. They fail to understand that initiatives may be challenged along procedural as well as content grounds. As one activist put it, "If it's in the Constitution, it must be constitutional (Interview #57)." Similarly, "It doesn't matter what the lawyers say, because if I win, it's automatically legal (Interview # 51)." Unfortunately (for the activists), these beliefs are incorrect. Even constitutional amendments may be declared unconstitutional if they violate constitutional procedural requirements.

It is common for amateurs to make simple and technical errors. This is usually the result of failing to get appropriate legal and content review of the initiative. The extent of legal review for most amateurs is to get a friend or a family member who is a lawyer to look at the initiative. Most of the time, the lawyer does not specialize in the field of law that the initiative requires.

However, amateurs can have money. Some amateurs are wealthy people who want to "buy" a policy. Some have special financial circumstances that allow them to support the cost of a campaign. There are plenty of examples. Gordon Miller, an Oregon doctor, financed four initiatives with his own money. Helen Hill, who supported an open adoption initiative, used inheritance money to back her initiative. Mike Reynolds, the chief petitioner of California's "three-strikes" initiative used his retirement account to pay. Other amateurs are independently wealthy. Examples include Tim Draper, who backed a voucher initiative in California, or Ron Unz, who passed an initiative banning bilingual education in California.[11]

The Lawyer

It is increasingly common to see lawyers as the primary drafters of initiatives.[12] As the initiative process becomes more fraught with legal challenges and the courts are more strictly enforcing procedural rules, lawyers are increasingly naturally suited to be initiative proponents. Their knowledge and skill in the legal profession helps them anticipate potential challenges and avoid some of the simplistic procedural errors that amateurs will make. Typically, lawyers are gradually drawn into the initiative system along one of two paths. In the first path, they start as consultants for other initiative elites. Eventually they get drawn into a controversy due to a client, and then adopt the issue as their own. Often, they become partners with an initiative drafter. The "lawyer and zealot" team was the most common pairing of initiative elites in the data set.

In the second path, lawyers are already activists on their own. They are deeply involved in politics, having either run for or held elective office. The initiative process provides an opportunity to stay involved in politics after leaving office, or provides access to politics after failing to achieve elective office. As an example, Terry Considine, who helped lead the term limits movement in Colorado, began his career in politics in the Colorado Legislature. After leaving the legislature, he remained active in politics via the initiative process. Conversely, Ron Natelson, a Montana anti-tax activist, started his career as a law professor followed by an unsuccessful run for governor. Afterwards, he pursued CI-75 an attempt to require public votes on all tax increases.

Although this subset of the typology is labeled "lawyer," the reference is more an indication of their worldview than their profession. The label comes from the fact that this group of initiative drafters is very concerned about the legality of their initiative. They are very concerned about technicalities, the likelihood of judicial nullification, and focus on how "defendable" an initiative will be. There are individuals in this subset, particularly law and social science professors, who are not lawyers. But because so many of the interviewees who had these characteristics were lawyers, that became the label for this subset.

Lawyers are more aware of the legal problems that initiatives face. When working with a group, they tend to be the "voice of reason" in the drafting stage. As such, they are much more likely to compromise. Coming from a legal background, the lawyer adopts the attitude that "it is better to get some of what you want than nothing at all." Like a figurative "catcher in the rye," the lawyer deflects many of the demands coalition members have for inclusion into an initiative, and in essence, prevents or attempts to prevent an initiative from going over the "constitutional cliff."

As Mansbridge (1986) shows, "institutional maintenance" is a concern of any coalition. When coalitions become too diverse they are pulled in too many directions to maintain an effective focus. Within initiative coalitions, at times it is the "lawyer" drafter that will eject members from the coalition of initiative elites in order to protect the legality of an initiative. An initiative experience that highlights this phenomenon is Oregon's Death with Dignity Act. Originally drafted as Measure 16, there were several interested groups involved in the early drafting stages. One of the involved groups was the Hemlock Society. The Hemlock Society wanted to push Measure 16 to include the right to euthanasia. A lead lawyer involved with Measure 16 knew these provisions would drag the initiative across the unconstitutional threshold. As a legal move more than a political move, he ejected the Hemlock Society from the drafting committee to protect the initiative from potentially devastating legal challenges. He commented, "In general I work with very pragmatic people, but sometimes you have to tear an issue away from the radicals. That's what we did with Measure 16. The radicals [the Hemlock Society] had the issue, and we tore it away from them (Interview # 84)."

However, being a lawyer does not ensure success in post election initiative court battles. Many initiative activists who have legal experience still suffer judicial nullification of their initiatives.

The Professional

Professionals are initiative elites who have developed an institutional structure to better navigate the initiative process. Included in the institutional structure are any combination of professional signature gatherers, pollsters, legal counsel, fundraising mechanisms, and central offices. Most often, but not always, professionals make a living with the initiative process.[13] People like Oregon's Bill Sizemore or Washington's Tim Eyman are well known initiative professionals who make a living out of the initiative process.[14] In contrast, there are professionals such as California's Ward Connerly, Lewis Uhler, and Ted Costa who have institutional structures to work with but do not make their living with the initiative process.[15] Sometimes, the professional does not have his own organization, but is closely tied to some other type of institutional structure such as a PAC, an ideological organization, or a non-profit advocacy group.

Professionals are repeat players. They have the time, the motivation, and the money to participate in every election cycle, if they so choose. This fact helps and hurts the professional. As repeat players, professionals learn from their mistakes. If the specific wording of an initiative causes judicial nullification, the professional has the resources to submit the same initiative with minor changes in the next election cycle. They also have the benefit of experience. They learn how certain judges rule, how Attorneys general behave, and how to react to new procedural rulings by the courts.

Professionals also have some disadvantages. They can collect a lot of "political baggage." Because they are repeat players, voters and activists can identify their names as information cues regarding the content and ideological leaning of the initiatives. This allows opponents of initiatives to attack the person drafting the initiative rather than the content of the initiative. Oftentimes a professional will ask a lesser-known person to act as the chief petitioner to avoid attracting negative publicity (Interview # 92).

Contrary to what some might expect, professionals still suffer ballot measure nullification. Some explanation for these numbers can be found in the fact that many professionals are also zealots, or at least they have some zealot characteristics. Many professionals have an ideological agenda. As repeat players with resources, they gain the institutional knowledge to avoid *procedural* challenges. But at the same time, they maintain an ideological bent that leads to successful court challenges of the *content*. An excellent example would be Oregon's Lon Mabon. Mr. Mabon runs the Oregon Citizen Alliance (OCA). The OCA has all the institutional advantages to ensure that their initiatives will make the ballot. But because the OCA pursues issues such as limiting homosexual rights and stopping abortion, they still have a very high nullification rate.

To understand this apparent political recalcitrance, it helps to understand the mindset of professional initiative elites. Many times, professionals have been failures at other endeavors, especially in business, or have been "little fish in a big pond." After passing a statewide initiative, they suddenly find themselves the center of media and political attention. After a taste of success or popularity, they decide to engage in the initiative process full time. The sudden jump from obscurity to being a statewide (sometimes national) figure has an effect upon their ego. Some professionals find themselves running a successful organization for the first time. Powerful politicians want to speak to them. The attention they receive leads them to see themselves as significant players in the political area, on equal terms with the legislature or the governor (Interview # 101). Subsequently, they are less inclined to compromise with the content of their initiatives.

Therefore, when professionals have their initiatives nullified by the courts, they also tend to take it more personally. They begin to view legislators, the courts, and political opponents as being personal enemies (Interview # 30, 91, 92,

93). The escalation of bitterness results in continued determination to pursue their agenda even after repeated defeats. Of course this leads to a cyclical escalation. The more initiatives they write, the more that are nullified. The more nullifications lead to greater resentment and more initiatives. In frustration, professionals will sometimes begin to use the initiative process as a tool to attack other institutions or political enemies. As one drafter put it, "If they strike down Measure 7, it's war. We're going to go after the judges with everything we've got. We found out he let a child molester go on a technicality. We're going to use that against him (Interview # 92)"

The Politician

Initiatives are seen as a tool for political outsiders (McCuan, 1998). People who can't get access to the established political institutions will resort to the initiative process. Of the 45 initiative elites interviewed, all 45 indicated they use the initiative process because they cannot get access to the legislature, or because the legislature has been non-responsive to their desires. Given this data, one would not expect sitting politicians, people who have the most access to the legislature, to be initiative drafters. However, this is not the case.

The legislative process is encumbered with many "minority vetoes."[16] Powerful committee chairs can pigeonhole bills. Intense minority factions can filibuster bills. Governors can veto bills. The initiative process offers an appealing outlet to frustrated legislators. The initiative process has no "minority vetoes" other than the court system. Governors cannot veto an initiative. Powerful committee chairs cannot remove an initiative from the docket. And with the initiative process, an apathetic 51% of voters always defeats an intense 49% of voters.

Given the different rules direct democracy offers, politicians use the initiative process to pass legislation. They are not interested in symbolic gestures, or sending political messages. As legislators, they already have the ability to do these things. Because policy creation is their primary goal, they are willing to modify bills to ensure legality. However, they are less likely to amend bills for political reasons. The reason they use the initiative process is to avoid all the compromises they are typically required to accept in the legislative process.

Because the initiative process has only one minority veto (the courts), politicians are very active in the initiative process. Politicians who directly participate in the initiative process have one of four goals.[17] They use the initiative process to disentangle themselves from the complexities of legislative politics, avoid gubernatorial vetoes, set the statewide political agenda, and increase their political name recognition throughout their state.

One reason they become involved is because they are frustrated with their own legislature, which they feel is non-responsive to an issue of personal importance. A good example is Doris Allen, who was a member of the California Legislature. After years of unsuccessfully trying to get an anti-gillnetting bill passed through the legislature, she drafted an initiative, and on the second try was successful.

Politicians also draft initiatives to avoid gubernatorial vetoes. According to Henkels (1999) the number of legislative initiative referrals goes up when different parties control a state's governorship and legislature. Henkels concludes that the main reason for this jump is because frustrated legislators see the initiative process as a way to sidestep governors.

The third reason politicians get involved in the initiative process is because it allows them to set the agenda. It is already established that the ability to set the agenda strongly affects the ability to set policy (Riker, 1980). Representative Kevin Mannix of Oregon provides an excellent example. After failing to pass his victims' rights bills in the Oregon Legislature, he successfully used the initiative process to achieve his political goals. When asked why he, a legislator, would need the initiative system, he responded:

> I have been an extremely successful legislator—sponsoring or co-sponsoring 135 bills that were signed into law. I know how to get bills through the process. However, in other instances as an individual legislator, I could not always overcome special interests (in this case the trial lawyers). I used the initiative process exactly as it is intended: as an escape clause. I did so with Measure 11, Measure 17 and Measure 40.

Representative Mannix understood he had the popular support to pass his legislation. However, in the context of the legislative process, he did not have the ability to control the agenda. Lacking the opportunity to get a vote on his legislation, the popular support for the bill became meaningless. However, the initiative process allowed Mannix to set his own agenda. The initiative process guaranteed him a yes or no vote on his proposals.

And finally, a successfully passed initiative increases a politician's visibility and thus their chances for higher office. Of the ten initiative elites that were classified as politicians, five went on to run for higher office. In fact, Representative Mannix ran for the Oregon governorship in 2002, narrowly losing to Ted Koolengoski, the Oregon Supreme Court Justice that sided with the majority that invalidated many of his initiatives.

The Victim

The victim initiative elite drafts initiatives to "take on the system." They view the state as unresponsive to their plight and use the initiative process to "go over their heads." Victims usually draft anti-crime initiatives. Typically, they or some close member of the family have been a victim of a crime or governmental injustice. Victims use the initiative process to right the wrong and are often seen as sympathetic characters.

The best examples of victims are Mike Reynolds and Collene Campbell, both from California. In both cases, these initiative drafters had close family members killed in violent crimes. Reynolds went on to successfully pass Proposition 184, California's "three-strikes" bill. Campbell paired up with two state politicians to draft and pass Proposition 115, a "victims' rights" bill.

Victims have many of the same characteristics as the amateur and the zealot. However, they merit their own classification. Like zealots, they are passionate about their issue but they are not blind to the practicalities of the law. Victims are not interested in just sending a message like a zealot. The victim initiative drafter does care whether their initiative becomes law. They are willing to compromise in order to maintain its legality.

In addition, victims differ from amateurs in the sense that victims are aware they are unqualified to draft legislation. The victim will find qualified people to work with. What truly differentiates the victim from the amateur and the zealot is that their passion is tightly focused on making noticeable change. Therefore, they are not interested in wasting resources to lash out at the system, like a zealot. And they are not willing to waste resources on their own incompetence, like an amateur. Because victims usually see themselves as fighting for someone else (a lost loved one, for example), they are driven to get results. For a victim, nothing is accomplished if the law is not upheld in the courts.

The victim initiative drafter is rare. Only four interview subjects were classified as victims. However, at the time of writing, none of their initiatives had been completely nullified. Some had faced partial nullification of subsections of the initiative, but in general, the majority of their original legislation was still in effect.

Combinations and Causal Relationships

Not every initiative elite fits neatly into one of the six defined categories. Many can have overlapping characteristics from several classifications. For example, many politicians are also lawyers. Many amateurs and professionals have some characteristics of the zealot. The victim is usually new to the initiative process and has many of the flaws of an amateur.

It is also important to note that very few initiative elites work alone. Individuals may fall into one of the six categories, but groups that form to draft initiatives may have representatives from many or all classifications. This can have a variety of effects on initiative drafting. Zealots and lawyers tend to pull groups in different directions. Amateurs that finance professionals sometimes make demands that are politically or legally untenable. As discussed further in Chapter 6, an examination of the initiative drafting coalition provides significant insight into why some initiatives fail to survive court challenges.

It is important to note that the above typology was not developed as a way of providing a causal relationship. That is, I am not arguing that the typology represents variation in an independent variable and that some types of initiative elites have their measures nullified while others do not. Instead, the typology suggests that different types of initiative elites have their measures struck down by the courts for different reasons. Both amateurs and zealots have limited success with the courts but the reasons for their failures differ. By offering a glimpse into the mindset of various initiative elites, one can see the various reasons why they suffer such high rates of judicial nullification. Subsequent chapters explain how the behavioral characteristics identified here commingle with institutional aspects of the initiative system and contribute to high levels of nullification.

---

[1] See *Hern, et al. v. Beye*, 57 F.3d 906 (10th Cir., 1995) overturning Colorado's Measure 3 (1984) and *Planned Parenthood v. Owens*, et al., 287 F.3d 910 (10th Cir., 2002) overturning Colorado's Measure 12. Measure 3 denied public funds for abortions, and Measure 12 required parental notification prior to abortions.

[2] Measure 8 was a more moderate attempt to restrict abortion in Oregon.

[3] A 19th century English abolitionist.

[4] See *Crosby v. National Foreign Trade Council* (2000) at US 120, S.Ct L.Ed 2d.

[5] Both Robert Axelrod and Marc Galanter have explored the behavior of repeat players. Axelrod (1984) concludes repeat players develop the ability to cooperate despite a lack of coordinating mechanisms. Galanter (1974) suggests that repeat players have the ability to influence the way rules are created so that the rules become advantageous to repeat players.

[6] The belief that judges should rule based on the original intent of the Constitution's drafters.

[7] The doctrine that some types of government classifications (race and sex) must meet a higher standard of justification or "state interest" than other classifications (age and disability).

[8] Organic law is constitutional law, or law about how to make statutory law. Statutory law is less permanent. It is easy to change and simply reflects the current preferences of the legislature. In speaking with one initiative drafter I classified as a zealot, I asked him why he did not pursue his initiative as a constitutional amendment instead of a statutory amendment. I asked because he had successfully passed his initiative only to have it altered by the state legislature. He responded that he felt his initiative was a statute, and did not rise to the level of constitutional change. As a result, it was not appropriate to embed in the constitutional fabric of the state.

[9] There was some luck to Bruce's success. The bill was passed before Colorado voters amended their constitution barring initiatives that contained multiple subjects. If the amendment had been in effect in 1988, the courts would have nullified Bruce's initiative.

[10] *US v. Cannabis Cultivators Club*, 5 F.Supp. 2d 1086, 100 (1998) made it clear that, "a state law which purports to legalize the distribution of marijuana for any purpose, even a laudable one, nonetheless directly conflicts with federal law, 21 U.S.C. 841(a)."

[11] Being an "amateur" in one's initial initiative campaign does not mean an initiative drafter will stay an amateur. I list Ron Unz here as an example of an amateur based upon his first initiative campaign. However, in subsequent campaigns, Ron Unz had more characteristics of a professional.

[12] I include law professors in this classification.

[13] Because professionals engage in the initiative process for a living, they sometimes work for other initiative drafters. However, professionals maintain an ideological slant. If the initiative is close to their philosophy, or at least does not conflict with their values, they will work for other initiative elites.

[14] Bill Sizemore runs an organization called Oregon Taxpayers United and Tim Eyman runs an organization called Permanent Offense.

[15] Ward Connerly has an organization called America's Civil Rights Institute, Lewis Uhler runs the National Tax Limitation Committee, and Ted Costa directs The People's Advocate. However, none derives their income from these organizations.

[16] Robert Dahl provides an extensive description and explanation of minority vetoes in his seminal work, *A Preface to Democratic Theory* (1956). In a more recent work, George Tsebelis (2002) argues that the only difference between political systems is how the system distributes minority vetoes to interested political actors.

[17] By "directly participate" I mean that they actually draft and submit initiatives. Many politicians become tangentially involved in the initiative process by actively supporting or opposing initiatives via their campaigns for election or non-election media campaigns.

Chapter Four

Initiative Elites and Institutional Learning

Can institutions learn? That is, can they adapt to changing environments? Can they alter strategies to increase the likelihood of victory over other institutions? Can they attack other institutions? Can an institution defend itself from other hostile institutions? Typically, one associates the concept of "learning" with humans, not impersonal institutions. However, there is considerable evidence to suggest that institutions can adapt to fluctuating circumstances. Taking special care not to reify institutions, it is important to understand how institutional learning, or a lack of it, can affect the competitive relationship between courts and initiative activists.

Before engaging the question of how courts and initiative activists "learn" it may be helpful to examine how institutions, in general, "behave" in a multi-institutional, competitive environment. Previous research, which falls under the general heading of "the positive theory of institutions" (PTI) sheds light on how institutions adapt to one another.

Institutional Theories of Competition

One aspect of the positive theory of institutions suggests that institutions react to other institutions' actions. More accurately, individuals within institutions, working in the context of some aggregation rule (voting, for example), act to prevent the encroachments of other individuals acting within an institutional setting. Some political analysts refer to this as the "political systems" or "separation of powers" approach to PTI (Clayton, 1999; Ferejohn and Shipan, 1990; Gely and Spiller, 1990). The general argument is relatively Madisonian in nature. The theory argues that institutions strategically react to one another in order to maximize institutional autonomy. When one institution intends to encroach upon the powers of another, the theory predicts that the first institution will react to countermand such an encroachment. However, institutions are not necessarily engaged in a zero-sum game over finite political resources. Instead, it suggests that institutions, or individuals acting within institutions, adopt strategies based on current institutional relationships. When those relationships change, we expect the strategies to also change. For example, if the Supreme Court continually strikes down Congressional enactments, PTI theory suggests that we will observe actions in Congress either to restrict the Court's power or to alter their legislative drafting process in such a manner as to prevent the courts from legitimately nullifying a law. PTI borrows much from rational choice institutionalist models which focus on individual strategic decision making. Institutional models expands differ from individualist models by making institutions the primary unit of analysis (March and Olson, 1984). In the context of PTI institutions serve to constrain behavior, catalyze action, or endow power (McCann, 1999). The models' general outline suggests that individual actors pursue their goals within the constraints set up by political institutions.

Given the theoretical predictions of PTI, coupled with the fact that we have observed consistently high rates of judicial nullification of ballot measures, we should be able to make some predictions about the way initiative elites will behave within their institutional arena. PTI predicts that initiative elites should react in a variety of ways to maximize their own autonomy and limit the autonomy of the courts or other institutions which might seek to limit the ability of initiative elites to pursue their political goals. Specifically, in the context of direct democracy and public law, we should expect to see initiative elites taking steps to reduce initiative invalidation rates. Concurrently, we would also expect courts to assert their independence and limit the role of initiatives that affect public policy. Clearly, the type of interaction anticipated is not a single step process. Each action causes a reaction. In essence, we can safely assume that if the initiative elites do respond to judicial actions, the courts respond to those actions by initiative elites.

PTI, with respect to the courts, notes that individual justices pursue their policy preferences subject to both endogenous and exogenous constraints (Maltzman, Spriggs and Wahlbeck, 1999). For example, justices cannot simply strike down any initiative to which they object. Precedent acts as an internal constraint. With most state courts, reelection pressures act as external constraints (Hall, 1996). PTI effectively models the behavior of initiative elites. Initiative writers' internal institutional constraints include the single subject rule and other constitutional limitations. They are also subject to external constraints such as the values of the voting public and other institutions, especially the courts. Given the model of PTI and two prominent political actors, initiative elites and the courts, we expect both institutional actors to behave in a way that maximizes their political autonomy given the constraints on the other political actor. Assuming a court or individual justice opposes a ballot measure, institutional models predict that courts will strike down initiatives if they can find any previous legal precedents or if they can cite at least a tangential constitutional provision. We can observe such a phenomenon in the form of the courts narrowly interpreting the single subject rule, narrowly interpreting the "amendment vs. revision" clauses of state constitutions, or upholding various strict scrutiny doctrines of citizen enacted laws. In addition, such a model also predicts that the courts will be more hesitant to strike down initiatives that pass with a wide popular majority. On the flip side, we can expect initiative elites to draft initiatives that conform to the narrow precedents set by previous rulings and have the backing of at least a majority of the populace. We might also expect to see initiative elites attempt to undermine the authority of the courts through other avenues. Such actions might occur in the form of increasingly partisan judicial elections, drafting and financing candidate challenges to sitting justices, or seeking to amend the state Constitution in order to allow the initiative process more flexibility. Institutional models also offer insight into why the level of judicial nullification of state ballot measures remains so high. Simply put, success breeds success. Marc Galanter (1983) notes that the courts affect political games "primarily through communication of symbols -- by providing threats, promises, models, persuasion, and so on." Courts have the ability to signal which "players" will be winners and which will be losers. Once the court signals which actors will be losers, those actors will most likely remove themselves from the game. And conversely, once the court identifies winners those political actors will choose to play over and over again. Therefore, because those political actors who seek to overturn ballot initiatives have been so successful in the courts, it is only logical that they will continue to seek that venue to achieve their political goals.

Also to be considered is the institutional catalyst of counter-mobilization. McCann (1999) notes that controversy over judicial decisions can serve as a spark for counter-mobilization efforts of losing groups. Rosenberg (1991) highlights several examples that include the anti-segregation movement, which occurred after *Brown v. Board of Education*, and the pro-life movement, which occurred after *Roe v. Wade*. It is the counter responses of the initiative institution that this book seeks to explain. Assuming for the moment that initiative drafters are sincerely interested in enacting policy, institutional models of political behavior predict that initiative elites will react to the consistently high level of judicial nullification of successful ballot measures. Therefore, if the research shows that counter response is not taking place, then political scientists need to question or refine some of their institutional models. Or, if the research shows that counter response is taking place, but failing to have an overall effect, political scientists need a detailed analysis of how that counter response is occurring and why it is not affecting the final result.

One of the primary concerns of this book is to examine why state ballot measures face an inordinately high rate of judicial nullification. Because courts nullify state and federal statutes far less frequently than ballot measures, two questions are posed: (1) Does initiative elites do not behave according to the dictates of PTI? (2) If initiative elites do, in fact, behave according to the dictates of PTI, then what other factors present in the relationship between the courts and initiative process explain the high rates of nullification? The purpose of this chapter is to argue that the answer to the first question is "yes." Chapters 5 and 6 examine the second question.

Given the theoretical predictions of PTI coupled with the fact that we have observed consistently high rates of judicial nullification of ballot measures, institutional theories suggest that initiative elites will react in a variety of possible ways. At minimum, we should see initiative elites altering their strategies in light of court rulings. But we should also expect to see initiative drafters protecting their own institutional prerogatives and autonomy by proactively limiting the powers of the courts. However, given the fact that the courts reject initiatives so frequently, we might question how accurately PTI explains the behavior of initiative elites. Are there high rates of nullification because initiative elites are not engaged in institutional competition/reaction at the same level as other institutions? Or is there something unique about the interaction of initiative elites and the courts which limits how much insight can be gained by viewing this institutional arrangement through the lens of PTI?

A simplistic approach to explaining high rates of judicial nullification is to blame amateurism. In fact, a lot of amateurs do participate in the initiative process.[1] Because of their inexperience they make simple mistakes that lead to nullification. However, as the typology in Chapter 3 indicates, a large majority of initiative elites are strategically savvy (professionals), legally knowledgeable (lawyers), and/or experienced political actors (politicians). Therefore, we must seek a richer understanding of why initiative elites fail in front of the courts, an understanding that goes beyond simply blaming amateurism. Although I refer to the initiative process as an institution, aspects of the initiative process separate it from more typical institutions. The initiative process, despite having established rules and inter- and intra-institutional procedures, is also a collection of disunited individuals who are often single-shot players. As such, they often fail to appreciate the historical and legal context in which they participate. The main focus of this chapter is to demonstrate that initiative elites, despite suffering from a lack of institutional cohesiveness found in other, more established institutions, are capable strategic actors whose behavior is predictable based on what we know about institutional competition.

The case of Rob Natelson, the Montana activist who successfully passed the tax reform Constitutional Initiative 75, helps refute the simplistic argument that amateurism is the sole cause of ballot measure nullification.

Chapter 1 leaves the story of Mr. Natelson's crusade at the point the Montana Supreme Court invalidates his initiative. However, the story does not end there. Natelson did not give up the fight when the courts overturned his initiative. As institutional theories predict, Natelson took actions to protect the autonomy of the initiative process and to limit the autonomy of the courts. After the court ruling, he became involved in judicial politics. He spoke out and wrote several articles criticizing the court's decision. He also campaigned for one of his former teaching assistants to unseat a sitting justice. Since the ruling, he has been involved in politics, seeking to change the makeup of the Montana Supreme Court.[2]

Second, his organization *Montanans for Better Government* considered pursuing plans to petition for a constitutional convention, sue the Supreme Court justices who ruled against CI-75, and seek a change-of-venue law to get constitutional decisions out of Lewis and Clark County.[3] In 2002, the group drafted (and is currently seeking signatures) for two subsequent constitutional initiatives. According to the Secretary of State:

> Both proposed ballot measures would revise Article XIV, Section 11 of the constitution, which currently requires that voters vote on every constitutional amendment separately. MBG's proposals define 'one amendment' as including 'the entire content of a single constitutional initiative petition or legislative bill proposing constitutional revision.' If the proposed ballot measures pass, voters would be able to amend multiple sections of the constitution with the passage of a single initiative. Both proposals also prohibit the courts from using Section 11 to review the validity of constitutional amendments based on their content or structure. One proposed initiative would become effective upon passage. The other would be retroactive to Jan. 1, 1991.[4]

Natelson's case highlights the fact that theories of institutional competition can accurately predict how initiative elites will behave. In this case we see a sophisticated political actor reacting to previous changes in his political environment, and pursuing actions that protect his autonomy while also restricting the autonomy of his "competitor institution." There are a variety of reasons why the court nullified Natelson's bill, but it is clear that amateurism is not one of them. Natelson, like other initiative elites around the country, is engaged in institutional learning. It is clear from his behavior that he did anticipate the Montana Supreme Court as a strategic actor, and sought to alter the makeup of his initiative based on previous strategic cues set down from the Montana court. And in defeat, he pursued actions that would prevent the same result in the future.

The remainder of this chapter provides further detail and more examples of the types of institutional learning Natelson's case highlights. I look at the three ways institutional theories predict that initiative elites will strategically react to court behavior: reacting to courts' encroachments by altering their strategic behavior, protecting their own institutional autonomy, and seeking to limit the autonomy of the courts.

Reacting to the Encroachments of the Court

This section identifies several ways in which initiative elites react to court rulings which invalidate ballot measures. Their actions include: professionalization of grass-roots organizations, altering the language of measures to meet current legal requirements, incrementalism, using previously upheld legal language, keeping initiatives very short, drafting constitutional amendments rather than statutory initiatives, the development of nonprofits and political action committees (PACs), judicial forum shopping, seeking intervener status when an initiative is challenged, and drafting multiple versions of the same initiative. The behavior noted above is not only manifested in repeat players; single shot players also engage in some of the strategies outlined. In a process of what can be termed "vicarious institutional learning," single shot players often identify the "mistakes" of previous initiatives' campaigns and adapt accordingly.

Professionalization

As part of the interview process, subjects were asked what steps they are taking to prevent future judicial nullification of their ballot measures. The most common response was that they were professionalizing their methods. In the process of examining how initiative elites pursue their agendas, it became very clear that the initiative process is not dominated by the lone activist who writes his measure in isolation. Many repeat players admitted that when first involved in the initiative process they worked in isolation or semi-isolation, without the benefits of more sophisticated political tools. However, most soon realized that in order to successfully navigate the initiative process they needed to hire legal counsel, subject their initiatives to qualified peer review, submit their measures to legislative council, and ensure that signature gathering was conducted in a legal manner. The most obvious cases of professionalization are initiative drafters who build up organizations around their efforts. Men such as Ward Connerly, Bill Sizemore, Tim Eyman and Ron Unz all have sophisticated and well financed organizations that conduct polls, hire legal counsel,[5] have extensive fund raising mechanisms, and have access to a web of professional resources.[6]

However, even the initiative drafter with fewer resources shows signs of professionalization. In one of the more interesting examples, an initiative drafter submitted his measure to ten retired appeals court justices. He asked each justice to act as a "devil's advocate" and pretend to be the lawyer challenging the constitutionality of the bill. To this date, his measure has been challenged multiple times in both state and federal court, each time surviving the challenge.

It is also common for initiative elites to draw from existing professional organizations. Most of the term limit, campaign finance reform, and abortion advocates submitted their initiatives to their national parent organizations or think tanks. Term Limits, Inc., Right to Life, and various think tanks all have permanent legal staffs. The sympathetic national groups were more than willing to provide their services to state level initiative advocates who were pursuing compatible agendas. Although the move to utilize national organizations arose from multiple motivations (fund raising knowledge, political sophistication) the ability to survive legal challenges was a principal reason for doing so. Because national organizations have a history of engaging in legal battles, they can help local elites anticipate expected challenges.

Incrementalism

As explored in Chapter 2, the legislative process is much easier, cheaper, and simpler than the initiative process. As a result, individuals who use the initiative process are usually doing so because they could not get access to traditional lawmaking institutions. Access is denied because they are pursuing agendas that arouse the passionate opposition of people or groups who wield "minority vetoes." Or, they are challenging the authority of the legislature itself. Having been rebuffed in the legislative arena they transfer their resources to the initiative arena. However, often overlooked in this "political natural selection" is the fact that initiative drafters are passing laws that have either been rejected by or never introduced in the legislature. Consequently, this leads to situations where initiative elites are passing measures that have little or no case law indicating what is, or is not, constitutional. Because legislatures will not pass term limits, campaign finance reform, and Indian gaming bills, courts have not had to consider their legality very often. The dearth of constitutional guideposts encourages initiative drafters to adopt a strategy of incrementalism.

Incrementalism is the process of attempting to pass a scaled back version of a similar bill that has been nullified. The term limits movement provides clear insight into the incremental strategy. Beginning in the 1990s, the term limits movement began to sweep the states. Because there was little chance legislatures would enact self-restrictive limits, most term limits bills came about via the initiative process.[7] By 1995, twenty-three states had imposed term limits on federal candidates. However, in *US Term Limits v. Thornton* (1995), all federal term limit bills were declared unconstitutional by the US Supreme Court. In response, many term limit advocates re-entered the battle over term limits with "scarlet letter" initiatives. The scarlet letter bills sought to put the phrase "disregarded voters' instruction on term limits" on the ballots next to the names of

any candidate who didn't vote for term limits in Congress.[8]   These groups
reasoned that if they could not get outright term limits because of the Supreme
Court's ruling, they would achieve de facto term limits through political pressure
imposed by their initiative (Interview # 20, # 41, #81).   Therefore, they
incrementally took a small step back from their initial goal of an outright term
limit.   By drafting a "scarlet letter" initiative they could achieve their political
goals, while avoiding the new constitutional restrictions on outright limits.
However, these initiatives were also struck down by the courts.   So term limit
activists incrementally took another step back.   In 1998, the same term limit
activists, having been twice rebuffed by the courts, attempted a "self limitation"
approach to term limits.   According to the bill, candidates could voluntarily agree
to term limits and then have that information placed on the ballot. Rather than a
"scarlet letter," candidates would be getting a "gold star."   This approach was
taken because the courts had ruled that the scarlet letter bills were pejorative in
nature. The exact language asked,

> Shall there be an amendment to the Colorado Constitution concerning
> term limits declarations that may be voluntarily submitted by candidates
> for the U.S. Congress, and, in connection therewith, specifying when such
> declarations must be submitted to the secretary of state; providing that a
> candidate shall not be refused placement on the ballot if the candidate does
> not submit a declaration; providing that candidates may voluntarily
> declare that the candidate will not serve more than three terms as a U.S.
> Representative or more than two terms as a U.S. Senator or may
> voluntarily declare that the candidate has chosen not to accept term limits.[9]

In this case, the initiative was passed and upheld. It is clear that in a unique
environment with few legal cues to follow, initiative drafters strategically take
minimal steps backwards from their preferred policy position in hopes of avoiding
judicial nullification. Of course, this strategy is most amenable to professionals
who are repeat players. A group needs considerable resources and "institutional
memory" in order to adapt over time and incrementally adjust the scope of an
initiative.   That is not to say only professionals engage in incrementalism.
Lawyers tend to focus intently on the outcome of earlier court battles before

drafting legislation. By examining the rulings of cases that came earlier, they too, can adopt an incremental approach.

This strategy is not unique to term limits activists. Campaign finance reform advocates typically start by passing extremely low contribution limits, but after losing in court, they return with slightly higher levels each time until they are upheld (Interview # 23, #45). Or, as another example, abortion opponents often begin by attempting initiatives that clearly violate *Roe vs. Wade.* But after meeting with defeat in court, drafters return with less obtrusive measures, such as requiring abortion seekers to receive medical information before moving forward with the procedure (Interview # 43).

Initiative activists have a mixed record when it comes to scaled back versions of term limit restrictions, campaign finance initiatives, and abortion laws. Many of the second attempts are also struck down by federal and state courts.[10] However, the immediate point is not to identify the reasons why these particular initiatives are struck, but to show that initiative elites are indeed strategic players who behave according to the predictions of PTI theory. As Brace and Langer (2002) show, state supreme courts have "preemptive power" only when other actors have the ability to interpret and respond to the earlier signals the courts have sent. The evidence suggests that initiative elites qualify as such actors.[11]

Using Existing Legal Language

One of the most common reasons an initiative is struck down is that the courts identify specific legal language that violates some procedural principle. The statement seems almost tautological. However, leaving out seemingly insignificant single words from an initiative can lead to nullification. For example, leaving out words such as "notwithstanding section xx," or "subject to" can doom an initiative upon legal challenge. Failing to provide necessary exceptions for extreme cases,[12] or failing to provide specific definitions of terms used, can open the doors for courts to nullify entire initiatives (Interview #84, # 92).

In addition, some initiative drafters use language that fails to meet constitutional requirements. Miller (2001) shows that many initiatives run afoul of the 1st and 14th amendments, the Supremacy Clause and other federal civil rights laws. He also shows that initiatives are equally likely to come up against state constitutional provisions. One way that initiative elites are adapting to this problem is to adopt language from other laws, especially laws that have already survived legal challenge.

An enlightening example of such behavior involves the case of the initiative to ban the teaching of homosexuality in the schools. The bill sought to regulate any teaching that "would express approval of, promote, or warrant the behaviors of homosexuality or bisexuality." Not surprisingly, this bill was strongly opposed by teachers' unions and other teacher professional organizations. Therefore, it came as a surprise that the enforcement of the bill, if it had passed, would have been delegated to the state Board of Education—the very people who opposed the passage of the bill. I asked the initiative drafter why he chose that specific enforcement language. It turns out the language he adopted came word for word from a bill the ACLU had written with respect to the practice of teaching religion in school. The initiative drafter informed me that the reason he chose such language was that the ACLU was one of the more vocal opponents of his initiative. By using their language, if they challenged the bill they would in essence be challenging their own law (Interview #91).

As another example, initiative elites who were intimately involved with the drafting of California's Proposition 209, which sought to eliminate affirmative action in California's public colleges, were acutely aware of possible legal challenges. When questioned about the possibility of legal challenges, they pointed out that they had co-opted language from the 1964 Civil Rights Act (Interview # 22). This landmark civil rights legislation had been upheld in the Supreme Court a number of times. Thus, they were employing the same logic as the initiative elites seeking to ban the teaching of homosexuality in public schools. If someone were to successfully challenge Proposition 209, they would also be throwing into doubt the constitutionality of a 40-year-old civil rights bill.

In this case the strategy worked. The Ninth Circuit Court of Appeals, the most liberal of courts, upheld the initiative.

In all, 12 of the 45 subjects who constituted my data set noted that they had adopted pre-existing legally upheld language for inclusion in their initiatives. And in each case, the reason for such a move was to prevent judicial nullification.

Drafting Constitutional Amendments

Initiatives written as statutory law do not have the same staying power as initiatives written as constitutional amendments. A statutory initiative can be overturned by a simple majority vote of the state legislature (Waters, 2001). It can also be nullified if it conflicts with the state's constitution on procedural or content grounds. Constitutional amendments avoid two of those pitfalls because they are only subject to constitutional procedural restrictions. This fact has led many initiative drafters to stop pursuing statutory initiatives.

Constitutional amendments require more signatures and therefore more money. However, to many initiative drafters, the benefits of passing a constitutional amendment outweigh the marginally higher costs of acquiring a few thousand more signatures. In many cases, initiative activists are using the initiative process because the state legislature is adamantly opposed to their agenda. Therefore, pursuing statutory initiatives becomes almost self-defeating. They face a situation of spending hundreds of thousands of dollars and months of time to pass a bill that can be overturned by the legislature in a day. Consider the following comment:

> These are the very people [the legislature] that I'm going up against. If I'm going to go to all the work and expense to pass an initiative I'm sure not going to dump it back in their lap...furthermore, why should I give anyone two bites at the apple. With a Constitutional bill, they [the legislature] can't touch it (Interview # 60).[13]

More succinctly put by an initiative drafter whose statutory initiative was struck down on state constitutional grounds: "Never again!" (Interview # 85)

The empirical data supports the anecdotal evidence. In reexamining Miller's (2000) data, I compiled statistics measuring the number of constitutional amendment initiatives versus statutory initiatives. Table 5 summarizes data from California and Oregon.[14]

Table 5: Use of Constitutional Initiatives over Time

	1960 – 1999	**2000 - 2002**
	% of Initiatives that were Constitutional Amendments	% of Initiatives that were Constitutional Amendments
California	16/55 (29%)	6/12 (50%)
Oregon	14/42 (33%)	21/33 (63%)

The data clearly shows that initiative drafters have been moving away from drafting reversible statutory initiatives, and instead drafting "safer" constitutional initiatives. In California, we see a 21% increase and in Oregon, we see a 30% increase in the number of constitutional amendments. Despite the fact that constitutional amendments are more expensive and time consuming, initiative elites appear willing to bear that cost in order to insulate their initiatives from the courts and the legislature.[15]

Keeping Initiatives Very Short

Initiative drafters have not always been concerned with keeping their initiatives short. Many of the initiative elites interviewed, who were involved in politics only during the 1980s, said they were never concerned with single subject and separate vote restrictions (Interview # 17, 20, 9). Those veteran initiative elites who are still involved in the process note they only became concerned with such restrictions quite recently. When questioned about the role single subject and separate vote restrictions have upon strategy, the older drafters responded with comments similar to: "We never cared about the single subject law at the time. It was in the Constitution, but it was a dead letter of the law (Interview # 17)." Or, "Well, the damn thing [single subject rule] is construed so broadly now.

Until just recently, the courts never bothered us with this. My new initiative used the case law handed down as a result of Prop 8, but back then we didn't care" (Interview #9).

As Miller (2001) and Tushnet (1996) show, courts either have an "accommodationist" attitude or a "watchdog" attitude.[16] It appears that the accommodationist attitude was more prevalent until the late 1990s. About that time, a series of court decisions were handed down that altered the legal environment for initiative drafters. In California, *Senate v. Jones* (1999) put teeth into the state's single subject rule. In Oregon, *Armatta v. Kitzhaber* (1998) and in Montana, *Marshall v. Cooney* (1999) accomplished the same thing. Lowenstein's (2001) comprehensive examination of single subject rulings throughout the United States concludes that state courts are taking a more aggressive approach to single subject restrictions. He, along with Feeney and Dubois (1998), also notes that the courts are aiming these more restrictive standards at initiatives alone. Older case law not only had a more deferential standard, but held legislative law to the same standard as initiatives. Newer case law only applies the stricter standards to initiatives.[17]

Consistent with what PTI suggests, initiative drafters are reacting accordingly. Anticipating more hostile reviews of initiatives, drafters are limiting the scope of their initiatives, removing enforcement, punishment, and funding clauses, and drafting very short bills. An advocate of an education reform initiative wanted to put a funding clause in the measure, but removed it after *Senate v. Jones* was issued (Interview # 18). An Oregon activist working on a government reform initiative wanted his bill to deal with both civil and criminal penalties. But after the *Armatta* decision, he removed the criminal penalties half of the bill (Interview # 84). Several other activists limited their initiatives to three sentences or less, solely for single subject reasons (Interview # 80, 12, 31).

There is a counter tension that limits how far initiative drafters can take this strategy. As Gerber, et al (2001) has shown, state actors such as elected officials and appointed bureaucrats can "steal the initiative." By "stealing," they mean that other state officials can prevent or limit the implementation of an initiative even if it is upheld in court. The reason is that many initiatives "specify a policy goal without describing how to achieve it (p. 20)," and they fail to identify how to fund it. As a result, other state officials, often officials who opposed the initiative, become responsible for interpreting the law and determining funding and enforcement actions. Thus, initiative drafters are caught in a catch-22. If they provide specific funding and enforcement language they run the risk of violating single subject and separate vote standards. But if they do not provide such language, the intent of the initiative may be thwarted by other political players.

An alternative strategy to writing short initiatives involves breaking up an initiative into several shorter initiatives. Representative Kevin Mannix of Oregon successfully pursued this strategy when he passed Measure 40, a "victims rights" bill, in 1996. The bill implemented a number of changes to the Oregon Constitution. Among the changes were allowing 11-1 jury verdicts of guilty, barring felons from juries, requiring that full sentences be served, and more. The Oregon Supreme Court found Mannix's entire bill unconstitutional when the court manufactured a new "separate vote" requirement in *Armatta*. Undeterred, Mannix resubmitted his measure as seven separate measures in the next election. Of those, four passed.[18] Apparently, word of Mannix's success has spread to other initiative elites. Different activists from other states noted Mannix's strategy in their interviews and implied they were considering adopting his strategy (Interview # 51, 31). There is one obvious limitation to this strategy. It only works if each separate submission stands alone as its own law. The fact that three of Mannix's resubmissions did not pass did not have any effect on the four that did. One Montana activist considered submitting his initiative one sentence at a time (Interview # 31). Of course, all the sentences were interconnected. If only six of the seven sentences passed, he realized all the other sentences/laws would be nonsense. The comments of the Montana activist highlight the two levels at which institutional learning takes place within the initiative process. Clearly, some professional elites learn based on the iterated encounters they have with the process. Others, such as lawyers, learn from the experiences of others. In this specific case, the drafter was learning from a combination of the two. As a repeat player in the Montana initiative process, he had experienced the frustration the separate vote rule causes and had considered many potential remedies. However, he was also willing to learn from the experiences of other elites.

Changes in Judicial Strategies

One of the most significant changes in initiative elite behavior in the past decade is the increased focus on judicial strategies. This became evident after speaking with a number of long-time professional initiative drafters. When the strategies of initiative elites today are compared with those of a decade ago, it becomes apparent that there is more focus on post election judicial challenges now. In the 1980s, the strategic focus of initiative campaigns was to garner a majority vote. This meant initiative backers focused on tailoring their political messages to fashion a majority collation. Today, the focus is as much on potential post-election judicial challenges as on pre-election campaign strategies.[19] This behavior manifests itself in three ways. Initiative elites are "shopping" for sympathetic judges, demanding intervener status as defendants of initiatives, and they are drafting multiple versions of similar initiatives in hopes that opponents will "tip the hand" of their legal strategy.

Surprisingly, many of the initiative proponents that I met who had lost in court were unaware of the tactic of "forum shopping" for friendly judges. The following comments highlight this experience:

> "We were sued by five different groups, including the unions and both political parties. And all five lawsuits ended up in front of [the same judge]. This guy was known as the anti-campaign finance reform judge. It turns out he was the campaign finance reform specialist in this district, so he had the power to collect them all in his docket. We were completely ignorant on this issue. After a three-week trial, the proposition was enjoined. We tried to appeal to the Ninth Circuit. But because our judge never made a ruling, he just enjoined it, the Ninth Circuit wouldn't take our appeal. Our judge just held it for four years (Interview # 23).

This case provides some interesting insight into the ability of initiative drafters to engage in institutional learning. One of the backers of the initiative above was also involved in a subsequent initiative campaign. After a victory at the polls with his new initiative, he was faced with the same situation. Opponents of the measure filed 18 suits with judges they felt would be most sympathetic to their claims. This time, expecting such a move, he responded by filing to consolidate all the suits with the judge most sympathetic to his cause (Interview # 18). In the first example, the initiative was only in effect for three weeks. In the second case, the initiative is still in effect today.

It has also occurred to initiative drafters how important it is to achieve intervener status when an initiative is challenged. Technically, the defendant of any challenged initiative is the state. As soon as an initiative is adopted by the people, it has the force of law. It then becomes the attorney general's responsibility to defend the law. Sometimes this creates a situation where "the fox is watching the chicken coop" (Interview # 11). Obviously, attorneys general, and the governors who appoint them, are intimately involved in state politics. Most of the time, state administrations take public stances on initiatives during elections and actively oppose many of them.[20] This creates the awkward situation where state officials are put in the position of defending laws they actively oppose. Chapter 5 shows how attorneys general often take steps to weaken the state's defense of such initiatives.

As initiatives increasingly end up in court, initiative elites have become aware of the influence attorneys general have over the fate of their initiatives. When speaking with initiative drafters who had met with judicial nullification, I would either ask them what they did differently in subsequent campaigns, or what they would have done differently given the benefit of hindsight. Most often, the response was that they did, or should, have sought intervener status. Comments concerning the behavior of attorneys general defending initiatives ranged from the mild to the more visceral. "They're not as motivated as we [initiative backers] are" (Interview # 81) was one response. A more critical assessment was "He hated Prop 208...he was known as the eviscerator of 208" (Interview # 23). The most extreme response was, "That bastard screwed us. He threw the case and everyone knows it" (Interview # 12).

By becoming an intervener, elites (or their attorneys) have the ability to argue their case directly in court, rather than simply filing an amicus brief. Without intervener status, representatives from an initiative campaign may consult with the attorney general, but not dictate the arguments made before the court. In addition, by becoming an intervener, attorneys for an initiative can appeal unfavorable decisions made by lower courts. Without intervener status, if the attorney general (especially an apathetic one) decides not to appeal, the initiative elite is left without legal options.

In interviews, initiative elites implied that they are savvy enough to know when they should become interveners, and when not to. Many times, initiative backers are out of funds by the time the election is over, so experienced elites do not always chose to shoulder the extra expense in becoming an intervener. Often the decision was made based on the political disposition of the attorney general and/or governor. The people interviewed had a very accurate assessment of the political dispositions of their state's attorney general and they often knew whether the attorney general was supportive of their bill or not. In most situations, given the expense involved, initiative elites would only seek intervener status when they knew the attorney general to have political views detrimental to their initiative.

In other cases, time is a factor in determining whether to become an intervener. If elites are fearful of a change in the ruling political party before the legal battles are finished, they may seek intervener status regardless of the support of the current attorney general.

However, some elites seek intervener status regardless of the political leanings of the attorney general, since the defense of initiatives can take many years. The appeals process in American courts is slow. In some cases, the attorney general, *at the time the initiative was challenged*, was supportive of the bill. However, during the appellate process, there would be a change in administrations. The new attorney general sometimes did not have the same level of support for the defense. Such an event put the fox back in charge of the chicken coop.

In other cases, the initiative supporter had more expertise than the attorney general. As a result, they sought intervener status even if the attorney general was friendly. It is common to find initiative drafters who have spent considerable effort becoming legal experts in their narrow field. These elites simply felt they could do a better job defending the initiative.

More empirical evidence pointing to the effectiveness of this strategy will be presented in Chapter 5. For the purposes of this chapter, the simple fact that elites are seeking intervener status demonstrates that they are reacting in logical and strategic ways to defend their initiatives.

One of the more interesting cases of institutional learning, with respect to judicial strategies, comes in the form of drafting multiple versions of the same initiative. This strategy is best described in the following interview (my apologies to non-sports fans).

> Have you ever watched a basketball game when it's close and everyone is calling timeouts? Here's what coaches do. They call timeout, call up a play and then put their team back on the floor. But before inbounding the ball, he calls time out again. His real interest was not in calling a play. He just wants to see what the defense is going to be. You see…he forces the other coach to tip his hand. I do the same thing with my initiatives. I write sometimes ten versions of the same damn bill. When it leaks out (or is filed with the state), opponents start talking about how it's unconstitutional and all that B.S. But what they don't realize is that they're telling me their plan. Of course I go with the version that has the weakest arguments against me. But more importantly, if I do win, I already know what their arguments are gonna be (Interview # 92).

As indicated by the drafter's comments, initiative elites are anticipating challenges at the earliest stages of the initiative process. More importantly, it is clear that they are developing procedures to insulate their initiatives from encroachments of the court. In some states that have prior judicial review (pre-election review) of initiatives a similar strategy is adopted. Many times, drafters know they are "pushing the constitutional envelope" (Interview # 53). Therefore, they submit multiple bills, each one slightly more moderate and less likely to encroach upon constitutional restraints. They go to the public with the bill that is upheld by the courts but achieves the most of their policy goals. Notorious for this approach is Doug Bruce of Colorado. At times, he submits so many initiatives that are so similar to each other that the court becomes exasperated. At one point the Colorado court wrote,

> Initiative #40 is virtually identical to Initiative # 38, which we reviewed in re Proposed Initiative No. 38, 9777 P.2d 849. In fact, the only difference between Initiative #40 and Initiative # 38 is the amount of the annual tax cut. Therefore, for the reasons stated in In re Proposition # 38, we remand this matter to the Board with directions to strike.[21]

Creating Institutional Legal Support

Some initiatives attract vitriolic and unrelenting opposition. As noted earlier, Mike Reynolds' "three-strikes" bill has been challenged continually since its passage.[22] Oregon's "Death with Dignity Act" (doctor-assisted suicide) has been challenged at state and federal levels for the past decade.[23] Many initiative elites have come to realize that defending initiatives can become a full time job that lasts for years after the initial election victory. For professionals (See Chapter 3) this is not a serious problem. They already have an organizational structure to support appeals and defenses. However, for initiative elites who do not have such a support structure, something needs to be created. In many cases, initiative elites are not permanent players in the political arena. They pass their initiative and then get out. They are not prepared to spend years defending an initiative. This puts activists in the position of either delegating the protection of their initiative to the state attorney general, or remaining in the legal process far longer than they would like or longer than their other career commitments allow. A few initiative activists responded to this problem by created non-profit organizations or political action committees (PACs) to defend their initiatives. These organizations were used to raise funds, maintain legal counsel and support the ongoing defense of their initiative.

The supporters of Oregon's Death with Dignity Act (Measure 16) created both a PAC (Oregon Right to Die) and a non-profit (Oregon Death with Dignity Political Action Fund). In all, they raised $1.3 million to maintain the defense of their initiative (Interview # 99). According to one of the individuals behind the development of the non-profit,

> Enthusiasm and money was the issue. There were no volunteers. We [individuals who drafted Measure 16] were all paid. We couldn't put aside our "real" jobs for this initiative. We either had to be paid, or we needed to pay someone else to do it [defend the initiative]. Keep in mind, ten years is a long time to do anything. If we didn't treat it like a job, then our enthusiasm and professionalism would have waned (Interview # 84).

This strategy has worked so far. Measure 16 is one of the most challenged initiatives ever passed. And yet, it is still completely in effect today.[24]

Initiative Elites Protecting Institutional Autonomy

PTI predicts that institutions will do more than passively react to the encroachments of other institutions. There is also the argument that institutions will go on the offensive to defend their own autonomy (Epstien and Knight, 1999; Zorn, 1995; Spiller and Gelt, 1992). Not surprisingly, initiative elites do not stop at altering their own strategies to anticipate judicial nullification. They also proactively seek to protect the institutional autonomy of the initiative process. By "institutional autonomy," I mean they have taken steps to defend and expand the rights of individuals participating in the initiative process. This has meant protecting procedural rights, such as the ability to gather and count signatures. But it also means protecting the ability to put content into initiatives. There is a growing movement to limit the scope of the single subject rule so that initiatives can cover a wider area of content. Much of the focus is on defending these rights from the encroachments of the legislature and the courts.

As might be expected, it is repeat players in the initiative system who seeks to protect the autonomy of the process. As a result, 'professionals' have taken the lead in protecting the initiative process. The professionals use two tools to insulate the initiative process: one is the initiative process itself. More surprisingly, professionals also use the court system to protect themselves. Along the way, initiative elites have achieved many successes.

At the heart of the initiative process is signature gathering. Without signatures, no initiative elite can get a bill on the ballot. In protecting the signature gathering process, initiative elites have focused on three issues. First, they have fought for legal protection to gather signatures in public places, such as the Post Office and local supermarkets.[25] Second, they have successfully protected their right to pay signature gatherers.[26] In large states with high signature requirements, it is almost essential to have paid signature gatherers. In fact, opponents of the initiative process have attempted to use laws banning paid signature gathering as an indirect way to cripple the process. And third, initiative elites have rebuffed attempts to require that a certain percentage of signatures come from every precinct or county in the state.[27] Such a requirement would require sending signature gatherers to the far ends of the state, where population density is minimal, increasing the costs of the process.

Initiative activists have had mixed results trying to protect their right to count signatures that have been collected. For example, in Massachusetts, a mere coffee stain on a petition sheet may invalidate all the signatures on the page.[28] However, in Nebraska, the courts struck down a law requiring that the information that petition signers put on the petition is exactly the same as what is on their voter registration card.[29]

Initiative drafters have had more success protecting their right to raise money. Money is the lifeblood of most political processes, and the initiative process is no exception (Gerber and Garrett, 2001). In two landmark political speech cases, *Citizens Against Rent Control vs. Berkeley* (1981) and *First National Bank of Boston vs. Bellotti* (1977), the Supreme Court upheld the right of initiative supporters to raise money.[30]

Initiative elites have also tried to use the initiative process itself to protect the initiative process as a whole. Most of these attempts come in the form of "Initiative Bill of Rights" terminology. In 2000, Oregon Measure 96 was titled, "Prohibits Making Initiative Process Harder, Except Through Initiative." The measure failed before the voters, but it is likely that similar initiatives will appear in the future. In 1994, a Montana group calling itself the Tax Equity Action

Movement drafted an initiative that would eliminate the legislature's right to repeal or amend passed initiatives. Earlier (in 1990), Missouri activists attempted an initiative along the same lines.[31]

The actions noted above were designed to provide procedural protections for those who use direct democracy. However, just as important to activists is the ability to put content into initiatives. The biggest hurdles they face in this area are the single subject and separate vote requirements. As noted in a previous section of this chapter, initiative drafters are limiting the scope of their bills to conform to these rules. But more importantly, in the eyes of initiative elites, the single subject and separate vote rules give judges the ability to act like a supra-legislature, striking bills with which they simply disagree.

We should expect to see initiative elites using their institutional powers in attempts to limit the power of the single subject and separate vote rules—and we are. In Montana, Paul Befumo submitted a constitutional amendment to repeal the separate vote rule. However, in a case of interesting irony, Montana Attorney General Joseph Mazurek rejected the amendment on the grounds that it violated Article XIV, the state's separate vote rule! Also in Montana, Rob Natelson, whose CI-75 was the first victim of the state's new interpretation of Article XIV, also filed an initiative to repeal the rule. The initiative defines "one amendment" as including "the entire content of a single constitutional initiative petition or legislative bill proposing constitutional revision."[32] In Colorado, Dennis Pohill, a repeat player in the initiative process, is seeking to overturn the state's single subject rule. Filed as Initiative 43, it would add the following language to the state's constitution,

> Such ballot titles and all challenges to initiatives on single-subject grounds shall be appealed to the Supreme Court only within 5 days of the setting finally decided only within 14 days of the appeal, and broadly construed to aid initiatives. If the Supreme Court does not timely decide the petition is multiple subjects, it is conclusively a single subject. No later single-subject challenge is legal. Any petition adding, repealing, or rewriting within only one article of the constitution, one title of state statutes, one charter article, or one ordinance is conclusively a single subject and not subject to appeal.[33]

Like Paul Befumo, Pohill's bill was struck by the state Supreme Court as a violation of the state's single subject rule.[34] At the time of writing, he is still actively pursuing this agenda despite the legal setbacks.

Limiting the Autonomy of the Courts

In the eyes of many initiative elites, the courts are a "competitor institution." They see the courts as openly hostile and looking for any legal reason to strike down initiatives. Establishing new precedent for stricter single subject and separate vote rules has convinced many initiative drafters that the power and discretion of the courts needs to be limited. One interview subject's office has a large poster reading, "Judges Are Not Above the Law!" At the time, he was pushing an initiative that would require judges to take a new oath. The oath would bind judges to an "originalism" approach to interpreting the state and federal constitutions. This initiative activist, and others like him, feel that the only way to effectively protect the initiative process is to weaken the authority of the courts. As initiatives continue to be nullified by the courts, evidence suggests more initiative elites are challenging the courts' autonomy.

Challenging the autonomy of the courts is complicated by several factors. Historically, courts have been the institution most insulated from public and political pressures (Segal, 1997). As a result, initiative drafters have few tools with which to reign in the power of the courts. However, in most states, judges must face some type of retention election. Unlike federal judges, who are appointed for life, state justices do need to heed public opinion to some extent (Hall, 1999). It is this political opening that initiative elites use to limit the autonomy of the state courts.

Antagonism towards the courts is relatively new among initiative activists. However, there were some exceptions. Lewis Uhler, a member of a California-based group called the National Tax Limitation Committee, participated in the campaign to remove Justices Bird and Cruz from the California Supreme Court after the court removed one of his initiatives from the ballot. However, he openly admits that initiative supporters alone could never have removed a sitting justice.

Uhler notes that a combination of unpopular anti-death penalty rulings in conjunction with some anti-initiative rulings created a unique environment where public sentiment allowed them to successfully pursue the justices. Ed Jangles, another initiative advocate who participated in the coalition to remove Bird and Cruz, agrees with that assessment. He notes that in most cases, "The Bird option is just too hard. You need a bigger issue than just one overturned initiative to get the people to throw out Supreme Court Judges. Everything just came together at once with her. But that rarely happens."

Based on most of the interviews I conducted, most initiative elites agree with Jangle's assessment. However, initiative activists of the 1990s seem much more prepared to challenge the courts than their earlier counterparts. One obvious success occurred in Idaho. Justice Salik, an open critic of the initiative system (Salik, 1996), was removed from office in 2000. Although not claiming all the credit, an Idaho initiative activist made it clear why he supported her removal.

> These guys need to know we can get them. They sit down there in Boise thinking they're above the law. Hell, they think they are the law half the time...we only need to pick off one. The rest will get the message. I've worked on seven initiatives in my life, some in California and some here. I don't know if I'll do another one, but I thought, if I do, I need a better court. So I helped when they asked (Interview # 60).

As a repeat player, the Idaho activist clearly felt the court needed to respect his work. However, in this interview it was difficult to determine if he was a strategic actor trying to create a more advantageous environment for initiative drafters, or if he was just "anti-government" on all levels.

Other elites provide clearer evidence. One activist, pursuing an initiative he was sure would be challenged, took the unusual step of sending letters to all the state justices that were up for re-election in the next two years. Noting in his interview, "They're politicians too," he explained that he sent a letter to the judges explaining that he had a controversial initiative on the ballot, but that he was also aware that they were up for re-election soon. In his words, "We wanted to let them know we were watching them. I don't know if it had any effect...but it probably didn't hurt" (Interview # 12).

A more common approach has been to attempt to influence judicial elections. From Florida to Colorado to Oregon, angry initiative supporters have been pushing policies that would allow voters to vote for "none of the above" in judicial elections. Most of these bills have not made the ballot, but in Oregon, Don McIntire has been successful. In the 2002 Oregon election, voters had to decide if the "none of the above" option would be added to judicial ballots. They rejected the initiative. However, the fact that the issue made the ballot indicates a partial success on McIntire's part.

Other elites take the simpler approach of campaigning in judicial elections. Rob Natelson actively participated in campaign events to remove the justices that nullified his Initiative CI-75. An Oregon activist is compiling "opposition research" on the background and rulings of an "enemy judge" to use in the next election. He notes he will use the research in the next judicial retention election, "if he screws us one more time" (Interview # 92). In all, of the 45 interview subjects, 11 initiative elites took some action to limit the power and discretion of their state courts. This number is higher than it first appears when one considers that first-time initiative drafters normally don't challenge the courts. Repeat players have a stake in limiting judicial autonomy, and in no cases, in any state, did I encounter an initiative drafter whose first foray in the initiative process involved an attempt to limit judicial autonomy.

Conclusion

The purpose of this chapter was to examine the possibility that initiatives are nullified by the courts at a higher rate than legislative statutes because either (1) initiative elites are amateurs, (2) fail to engage in institutional learning, or (3) simply do not anticipate, retroactively or proactively, judicial actions. As previously indicated, some initiative activists are amateurs, or first time participants, who fail to benefit from institutional learning. Other activists, such as zealots, simply choose to ignore judicial signals. However, the larger body of empirical evidence suggests these three hypotheses cannot fully explain why measures are invalidated so frequently. The evidence does indicate that most initiative elites, such as professionals, politicians, lawyers, and victims are rational, strategic political actors, behaving in a way that theories of institutional competition predict. Given the evidence, an explanation for high rates of judicial nullification must be found outside the simplistic suggestion that initiative drafters are simply amateurs. However, if initiative supporters are rational, strategic actors, we are still left with the question of why so many initiatives eventually fall before the courts. The next two chapters seek to answer that question.

---

[1] See data presented in Table 3 in Chapter 3.

[2] See "Professor Hopes to Change Montana's High Court Base," in The Spokesman-Review (April 2, 2002) pp. 1a.

[3] See "Montanans for Better Government Sets Political Agenda," in Montana Human Rights Network Press Release, June 22, 1999.

[4] Analysis of Montana Secretary of State Bob Brown, accessed at: http//:sos.state.mt.us/textonly.

[5] In one of the more advanced cases of professionalization, an initiative drafter hired a lawyer who specialized in single subject case law (Interview #93).

[6] Connerly maintains the Civil Rights Institute, Sizemore has Taxpayers United, Eyman runs Permanent Offense, and Unz maintains the group English for the Children.

[7] Twenty-one of the 23 states that enacted term limits did so by the initiative process. Two states adopted term limits via the legislative process. See Danielle Fagre (1995), *Microcosm of the Movement: Local Term Limits in the United States*.

[8] This was the language used in California's 1998 Proposition 225. However, language varies from bill to bill. In Maine, the language read, "Failed to actively support term limits."

[9] Accessed at http://www.sos.state.co.us/amendment18.html.

[10] California's state Supreme Court struck down Proposition 225 in *Bramberg v. Jones*, S076784, but the 8th Circuit Court of Appeals struck down Missouri's similar law in *Cook v. Gralike* 996 F. Supp. 901 (W. D. Mo. 1998).

[11] Tim Nesbitt, an avid opponent of the initiative process, qualified Measure 26 for the Oregon ballot. However, in challenging the initiative system, he apparently learned from the incremental approach and is heeding the strategic cues sent by the courts. Measure 26 seeks to ban the process of paying signature gatherers per signature. *Myers vs. Grant* (1988) has already established that signature gatherers can be paid. However, he is seeking the incremental step of only banning payment based on a per signature basis. Since *Myers vs. Grant* did not specifically address this issue, there is the possibility it will be upheld.

[12] For example, the drafter of a measure that prevents the police/state from seizing property until after the accused has been found guilty, had to provide an exception for animal

cruelty. Without the exception, the abused animal would have to stay with the abuser until he/she was found guilty.

[13] Although this statement reflects the attitude of many initiative elites and is representative of why they pursue constitutional amendments, it is important to remember I am only looking at why initiatives are rejected by the courts, not why initiatives are amended or repealed by legislatures.

[14] I break the data at 1999 because courts in both California and Oregon made it clear by then that they would be reviewing initiatives under a stricter standard. Therefore, we should not expect to see an adjustment in strategy by initiative elites until the subsequent 2000 election cycle.

[15] Initiative elites are rapidly becoming aware of the limitations of this strategy. By passing a constitutional amendment, activists are insulating their measures from the legislature. But at the same time, they are subjecting their initiatives to separate vote challenges. Separate vote challenges can only be levied against constitutional amendments. Therefore, drafters must either pass a statutory bill and face the legislature, or pass a constitutional amendment and face the courts.

[16] An "accomodationist" court reviews initiatives under a very liberal standard. The rationale is that because initiatives are passed by the people themselves, the courts should show more deference. A "watchdog" court holds initiatives to a stricter standard because initiatives do not go through the deliberative legislative process. Tushnet (1996) notes a similar dichotomy, but does not use Miller's terms. Eule (1990) argues all courts should be watchdog courts because they are the only "minority check" in a mostly majoritarian process.

[17] See *Oregon Education Assoc v. Feeney*, 727 P.2d 602, 609 (Or. 1986).

[18] The fact that voters only passed four of the seven provisions when they had the choice to vote on each separately indicates the need for the single-subject rule. . In this case, Oregon voters rejected the provisions that allowed 11-1 juries, gave plaintiffs the right to demand a jury trial, and limited immunity for individuals forced to testify.

[19] The night I-695 was passed, chief petitioner Tim Eyman started raising funds for the anticipated legal battles. He comments, "This is going to rock and roll real fast through the courts. A week ago we did a mailing to all our supporters to say that when we win, that battle has just begun. Legally, the attorney general's office is supposed to defend it. Let me just say that our team is there to help." See Church, Foster. "Washington car tag, tax initiative takes hefty lead," The Oregonian, November 3, 1999. A8

[20] For example, Governor Locke of Washington openly opposed Initiative 200, a sister initiative of California's Proposition 209, which banned racial preferences.

[21] See 977 P.2d 853: 1999 Colo CAR 1482.

[22] Although originally passed in 1994, the initiative is still under attack. A recent challenge, on cruel and unusual punishment grounds, has been granted certiorari by the US Supreme Court and will be heard in the 2003 session.

[23] Having survived legal challenges (See *Lee v. Oregon* 107 F.3d 1382), the measure is still being attacked by the federal government. An attempt to have the bill overturned in Congress failed and another attempt to have the FDA deny licenses to physicians who acted according to the law also failed. See Pain Relief Promotion Act HR 2260/S1271 (2001).

---

[24] This case raises interesting questions about the political economy of judicial review with respect to initiatives. Epp (1999) shows that it takes considerable resources for cases to make their way through the appellate process. He contends that the issues the Supreme Court hears depends a lot on how well financed certain groups are in pursuing multiple appeals. With Measure 16, we may be seeing the same process but in reverse. Well-financed initiative groups may have an advantage when it comes to defeating multiple appeals by opposing groups. In other words, money matters. Well-financed initiative campaigns have the ability to fight off multiple challenges that poorer campaigns cannot. However, based on this one case, I cannot draw wider conclusions.

[25] See *Initiative and Referendum Institute vs. United States Postal Service* (2000) at 116 F. Supp. 2d 65.

[26] See *On Our Terms 97 PAC vs. Sec of State of State of Maine* (2000) at 2000 US Dist Lexis 11937, and *Meyer vs. Grant* (1988) at 486 US 414; 108 S. Ct. 1886.

[27] See *Initiative and Referendum Institute vs. State of Idaho* (2001) at 00-668-SMHW.

[28] See *Thomas Walsh vs. Sec of Massachusetts Commonwealth* (1999) at 430 Mass. 103; 173 N.E. 2d 369.

[29] See *Stenberg vs. Moore* (1999) at 258 Nebraska 199 No. S-98-983

[30] Given the fact that initiative elites have had some success *in the courts* protecting their process, it appears that the contentions of some elites that the courts are seeking the destruction of the initiative process is exaggerated.

[31] A comprehensive search of all initiatives between 1992 and 2002 (western states) identifies the following initiatives that pursue the same goal. In Oregon, Measure 96 (2000), Measure 33 (1996), and Measure 10 (1994); in Colorado, Measure 13 (1996); in Arizona, Measure 105; and in Nebraska, Measure 410 (1996) all sought to limit the ability of other institutions to infringe on the autonomy of the initiative system.

[32] Accessed at http://sos.state.mt.us/textonly/News_release/04_22_02.asp

[33] See *Jones vs. Pohill* (2002) Case No. 02SA50 (Colo).

[34] See *Jones vs. Pohill* (2002) Case No. 02SA50 (Colo).

Chapter Five

Institutional Causes of Judicial Nullification

The main focus of this book is explaining the institutional competition between direct democracy activists and the courts. Covered so far is the theoretical context in which judicial and initiative institutions interact, a typological analysis of the actors who engage in the initiative process, and an examination of how most of these actors are sophisticated players who benefit from institutional learning. However, we are still left with an unanswered question: Why do the courts invalidate initiatives so often if, in fact, initiative drafters are strategic actors that benefit from institutional learning?

This simple question does not have a simple answer. In fact, the question cannot be solved with one answer. Consider the question, "Why do car accidents happen?" There is no singular answer to this question. Car accidents happen for a variety of reasons. Inattentive drivers, unskilled drivers, poor road conditions, mechanical failure, and design flaws can all lead to auto collisions. The same is true for ballot measures. Ballot measures fail before the court for a host of reasons. However, out of the many possible causes, a dichotomous pattern can be discerned. Ballot measures are struck by the courts for two reasons—behavioral reasons, and institutional, or structural, reasons. Return for a moment to the question about car accidents. It would be easy to categorize those causes into two subdivisions. Some causes are strictly behavioral. Inattentive or unskilled driving cannot be blamed on car manufacturers or poor infrastructure. They are simply the fault of the people driving the car. Other causes for auto accidents might be termed structural. A leaky brake line or a tire blowout is not the fault of the driver. The same dichotomy can be used to categorize the causes of initiative nullification.

In discerning between the two types of causes, the focus must be on an overriding question: did the ballot measure fail to meet legal standards because of the institutional rules of initiative drafting (i.e. institutional or structural reasons), or did the measure fail to meet legal standards because of the nature of the person (or people) pursuing the initiative (i.e. behavioral reasons)? Utilizing the typology created in Chapter 3 is helpful in drawing these distinctions.[1] For example, some ballot measures are nullified because zealots purposely seek to challenge existing law. In other words, they want to end up in court challenging existing precedent. In contrast, some ballot measures are nullified because initiatives cannot be amended in any way after the first signature has been collected—a problem that strikes even the most professional elites.[2] If there is a change in legal precedent during the campaign, there is little an initiative activist can do to "fix" his measure. Clearly, these two causes of nullification fall into different categories. The first example is a situation where the goals and attitudes of the drafter are the cause for nullification. In the second example, the clear reason for nullification is the institutional structure of the initiative process. Chapter 5 outlines the institutional reasons that ballot measures have high rates of nullification. Chapter 6 will outline the behavioral reasons.

The dichotomy of behavioral and institutional reasons for initiative nullification requires a clear distinction between "institutional" and "behavioral" causes. A solid basis for such a distinction follows Knight's (1992) definition that "Institutions are viewed as a structure of formal and informal rules that shape the strategic calculation of actors who are self-consciously pursuing a set of presumably fixed short-term preferences." Furthermore, as implied in Knight's definition, institutions are made up of multiple formal and informal rules, which can be referred to as institutional structures. Therefore, when a specific rule or informal procedure has the effect of increasing the likelihood that an initiative will meet with nullification, I refer to this as a structural cause of nullification. Inherent in this approach is also the understanding that a collection of structures, combining into an institution, may also have an effect on initiative invalidation. Just as an individual rule may have an impact on the survivability of an initiative, so too will institutional frameworks. However, from the larger institutional view, judicial nullification may occur because of inter-institutional conflicts, such as that between the governor/attorney general and the initiative process. It may also happen through intra-institutional conflicts, such as the multiple structures of the initiative process that require both a certain number of signatures and a limited amount of time to collect them. These types of causes fall under the heading of "institutional" causes of nullification.

Additionally, it is important to be clear about the definition of an "institution" because the claim that institutional structures cause initiative invalidation naturally invites a comparison to other institutions that do not suffer the same high rates of nullification. Embedded in the question, "Why do initiatives fail more often than legislative statutes?" is another question, "How is the institutional structure of the initiative process different from the institutional structure of the legislative process?" Part of understanding how the initiative institution invites invalidation is to understand how it differs, structurally, from the legislative process.

Chapter 2 presented a comprehensive description of the collection of structures that make up the initiative institution. To recap: the initiative process has specific rules with respect to signature gathering, a legal review process, limitations on both the scope of acceptable content and the amendability of measures, and procedures concerning how measures are defended in court. Like all institutions, the "rules of the game" that are incumbent upon the initiative process affect the outcome. The goal of this chapter is to determine how those rules (structures) influence the rate of judicial nullification of ballot measures, and to a lesser degree, which type of initiative elite they most affect. For example, procedural hurdles are less likely to impede professional or lawyer elites, and more apt to confound amateur drafters.

Three broad issues shed light on why institutional structures within the initiative system promote judicial nullification. Generally described, they are procedural issues, discretion issues, and guidance issues. Procedural issues refer to the actual rules of the initiative drafting process that make it difficult to meet constitutional standards. Discussing discretion issues focuses on how the legal defense of initiatives is often left to political actors with so much discretionary power that initiatives can be rejected on political grounds as often as legitimate legal grounds. Guidance issues refer to the fact that other institutions, especially the courts, provide very little guidance to initiative drafters on how to make future initiatives constitutional.

Procedural Issues

Two procedural aspects of the initiative process clearly stand out as contributing causes to high rates of judicial nullification. First, ballot measures can be challenged both on the basis of their content (do they violate federal or state constitutions?) and on whether or not the ballot measure violates procedural rules. These dual restrictions require multiple skill sets by initiative drafters. Lawyers are more able to navigate the constitutional requirements, but professional repeat players tend to be better qualified to navigate the procedural rules. Individuals or coalitions that lack one or both of these skill sets are more likely to face nullification. The second contributing procedural factor is that initiatives cannot be amended once the signature gathering process has begun. Given the amount of time that elapses between drafting and voting, this restriction leads to the possibility that a ballot measure is constitutional when it is drafted but is no longer constitutional when it comes before the voters, and because of the inflexibility of the process, changes cannot be made.

Challenges on Procedural and Content Grounds

Initiatives can be challenged on both content and procedural grounds. Initiatives are struck down because they violate specific clauses of the state and federal constitutions. Miller (2001) notes that over half of invalidated initiatives are nullified because they violate individual rights protected in state and federal constitutions. However, unlike legislative statutes, initiatives are also invalidated because they fail to meet procedural hurdles such as single subject and separate vote procedures, title hearing standards, and restrictions against revising, rather than amending, the constitution. These latter hurdles are non-existent for legislators. In essence, opponents of initiatives get two "bites at the apple" whereas opponents of legislative statutes typically only get one. An examination of Table 6 shows that of the 160 initiatives passed in California, Colorado, Washington, and Oregon between 1960 and 1999, 28 were challenged on procedural grounds. Of those, 11 were invalidated due to procedural restrictions.

Table 6: Nullifications Based on Procedural Grounds[1]

	Challenged on Procedural Grounds	Invalidated on Procedural Grounds
Initiative Statutes	28 of 160	11 of 28
Legislative Statutes[2]	0	0

There is no evidence that this practice is abating. Of cases since 1999, Miller (2001) writes, "several courts are more strictly applying technical state constitutional restrictions on initiative lawmaking, such as single subject rules and ballot title requirements, invalidating numerous initiatives on these grounds." His conclusion, along with Lowenstein (2001), is that courts are becoming more predisposed to invalidating initiatives for procedural reasons. In most cases, the procedural reason for nullification is violation of the single subject or separate vote rules.

Part of the argument of this chapter is that institutional rules, not the incompetence of ballot measure drafters, accounts for some of the difference

---

[1] Not included in the chart's data are the numerous Colorado initiatives that are rejected on procedural grounds *before* they can get to the voters. See Note 145 in Miller (2001) "Courts as Watchdogs," *Seattle University Law Review,* for a comprehensive list.

[2] A Lexis-Nexis search failed to reveal a single decision where a legislative statute had been overturned on technical, procedural grounds. There is one example from outside the data set. A New Mexico lottery and gambling law was invalidated by the courts on separate vote grounds. The New Mexico legislature repealed the Constitutional separate vote clause soon afterwards.

between legislative and initiative nullification rates. The Oregon term limits group that passed Measure 3 in 1992 is a useful example. The Court argued that the drafting of Measure 3 in 1992 violated the procedural rules established in 1998. A bill that was constitutional for 10 years was eventually nullified because the Oregon Supreme Court created new procedural rules for the initiative system in 1998 and then held initiatives that were passed before 1998 accountable under the new rules.[3] One can only imagine the number of legislative statutes that would be invalidated if the courts held legislatures to the same standard.[4] What the above example illustrates is that completely competent and rational initiative elites can experience judicial rejections on purely institutional grounds.[5] The most experienced professional or most qualified lawyer cannot anticipate ex post facto nullifications any better than the most inexperienced amateur or blinded zealot.

Single Subject/Separate Vote Rules and the Collective Action Problem

From the above examples, it is clear that the single subject and separate vote rules are significant institutional hurdles for initiative drafters. These two rules are such a hurdle that it is unclear why these rules have not been repealed by initiative elites themselves. Initiative drafters have access to the legislative and constitutional amendment process, and yet the single subject and separate vote rules continue to exist in most state constitutions. Why have initiative elites not used the initiative process to eliminate these two restrictions on their legislative autonomy?

The answer lies in Olson's (1964) classic work *The Logic of Collective Action*. In his seminal work Olson argued, and mathematically demonstrated, that the procurement of public goods is made difficult by the free rider problem. Public goods are by their very nature non-excludable and non-consumable. This means that once procured, no one can be denied the use of a public good, and the consumption of a public good will not decrease the availability of the good for others. Olson showed that public goods attract free rider behaviors, because each contributing individual knows that use of the good will not be denied even if no contribution is actually made. Olson argued that without some selective incentive to motivate individual participants, all members of a group seeking a public good will choose the free-rider option, and ultimately the public good will not be produced.

Olson's theory is relevant because the elimination of the single subject and separate vote rules is a public good to all initiative elites. If one initiative coalition commits resources to repealing the single subject rule, all initiative drafters benefit. In essence, the "service" provided is non-excludable. Naturally, the incentive for every initiative drafter is to let some other initiative elite or coalition bear the burden of repealing the single subject rule, while they still enjoy the benefits. Such an environment is the classic "collective action problem" described by Olson.

Formal theory also provides some insight into who might actually bear the burden of repealing the single subject rule despite the collective action disincentives. Both Marc Galanter (1974) and Robert Axelrod (1980) conducted research on "repeat players." Galanter concludes that repeat players are willing to engage in costly behaviors if it means that the rules, in the long run, will be changed to benefit repeat players. The thrust of Galanter's research suggests that initiative professionals, far more than first time amateurs or victims, will commit significant resources to overturn the single subject and separate vote requirements.

Players in the initiative process can be identified by their repeat player status. Some people engage in the initiative process only once in their entire life—typically amateurs or victims. These individuals are clearly "single shot" players. In contrast, some people habitually use the initiative process to achieve their political goals. It is unlikely that a "single-shot" player in the initiative process would dedicate resources to challenging a procedural rule. The benefits for repealing the single subject and separate vote rules only exist for repeat players. Therefore, if any initiative elite were to expend resources to repeal these rules, it would most likely be a repeat player.

What formal theory predicts, and what actually happens, is not necessarily the same thing (Green and Shapiro, 1998). Given this criticism, Brace and Langer (2002) suggested that the best way to develop formal theory is to empirically test the predictions of formal models. Although formal theory predicts free-rider mentalities will prevent the repeal of the single subject and separate vote rules, does the empirical data from initiative elites support such a contention? Adopting Brace and Langer's suggestion, repeat players were questioned about repealing the single subject or separate vote rules. Their responses supported what previous political theory already predicted.

The following examples represent attitudes from repeat players in California, Colorado, and Oregon. The first comment is from a professional/zealot.

> I hate the single subject rule. It's just a ploy by the courts to strike down what they don't like. But I don't have the time or money to do anything about it. My supporters and I are interested in lowering taxes, keeping the government out of our lives, and term limits. If someone wants to get rid of it, they have my support, but it's just not a job I can afford to take on right now (Interview #17).

Or consider this comment from a lawyer/politician:

> We all know the single subject rule is in our way. But it is so expensive to repeal and everyone wants to do their own thing...there are limited resources and that's not on the top of the list. And there is no direct benefit. Why should I ask my group to repeal the rule? Why not someone else? (Interview # 40).

Another professional comments:

> I tried to deal with this issue a few years ago. I tried to contact all the groups that used the initiative process on a regular basis and see if we could get some type of cost sharing agreement worked out. I had Common Cause, the PIRGs, some environmental groups, the tax limitation groups all interested. But not in the same room of course (Joking and as an aside). But in the end, nothing came of it. I had other things more important to do and so did they. And money issues were going to be a problem. Who pays and how much? I think the interest in repealing the rule was there, but not the willingness to give up their own limited resources (Interview # 41).

It is clear that Olson's predictions about group behavior were played out. Many initiative elites want the procedural rules changed for their benefit, but the temptation to be a free-rider is too strong to actually produce the results. Each interview subject above hopes that someone else will shoulder the costs of the repeal, knowing it will benefit non-contributors equally.

From a broader, more historical perspective, it is also apparent that the battles over the single subject and separate vote rules are part of a cyclical institutional battle. Initially, initiative drafters pursued statutory measures because of the lower signature requirements. However, two events caused drafters to move away from this approach. First, unhappy legislatures amended or invalidated statutory changes. Second, the courts began to use the single subject rule more liberally. In response, drafters moved towards constitutional amendments. The costs were higher, but the measures were insulated from inter-institutional attacks. After some initial success on the part of initiative drafters with this strategy, the courts are responding by using rigorous interpretations of the separate vote rule. At this moment, it appears the courts have once again gained the upper hand over the initiative process. However, it is likely that initiative elites will respond with attacks directed at the separate vote rule, or at the courts themselves. Regardless of the approach drafters take, collectively they will still be faced with the free-rider problems illustrated by Olson.

The Inability to Amend Initiatives

In the legislative process, it is never too late to make an amendment. Right up until the final vote, members can make adjustments to a bill.[6] In the initiative process, it is very unlikely that a measure will be amended once it has been filed with the Secretary of State's office because initiatives cannot be altered once the signature gathering process has begun (Miller, 2001). The rationale for the restriction is that it would be unfair to collect a citizen's signature, and then alter the document to which that signature had been affixed. If an initiative is altered in any way, all the previously collected signatures become invalid and the process must begin anew. Because the signature gathering process is so lengthy and expensive, initiative elites are loath to change their measures. Changing the language of an initiative means starting the most difficult and expensive part of the process from scratch.

The indirect effect of this institutional arrangement is that the courts find more initiatives unconstitutional. Courts are always in flux. Despite the concept of *stare decisis*, new members are always joining courts and new precedents are always being handed down. Therefore, the actual "rules of the game," with respect to initiatives, are continually in flux. In a legislative environment, this is not a problem. But in the initiative process, the time lapse between drafting a measure and the public voting on it can be up to two years, and so there it is a problem. Some initiative activists, typically lawyers or professionals, who were intimately aware of the legal restrictions facing their initiative, labor extensively to meet those restrictions, but still have their measures invalidated because the rules of the game change after the measure has been submitted. In some cases, the rules change so late in the process no changes can be made.[7] In other cases, there is time to make changes, but starting the signature process over is too expensive. Consider the following examples.

> Being a lawyer is not enough. You need to get lucky too. When we were done drafting Measure 3 we were confident we had anticipated all legal challenges. And then when *Sager* and *Dale* both came down one after another, everything was thrown into limbo. We had a few options and none of them were appealing. On one hand we could go back, re-draft the measure and start over. No one wanted to do that. It meant more fundraising. The other option was to fight *Sager* and *Dale* after the election. That's what we elected to do. After it passed, there was a separate vote challenge. Our legal strategy was to argue to the Supreme Court that the Appeals Court had erred in *Sager* and *Dale*. We won the case and Measure 3 is in effect today. But, it's not a strategy I would want to pursue often (Interview # 84).

The drafters in the above case chose between two difficult options and eventually prevailed.[8] However, other elites were not as successful. Permanent Offense, a Washington State group with a mixture of professionals and zealots, is interested in tax reform. Their initial involvement in the initiative process was a success. They passed I-695, which limited car tabs (a tax) and the ability of legislatures to increase other taxes. The bill was invalidated on single subject grounds, but not before they had already drafted and submitted the subsequent Initiative 722. Timing was again a central factor. Because drafting and submitting an initiative is such a lengthy process, Permanent Offense went directly to work drafting I-722, a few months after I-695 was passed. They wanted their initiative to be ready for the next election. However, after they drafted and submitted the bill, but before the next election, the Washington Supreme Court ruled I-695 invalid. At this point, the drafters were caught in the same dilemma as the drafters of Measure 3. They too chose to fight it out in court rather than re-draft the measure, but in their case, I-722 met the same fate as I-695. As one of the lead drafters noted, "I had an uneasy feeling after the [I-695] ruling, but what were we supposed to do?" (Interview # 100).[9]

In a related example, a California lawyer responsible for helping draft an Indian gaming initiative wanted to change the measure from a statutory initiative to a constitutional amendment initiative. He argued to the group drafting the measure that a constitutional amendment would be safer from judicial interference. However, because signature collection had already begun, his suggestion was rejected. In the end, the measure did pass the voters, but as predicted, it was invalidated on state constitutional grounds.

The most obvious conclusion drawn from the data and these examples is that institutions matter. In these cases, we see that rational elites can anticipate the behavior of other institutions, but because of the limitations imposed by their own institution, they cannot effectively react. The above examples illustrate serious initiative activists drafting measures that meet legal requirements *at the time they were drafted.* But because of the institutional structure of the initiative process, this is not enough. Nullification of ballot measures results, to some extent, because the rules of the game are different for initiative drafters and legislative drafters.

Discretion Issues

The recent research of Lupia et al (2001) provides some interesting insights about the institutional structure of the initiative system. In their book, *Stealing the Initiative: How State Government Responds to Direct Democracy*, they show that successfully passed initiatives "neither implement nor enforce themselves." Specifically, once an initiative passes, it is incumbent upon other state actors to ensure that the law is actually carried out. The authors note this is problematic. In many cases, the "other state actors" were adamantly opposed to the initiative. The end result is that "government actors must choose to comply with an initiative if it is to affect policy" and because "full compliance with initiatives is the exception, rather than the rule...under normal conditions, government actors' policy preferences displace initiative content (p.vii)."

Their research provides insight into why initiatives fail before the courts so often. In order for initiative elites to see their initiative upheld, they need the cooperation of two independent branches of government—the executive and the judicial branch. In the executive branch, although governors cannot veto them, it is the attorney general's responsibility to defend initiatives and to appeal previous initiative court losses. Therefore, it becomes the discretion of many attorneys general to decide who will defend initiatives, how much effort and resources will be dedicated to the defense, and whether to appeal losses to a higher court. Attorneys general who do not personally support an initiative may choose novice attorneys to defend a measure, or simply choose not to appeal a court loss.

Despite some similarities, this situation is different than the legislative lawmaking process. Although governors and attorneys general have discretion on how to defend judicially challenged legislative acts, the need to use that discretion is very rare. Legislative acts must face a governor's veto before they are enacted. Therefore, if the bill was signed by the governor, as all bills must be, it is very likely that a legislative bill being challenged in the courts has the support of the governor. It is very rare for a bill to be enacted over a governor's veto. The only way a governor would be called upon to defend a legislative act that she did not personally support would be if a bill was enacted over her veto and then challenged in court. Furthermore, legislators know their bills must face a governor's acceptance or rejection. Accordingly, legislators will remove offending provisions to avoid a veto. Governors, being an integral part of the legislative process, have the ability to shape legislation *before* it is enacted. This is not the case with initiatives. Because the process does not go through the governor's office, the only way a governor can influence an initiative is in the judicial phase.

In many cases, the judicial branch must also be a willing accomplice in order for an initiative to become law. Obviously, the courts can decide whether to apply a strict or liberal scrutiny standard to their review of initiatives. They also have discretion when applying procedural standards, severability clauses, and other vague constitutional mandates. However, their discretion has the most effect when dealing with initiatives that challenge the autonomy of the court itself. Many initiatives try to limit the power of the courts or impose duties upon the courts. None of these initiatives are upheld by the courts.

The Power of the Attorney General

Once the voters pass an initiative, it becomes the law of the state. As such, any time a successfully passed initiative is challenged in court, it becomes the attorney general's responsibility to defend the law, even if he or she does not personally or politically support that law. As one interview subject noted, this creates a situation where "the fox is watching the chicken coop" (Interview # 11).

In a number of interviews, respondents claimed the courts invalidated their initiatives not because they were poorly drafted, but because the state official defending the law "sandbagged the defense" (Interview # 70). Unfortunately, this type of claim is very difficult to measure empirically. Methodological questions naturally arise. How does one measure "effort," "sincerity," or even the "quality" of the defense? How does one differentiate between intentional poor performance, and unqualified attorneys? As a result of these methodological problems, it's difficult to do a systematic analysis of the role the attorney general's office plays in high rates of ballot measure nullification. Despite methodological issues, the subject does merit attention, and one can indirectly show that unsympathetic attorneys general influence the success or failure of a ballot measure defense.

To begin with, it is clear that despite the institutional title and powers conferred upon attorneys general, they are still political actors. In each of the states studied in this project, the attorneys general are elected. In addition, many have sought higher office after their tenure as attorney general.[10] In fact, Lupia et al (2001) highlights many examples where attorneys general blatantly sought to prevent the implementation of an initiative. For example, in 1986, California voters passed Proposition 63, which required all official state documents to be printed in English only. This included ballots. Since non-English speaking minorities are more likely to vote Democratic, the more liberal candidates and office holders objected. Lupia writes, "Attorney General Van de Kamp reacted in a different way: with defiance. [He] issued a nonbinding research memorandum defending the use of voting materials in non-English languages (pp.36)." As a result, Proposition 63 has never been implemented, despite a few challenges to Van de Kamp's move. The example of Proposition 63 illustrates that political motivations, and the discretion attorneys general have, blunts the effectiveness of initiative lawmaking.[11] In all, Lupia et al looked at 11 case studies where officials of the executive branch tried to prevent passed initiatives from being implemented. And because the rationale for the opposition is typically political, all types of initiative elites are subject to this impediment. Although zealots are most likely to draft legislation that will attract the ire of established political elites, so too can libertarian minded professionals, politicians from an opposing party, and lawyers trying to draft legislation that met with previous rejection in the legislature.

The larger implications of their research suggests that if attorneys general are motivated by politics in the enforcement of ballot measures, then it is reasonable to assume they act politically in the defense of ballot measures. Two cases stand out as examples that support this contention. One example is the defense of Proposition 187, a California measure that limited the privileges of immigrants; and Measure 7, an Oregon bill that strengthened the eminent domain clause. In all, seven respondents claimed that lackluster performances by the attorney general led to the eventual nullification of their ballot measure. However, it is understandable that initiative elites seeking to explain the failure of their measure want to find someone else to blame. The two cases below are included because the interview subjects were able to offer documentation to support their assertion that the attorney general's opposition was the cause for nullification.

In 2000, Oregon voters passed Measure 7. The declared purpose of the bill was to require the state of Oregon to pay landowners if state regulations had the effect of lowering the value of a given property. The measure was drafted by Bill Sizemore, but supported by other "property rights" interest groups. Opponents claimed that the passage of Measure 7 would cost the state billions of dollars in revenue and cripple the ability of the state to protect the environment. However, despite the opposition of numerous environmental and liberal interest groups, relatively little money was spent opposing the measure. Because there were 26 measures on the Oregon ballot in 2000, many of which were considered more threatening to liberal interests, opposition groups focused more of their resources on defeating anti-union measures, an anti-gay measure, and several tax reduction measures. The end result was that Measure 7 passed with a slim majority.

As with most controversial ballot measures, the bill was immediately challenged in court. The plaintiffs sought an injunction preventing the governor from canvassing the votes (declaring a winner). In this case, the plaintiffs were the League of Oregon Cities, the City of Eugene and a private citizen, Tom Christ. Deputy Attorney General David Schuman, an open critic of the initiative system,[12] appointed himself to defend the law.[13] The measure came before Marion County Judge Lipscomb, who enjoined the measure from going into effect and eventually, in a later ruling, declared it unconstitutional.

Despite the official record of the case, suspicions about the legitimacy of the process were raised by an investigative reporter William Merritt. Merritt, using the Oregon Open Records Law, obtained several documents written during a meeting between Governor Kitzhaber[14] and the attorneys who would eventually challenge the law, and attorneys from the Attorney General's office who may have to defend the law. Schuman did not attend the meeting. If he had, he would have been ineligible to defend the measure. In the documents, Merritt discovered two important facts. First, the meeting was about Measure 7 legal challenges, but took place before any challenges were filed. Yet, the people who attended the meeting were the very people who would eventually bring such a challenge. Unless one believes in powerful coincidences, such timing implies that the meeting was intended to coordinate a challenge to the bill.[15] The meeting notes outline how the bill would be challenged, which county would be most sympathetic to the challenge, and which judges would be most likely to overturn the measure. No one would challenge the legitimacy of the process if this were a strategy session *among* the people challenging the bill. However, this meeting also included the people who were responsible for *defending* the measure.

The second fact Merritt found notable was that the members of the meeting all agreed on which judge would be best for the case—Lipscomb. Again, if the only people in the room were those responsible for challenging or defending the bill, unanimity in selecting a judge would be reasonable. However, given that both opponents and "defenders" of the bill were in attendance, they should have desired different judges.

In the end, Schuman defended the measure against the combined challenges of all the people who attended the meeting with Governor Kitzhaber, and he lost. During the oral arguments Schuman conceded that if the court failed to enjoin Measure 7 the State would suffer "irreparable harm" and that plaintiffs were likely to prevail in the later trial.[16] Three weeks later, Governor Kitzhaber appointed Schuman to the Court of Appeals.

The second case study that offers evidence that unsympathetic executive branch officials can navigate initiatives to invalidation is the example of California's Proposition 187. In 1994 Ron Prince successfully passed an initiative that denied education and health care services to illegal immigrants.[17] The measure also required state and business officials to help identify illegal immigrants for law enforcement officers. After passage, the proposition was immediately challenged, enjoined and declared unconstitutional by the state courts.[18] At the time, Republican Governor Pete Wilson supported the measure and appealed the lower court's decision to the Federal Ninth Circuit.[19] However, courts can be slow to act. After Wilson appealed, but before the courts reached a decision, Governor Gray Davis was elected. Davis was an outspoken critic of Proposition 187 and vowed not to implement it. Despite his rhetoric, when Davis became governor, he also became the acting defender of the proposition. Davis chose to remove the case from the Ninth Circuit Court and move it to the Ninth Circuit's Mediation Office.[20] In the mediation, Davis agreed not to enforce the remaining provisions that had not already been declared unconstitutional.[21] The part of the process that frustrated the chief petitioners, and led to charges of "sandbagging the initiative," was that no one from their group was invited to participate in the mediation.[22] The mediation involved all the attorneys who had challenged the measure, as well as representatives of Gray Davis. This meant that there were not any supporters of the initiative involved in the mediation.

The above two case studies, when taken together with other existing literature, suggests it is possible, if not likely, that attorneys general and other executive branch officials use their discretionary powers to invalidate ballot measures they personally do not support. Although broader conclusions cannot be drawn from my data, due to the methodological difficulties associated with such research, it is clear that in specific cases, attorneys general and their associates obstruct the implementation of initiatives. Given the fact that a governor's veto power pulls potential legislative acts closer to his political orientation, it is uncommon to see this type of behavior with respect to legislative acts. However, in the absence of an "initiative veto," initiatives are not pulled towards the governor's political orientation. Thus the discretionary legal powers of the attorney general are more likely to be used against initiatives than legislative acts.

The Power of the Courts

Initiative elites, in general, do not like the courts. Amateurs see the courts as imperiously undemocratic. Zealots often see the courts as "godless abortionists," or "pro-government liberals." Politicians see the courts as "elitists," thwarting the will of the legislature. Victims often feel betrayed by the courts because they failed to protect a loved one, or handed down too lenient of a sentence. Their attitudes range from general contempt to open hostility. Given that over half of all initiatives end up in court, and half of those are invalidated, this is an understandable sentiment. Rarely does any institutional actor appreciate it when another institutional actor undoes his work. Majorities in legislatures do not applaud presidential or gubernatorial vetoes. Nor do they greet with enthusiasm judicial review of their bills. But for initiative elites, their opposition to the courts is twofold. First of all, they object to the fact that courts reject their initiatives at all. But, given the relatively conservative nature of many initiative elites, specifically professionals with libertarian values, they also object to what some term "judicial activism." When courts expand criminal and civil rights to new areas of the law, they attract the ire of many initiative drafters.

The response of many initiative elites is to turn to the tool they know best—the initiative system. Consequently, a number of initiatives try to limit the power of the courts, or require the courts to take on duties that courts do not want. Given what we already know about principal-agency theory (Mirrlees, 1976; Holmstrom, 1979), these initiatives are doomed to fail when brought before the courts.[23] Kiewiet and McCubbins (1991) observe that principals can delegate to agents the authority to pursue a policy initiative. However, in the absence of perfect oversight, agents can ignore the dictates of the principal. Calvert (1987) comments, "The leader can only influence members who want to be influenced, and exercises power only as long as he uses it to provide them with what they want." As Presidents and members of Congress have already learned, simply instructing a bureaucratic entity to carry out a task does not mean it will actually be carried out, especially if the bureaucratic organization is opposed to the principal's demand, or has some discretion as to how the task will be done.[24]

Initiative elites attempting to direct the courts run into the same problem. Once an edict is passed, it becomes incumbent upon the courts to enforce the edict upon themselves. Not only does principal-agency theory predict such behavior is unlikely,[25] judicial models such as the Positive Theory of Institutions (PTI) also suggest courts, like all institutions, will resist encroachments upon their sovereignty and autonomy (Hall and Brace, 1999; Marks, 1988).

The empirical data suggests such models help explain the inability of initiative drafters to affect the behavior of the courts, or more accurately, the tendency of courts to invalidate measures that seek such outcomes. Table 7 examines all the ballot measures from Oregon, California, Washington and Colorado between the years 1960-1999 that attempted to restrict judicial autonomy. Essentially, the data set is comprised of all the initiatives that, in some way, tried to dictate to the courts how they would run their own institution, or sought to overturn a ruling of the court. Included were initiatives that sought to restrict how courts admit evidence and impose sentences, and ones that were written to overturn a previous judicial ruling, such as unpopular busing or death penalty rulings. In one unique case (Proposition 24) the initiative seeks to impose a burden on the court it previously did not have.[26] Despite the many attempts by initiative elites to impose upon the autonomy of the courts, the results indicate, with one policy area exception, that such attempts have been relatively futile.

The data in Table 7 tell an interesting story. It is clear that courts resist dictates when they come via an initiative. Eleven of the 16 measures were either invalidated or re-written by the courts. This represents a near 70% nullification rate, almost 20 points higher than the nullification rate for initiatives in general. Courts appear more protective of their prerogatives in some cases, and less protective in others. For example, the courts seem unwilling to have their decisions second-guessed by the electorate. In cases where the court determined that busing was an essential remedy to segregation, or the court determined the death penalty was illegal, they nullified bills that sought to overturn their rulings. Courts seem equally resistant to attempts to change the way the courts function.

Initiatives that sought to restrict judges' ability to use personal discretion were nullified.

The electorate's attempt to alter jury instructions, change what precedent courts can follow, or change how the court itself function, met almost universally with invalidation. In the rare cases where the court did not invalidate, they essentially re-wrote the initiative in their rulings to return the court's discretion. The one area courts seem slightly more willing to accept guidance from initiatives is in sentencing. This may be the case because legislatures have traditionally set sentencing guidelines for the courts, and the initiative process being an extension of the legislative system, perhaps sentencing is considered an appropriate topic for initiatives. But even in the case of Proposition 184 (three strikes) the bill was upheld because it was not too intrusive upon court discretion.

Table 7: Measures Challenging Judicial Autonomy

Measure # and State	Measure Content	Invalidated	Upheld
Proposition 17 (CA)	Declare death penalty legal	X	
Proposition 21 (CA)	Declare busing illegal	X	
Proposition 7 (CA)	Changes rules for jury instructions	X	
Proposition 8 (CA)	Changes sentencing for criminals and how they pay restitution		X
Proposition 115 (CA)	Requires CA Supreme Court follow US Supreme Court (anti-Judicial activism clause)	X	
Proposition 184 (CA)	Mandatory sentences for three time offenders		Upheld because it preserved court's discretion to strike prior convictions. [3]

---

[3] In *People v The Superior Court of San Diego County* 13 Cal 4th 497; 917 P2d 628 the court noted that if the court read Proposition 184 as denying the court the right to "strike prior convictions," which according to the court "would be reasonable," it would violate the separation of powers doctrine and would therefore be unconstitutional. However, the court continued that by choosing to interpret Proposition 184 as not denying the court such a right, the measure could be upheld.

Proposition 24 (CA)	Requires courts to draw legislative districts to avoid gerrymandering [4]	X	
Measure 8 (OR)	Requires sentences proportional to offense and liberalizes circumstances for a jury trial	X	
Measure 6 (OR)	Death penalty not cruel and unusual punishment		X
Measure 7 (OR)	Mandatory death sentence for aggravated murder	Court re-writes to allow for "mitigating circumstances"	
Measure 10 (OR)	New rules for evidence, sentencing and parole	Court re-writes to limit the use of victim impact statements	
Measure 11(OR)	Mandatory sentences		X
Measure 40 (OR)	Seven changes to jury and legal system, mainly under the heading of "victims' rights"	X	
Initiative 350 (WA)	Declares busing illegal	X	
Initiative 593 (WA)	Life sentences for repeat offenders		X
Initiative 316 (WA)	Mandatory death penalty for first degree murder	X	

The initiative process is unique because there are few veto points and no power sharing among separate state institutions. The only minority veto present in direct democracy is that of the courts. It is not surprising that the courts protect the one minority faction they are most interested in—themselves. The empirical data bear this out. Courts have become more suspicious of initiative lawmaking in general in the past decade. But they appear to have always been suspicious of direct democracy when that democracy intrudes upon their institutional prerogatives.

This is not to say the courts are only protective of their autonomy when the attacks come from direct democracy. Courts have traditionally resisted encroachments from Congress, too. However, when looking at the larger picture,

---

[4] The courts actually nullified Proposition 24 before it went to the ballot, but after Ted Costa spent over $1.3 million collecting signatures to qualify the proposition.

it is necessary to look at all reasons for nullification—not just reasons that are unique to the initiative process.

The Lack of Institutional Guidance

It is well know that court decisions do more than simply adjudicate a legal conflict.   Court rulings also serve to act as "signals" to other political actors. Court decisions affect the way legislatures draft legislation, influence the strategies of attorneys, impact the way lower courts decide cases, and encourage and discourage various social movements.

When courts invalidate legislation they signal to legislatures how laws must be written in the future to avoid judicial review.   Relatively recently, scholars have begun to incorporate courts into their "separation of powers" games that model the signaling relationship between legislatures and courts (Rogers, 2001; Marks, 1988). In terms of a game, the relationship between the courts and legislatures is an iterated one. Legislatures continually draft legislation and courts continually rule on the constitutionality of the legislation. As Axelrod (1980) suggests, iterated games, even absent formal rules, tend to find equilibrium. One would expect, then, that an iterated game between courts and legislatures would eventually result in very few nullifications by the courts. Over time, using the interpretation of multiple signals from courts, legislatures will come to understand the limits of their lawmaking discretion in a constitutional system.   Empirical evidence appears to buttress this understanding of the legislative/court relationship. Landis and Posner (1975) illustrate that the nullification of federal statutes is in fact very rare, and Emmert (1987) reports similar findings for state statutes.

The exception to the above narrative is the nullification rate of state ballot measures. Unlike federal and state statutes, state ballot measures suffer an extremely high rate of judicial review. Miller (2001) demonstrates that 54% of all ballot measures are eventually challenged, and approximately 50% of those challenges subsequently result in partial or complete nullification of the statute. This data forces scholars to confront a question about the relationship between ballot measure drafters and the courts. In comparison to the legislative/court relationship, either the game between the courts and ballot measure drafters is different, or the players are acting differently. It is safe to assume that is unlikely, if not impossible, for courts to isolate signals sent to legislatures from signals sent to ballot measure drafters. Once a court issues a ruling on a point of law, any political actor has access to that "signal" and can use it to alter her behavior. Therefore, it is safe to assume that the game between ballot measure drafters and courts is the same as the game between courts and legislatures.

If the game is the same, the players must be playing differently. Under this assumption, inadequate signaling can contribute to high invalidation rates of ballot measures in three ways. First, it is possible that courts signal ballot measure drafters in the same manner as they signal legislatures, but that ballot measure drafters are amateur lawmakers who fail to interpret the legal signals correctly. Second, it is possible that courts simply don't send signals to ballot measure drafters. For this hypothesis to be correct, ballot measure legislation must be completely different than legislation enacted by legislatures. And third, it is possible that courts send incoherent or contradictory signals to ballot measure drafters.

The Courts as Political Signalers

When institutions share political power, especially if that power includes a veto over the others, each institution must inform one another what actions will be permissible. Luce and Raiffa (1957) called these "signaling strategies." Galanter (1983), speaking specifically about the courts, notes "the law articulated by the courts is better understood as complex signals rather than as a set of operative controls. It affects us primarily through communication of symbols—by providing threats, promises and so on." Brace and Langer (2002) take this logic a step further and suggest the courts have "preemptive" signaling power. They suggest that judicial scholars have too long viewed courts as "reactionary, responding to the law passed by the legislature." But in reality, "supreme courts also shape public policy passively or preemptively by their ideological composition." In other words, political actors make strategic decisions based on how they *assume* the courts will react in the *future.* Maltzman, Spriggs and Wahlbeck (1999) agree. They note that "Because the Supreme Court is embedded in a political system in which legislative and executive branches have the capacity to overturn, circumvent, or even ignore its decision, the Supreme Court will anticipate the reaction of Congress and craft its decisions not to be overturned."

Michael McCann (1999) identifies five ways in which the courts act as political signalers. He argues that courts act as a catalyst to encourage further litigation in specific areas of law, distribute "endowments" of power to specific "parties locked in prolonged patterns of conflict," while at the same time, constraining the options of other legal actors. He also argues that courts displace political conflict and encourage counter mobilizations. For the purposes of this chapter, the first three are the most relevant. He comments,

> After all, judicial decisions do not simply dictate particular types of behavior; rather, they identify potential opportunities and costs, resources and constraints, which become meaningful only in the diverse strategic responses from differently situated public and private actors in society.

The historical record is replete with examples of political actors reacting to the Supreme Court's signals. To identify them all would be impossible. However, consider the following examples as representative of how courts can signal other actors.

One of the most obvious examples of court signaling is the Supreme Court's decision in *Regents v. Bakke* 438 U.S. 265; 98 S. Ct. 2733 (1978). In the *Bakke* case, the court invalidated the UC system's affirmative action program. The Court could have stopped by simply noting that quotas violated the 14th Amendment. However, Justice Powell went further and explained that if the UC system had used the affirmative action program developed at Harvard or Princeton, the Court would have upheld the system. As can be expected, admissions programs around the country began emulating the Harvard/Princeton system to avoid judicial censure.

In *Miller v. California* 413 U.S. 15; 93 S. Ct. 2607 (1973), the Court tackled the issue of obscenity. In *Miller*, the Court meekly announced that it is not the place of the Court to "propose regulatory schemes for the States" and then proceeded to do exactly that. The Court writes,

> It is possible, however, to give a few plain examples of what a state stature could define for regulation under part (b) of the standard announced in this opinion. (a) Patently offensive representation of descriptions of ultimate sexual acts, normal or perverted, actual or simulated. (b) Patently offensive representations of descriptions of masturbation, excretory functions, and lewd exhibition of the genitals.

Not surprisingly, soon after *Miller* was decided, many states adopted the Court's wording verbatim when amending their obscenity statutes.[27] What makes *Miller* such an effective signal to other actors is that the case both identifies what type of legislation is impermissible but, like *Bakke,* also takes the additional step of identifying what *is* permissible.

If the signaling paradigm accurately describes the behavior of courts and legislative bodies, there is no reason to believe that it does not describe the relationship between ballot measure drafters and the courts. Ballot measure drafters, as one player in a multi-institutional system, are affected by the preemptive influence of courts. If they are rational actors, they would attempt to craft initiatives that avoid nullification.[28]

Most relevant to this chapter is the courts' ability to constrain the options of political actors. Judicial review is the process of telling lawmakers what they cannot do. Every time a court invalidates a statute, it sends a clear signal to lawmakers that certain strategic options are unavailable to them. In an iterated game, lawmakers absorb the signals provided by judicial review, and then alter the substance of future legislation. For ballot measure drafters, every time a court invalidates one of their initiatives, they should be able to amend future measures to navigate the constitutional restrictions erected by the court.

However, despite the hundreds of signals that courts send with each docket of cases, ballot measure drafters still have an extremely high rate of invalidation before the very institution that is sending the signals. If ballot measure drafters are not ignoring the signals, one contributing cause to high rates of ballot measure nullification might be that the courts' signals are unclear, contradictory, or in some cases, non-existent.

Blaming the Court for a Lack of Signals

The interview data revealed two complaints drafters have about the courts. Drafters complained that much of the law they were creating was new and as a result, there was very little case law for them to follow. Legal scholars identify these types of cases as "first impression" cases. [29] Second, they complained that courts "changed their minds" quite often, thus sending contradictory messages to drafters, and that the messages the courts sent were unclear and hard to use as a guideline for drafting legislation. The remainder of this section elaborates on the complaints ballot measure drafters have about the way courts signal.

In order to understand why the courts fail to provide effective signaling to initiative drafters, one must first understand who uses the initiative system. Initiatives are a tool for political outsiders. People who can't get access to the established political institutions resort to the initiative process. Of the 45 ballot measure drafters interviewed, all 45 indicated they use the initiative process because they can't get access to the legislature, or because the legislature has been non-responsive to their desires. Therefore, ballot measure drafters do not draft the types of legislation that have histories in legislatures. For example, legislatures are not generally friendly to term limit laws, campaign finance laws, medical marijuana laws, doctor-assisted suicide laws, and laws that limit their ability to finance public goods. Bills concerning subjects such as doctor-assisted suicide or medical marijuana are blocked by passionate minority interests (institutional minority vetoes). Term limit and campaign finance bills tend to threaten the legislature itself and find no support.

If certain bills have never made it through the legislature, then it is very unlikely that there will be any case law regarding the issue. As a prime example, there was no federal term limits case law until *Thornton* in 1995. [30] The reason is obvious. No legislature had ever passed a self-restrictive term limit law, and thus there was no need to challenge a non-existent law in court. Given that there was no case law about term limits, the pioneer ballot measure drafters who crafted the term limits laws had no signals to observe from the courts. Of course, every time a new law is drafted, whether by the legislature or by initiative, there may be some aspects that have not been dealt with in a legal setting. But what makes the initiative process unique is that many of the laws passed via this venue are completely new.

Indian gaming is another prominent example. Many Indian activists who want to promote Indian gaming run into dead ends when proceeding through the legislature. Gambling is an issue that conjures up a variety of social issues (some taboo), and is usually blocked by passionate conservative groups. As one activist noted, "I've worked with the legislature and governors of both parties on other issues. But this [Indian gaming] was a dead on arrival issue. We knew the initiative was the only way" (Interview # 61). When questioned about how they proceeded during the drafting stage of the process, this comment was insightful:

> Most of us in the drafting committee were lawyers. So we started with a basic WestLaw and Lexis search. It was almost funny. We got about five hits if I remember right. It was then that it hit us that we were doing something completely new. We ended up using a legal case about the state lottery as our guiding principle. It was the closest thing we could find (Interview #10).

Another activist pursuing the same goal in a different state had the same problem, but took a different tack.

> We searched for anything we could find. But there was nothing [no case law] in our state. We eventually looked to experts in other states that had successfully passed some similar legislation…it was interesting when we ran it by the AG. He had no suggestions for us. I don't think he knew if it was constitutional or not, either (Interview # 61).

In these cases we see a complete lack of signaling by the courts. Not that this should be taken as a criticism of the courts. Courts that deal with issues of constitutionality predominantly have appellate jurisdiction and therefore must wait for cases to come to them. Furthermore, most state courts refuse to issue "prior review" decisions. These are seen as "advisory opinions," and courts are loath to get involved in the political process this way (Arrow, 1992). As a result, institutional restrictions upon the courts prevent them from sending signals to ballot measure drafters who are crafting innovative law. Thus, when ballot measure drafters need legal signals from courts the most, they are least likely to receive them.

Just as complicating for ballot measure drafters is when courts send conflicting or ambiguous signals. Many ballot measure drafters express their frustration with how the courts hand down contradictory cases, or make rulings that do more to define what is unconstitutional than what is constitutional. Consider the following comments:

> Yes, I do pay attention to the courts. But they change their minds so often. I think it's because they change membership so often. For instance, they completely reversed themselves within five years with the *Whiffen* and *Sithranahan* cases.[31] Nothing really changed except for who was sitting on the courts. But the real problem is that courts only tell us what they don't like. They never tell us what is OK. So we just keep coming back with new attempts, and they keep coming back with new reasons why we can't do it (Interview # 92).

Another drafter expressed similar feeling about the lack of direction the courts provide. As an activist pursuing campaign finance reform, he wanted the courts to say what limits they would accept, but instead the court kept indicating what they would not accept.

> The judge came back to us saying our limits were too low. That's exactly what they said a few years before when [...] lost his measure in court. Well, where does that leave us? We know that $100 is too low, and now we know that $500 is too low. Of course they never tell us what isn't too low (Interview # 53).

However, another drafter was more frustrated with conflicting signals. As an environmentalist, he tried to pass protective legislation and kept running into single subject problems. He notes,

> The single subject rule is like pornography to judges.[32] They know it when they see it. They just can't seem to tell us what it is. I've watched Bruce's initiatives get struck down one after another on single subject grounds, and then watched that same court uphold initiatives that are twice as long and twice as complicated (Interview # 48).

An Oregon drafter made similar comments.

> *Armatta* came out of nowhere. We had been paying attention to single subject rulings and noticed they were getting tougher. But then they hit us with a whole new hurdle. They tell us, "OK, we know you've met all our single subject criteria, but now we have a new separate vote criteria. Surprise!" I think it's important to note that the Secretary of State certified our measure. So he obviously thought it was OK (Interview # 87).

In all these examples, initiative drafters are expressing their frustrations about the erratic nature of court rulings. Of course, "erratic" is in the eye of the beholder. But it is fair to say that courts have been adopting new case law with respect to initiatives. When initiatives were a relatively rare phenomenon, there was little opportunity to develop new initiative case law. But with the increased use of initiatives in the West (Waters, 1999), we have clearly seen a shift in the way the courts approach initiatives (Lowenstien, 2001; Campbell, 2000). Courts often seem to be torn with respect to protecting the democratic nature of the initiative process, while at the same time intent on reining in what they view as a process run amok.

Empirical Testing

Ballot measure drafters suggest courts are poor signalers. However, does the empirical evidence support such a claim? In order to test this hypothesis, every decision that ruled on the legality of an initiative between 1990 and 2000 in the states of Washington, Oregon, California and Colorado was examined. In all, there were 40 cases that either invalidated or upheld an initiative. Appendix B identifies each of these cases and examines how the court signaled ballot measure drafters with respect to their constitutionality. Specifically, all cases were classified into one of four categories:

• Cases that *"moved the target."* These are cases in which the courts ignored previously established precedent and created a new precedent.

- Cases that provided *"no future guidance."* These cases ruled on the constitutionality of a ballot measure but failed to provide any guidelines on how to make future initiatives on the same topic meet constitutional muster.

- Cases in which *"no prior guidance existed."* These are cases of first impression. Neither the courts nor drafters can rely on any previous precedent because none exists.

- Cases with *"well established precedent."* These are cases in which the courts handed down ruling on ballot measure and could rely on well established and clearly related precedent. Such cases also maintain a clear signal to future initiative drafters.

The following examples help flesh out the above definitions. Table 8 summarizes the cumbersome data contained in Appendix B.

An example of a case that "moved the target" is *Armatta v. Kitzhaber* (1998). Prior to *Armatta*, no Oregon initiative had ever been nullified on "separate vote" grounds. The reason was that the Oregon Constitution explicitly exempted initiatives from separate vote concerns. Article XVII of the Oregon Constitution, which sets out the separate vote requirements, concludes, "This article shall not be construed to impair the right of the people to amend this Constitution by vote upon an initiative petition therefor [sic]." Prior to *Armatta*, state courts had used the single subject rule to invalidate initiatives that covered more than one area of policy. The rationale of the single subject rule is to prevent logrolling such as ballot measure drafters including a divisive or harmful measure along with a popular tax cut. As Anne Campbell (1999) has shown, courts have increasingly relied on the single subject rule as a barrier of last resort to invalidate otherwise constitutional measures. She also notes that courts have been relatively erratic in defining what exactly constitutes a "single subject."

The erratic application of the single subject rule proved problematic for initiative drafters. Yet, through a series of adaptations (mainly shortening the length of ballot measures), drafters increasingly overcame single subject requirements as established by the courts. Therefore, it came as a great surprise to initiative drafters when the Oregon Court decided to ignore the last sentence of

Article XVII and apply the separate vote rule to initiatives. In rejecting an initiative (Measure 40, 1998) that altered several aspects of the Oregon judicial system, the Court ruled that the drafters had indeed kept their initiative to one subject, but failed to provide for a separate vote on each change. In essence, the Oregon Court abruptly created an entirely new hurdle for initiative drafters. In a case like *Armatta*, it is impossible for ballot measure drafters to anticipate such a ruling and draft their measures accordingly. Not only had a separate vote standard never previously existed, but also the application of the standard was clearly prohibited.[33]

Through a process of diffusion, other states began to adopt single subject rules and the new *Armatta* standard. In Washington, *Amalgamated Transit Union Local v. State* (2000) suddenly imposed the single subject restriction. In California, *Senate v. Jones* returned the single subject rule after almost 30 years of dormancy. In Montana, *Marshall v. Cooney* (1999) adopted *Armatta* as precedent and created a separate vote rule for the first time in the state's history.

More vexing to initiative drafters than the creation of the "separate vote" rule was the *ex post facto* application of the new standard. In 1990 Oregon proponents of term limits passed Measure 3. Measure 3 prescribed term limits to Oregon state legislators serving in the state government and the federal government.[34] The complete law was in effect until the US Supreme Court's 1995 *Thornton* decision invalidated the sections applying to federal term limits. However, the state-imposed limits continued to stay in effect after *Thornton*. In 1998, in a seemingly unrelated issue, the Oregon Court's *Armatta* decision nullified Measure 40 on the grounds that it required separate votes on each of its "victim's rights" provisions. Then in 2002, the Oregon Court found the remaining state limitations of Measure 3 unconstitutional based on their earlier *Armatta* ruling in 1998.[35] The Court argued that the drafting of Measure 3 in 1992 violated the procedural rules established in 1998. The end result is that a bill that was constitutional for 10 years was eventually nullified because the Oregon Supreme Court created new procedural rules for the initiative system in

1998 and then held initiatives that were passed before 1998 accountable under the new rules.[36]

A case that provided "no future guidance" for initiative drafters who wanted to revisit an issue is *California Pro-life Action Council v. Scully* (1998). This California case nullified a campaign finance reform initiative by simply ruling the contribution limits were "too low." However, the ruling offered little information as to what was high enough. Many of the ballot measure drafters expressed their frustration over this ruling. Wanting to draft a subsequent measure, they were unsure how to proceed because they had no information from the courts as to what limits would be upheld. These frustrations were most evident with campaign finance and term limit activists (Interview #23, #85, #44, #41). Without more specific signals from the courts, initiative drafters find themselves in an environment similar to the child's game of 20 questions. As one drafter put it,

> In 20 questions, one kid thinks of an object and everybody tries to guess what he is thinking of. Is it blue? No. Is it big? No. Is it in the room? No. In our case the courts know the "object" but won't tell us. So we draft one initiative after another that basically asks the question, "is the limit here?" No? OK. "Is it here?" No? Ok let's try one more time. Just with an initiative it takes a lot longer and costs a lot more (Interview # 70).

The approach to initiative drafting illustrated above is indicative of the incremental approach. It is also indicative of the "probing" approach. Many initiative drafters are looking for novel ways to achieve their policy goals. They don't know what the courts will allow, but they are purposely trying an approach that has never been attempted. Gordon Miller, an Oregon campaign finance reform activist, passed an initiative that required all campaign contributions to come from within the candidate's district. Miller's logic was that if he could not limit the amount of a contribution, he would limit from where contributions could come. Because there was no case law indicating whether this approach was constitutional or not, Miller felt the lack of precedent might work in his favor. It did not. The court rejected this type of contribution limit, ruling, "The [previous] court did not concern itself with a distinction between in-district and out-of-district corporations. Therefore, we conclude that the state interest defined in Austin does not support Measure 6." The court could have gone either way. Noting a lack of precedent, the court could have determined that because out-of-district contributions are not explicitly endorsed, Miller's approach is acceptable. However, the court's ruling simply notes they have never dealt with this issue and, as a result, they are not going to allow the restriction. It is the 20 Questions syndrome. Mr. Miller asks, "Is this type of limitation OK?" The court responds "No, it is not," but provides no further signal as to what limitation is acceptable.[37]

A case where "no prior guidance" exists is *Thornton v. US Term Limits* (1995). This is a classic case of first impression. There was absolutely no case law on federal term limits prior to this ruling. As a result, no initiative drafter pursuing term limits had any signals from the court as to what would be acceptable. It was only after *Thornton* that term limit activists could use the courts as a signaling mechanism. But even in this case, the courts only established that states could not impose term limits outright. The case did nothing to indicate what type of actions states could take. Into this vacuum stepped several initiative drafters testing what was acceptable. The result was several "scarlet letter"[38] measures that were all struck down.

A case of "well established precedent" is *League of United Latin American Citizens v. Wilson (1995)*. This case was a challenge to Proposition 187 which, among other things, denied education benefits to children of illegal immigrants. However, the body of law concerning regulating the education of illegal aliens was clearly established in *Plyer v. Doe* (1982). In *Plyer*, the US Supreme Court ruled that a Texas statute denying the use of state funds to educate illegal aliens violated the 14th Amendment's Equal Protection Clause. This case was well known to the drafters of Proposition 187 (Interview # 11). They simply ignored the precedent. And the initiative was immediately rejected by the District Court of California.

A case-by-case analysis is presented in Appendix B. The data reveal some important patterns. Drawing from the qualitative interpretation of the 40 cases, a summary of the data in Appendix B is presented in Table 8.

Table 8: Rates of Nullification per Type of Judicial Decision[5]

	Moving Target	No Prior Guidance	Established Precedent
Initiative Overturned	10	11	6
Initiative Upheld	0	5	11

* Chi-Square (two-sided) significance is .007

It is clear that court cases that establish a new legal doctrine, or in essence "move the target," will lead to ballot measure invalidation. Of the ten cases in which the courts established new doctrine, the courts overturned all the initiatives. Initiatives have only a slightly higher survival rate when courts had been unable to provide prior guidance or signaling in the form of earlier case law. These "cases of first impression" tend to result in nullification for ballot measures. Of the 16 cases, the courts rejected 11 and only five were upheld.[39]

The cases where there was a well-established precedent tell a more complicated story. The data show that initiatives that are drafted in this environment have the best chance of surviving judicial scrutiny. The courts upheld 11 of the 17 cases. This data supports the model presented here—that clearer signaling by the courts will lead to less ballot measure invalidation. However, seven cases remain in which there was clear precedent, yet the measures still met with nullification. The reason is that information or signaling deficiencies are not the only reason for ballot measure nullification. Although it is beyond the scope of this chapter, evidence suggests that even in the face of clear signals from the courts, some drafters still make "mistakes." These mistakes arise from the fact that ballot measure drafters are not always seeking to immediately achieve policy implementation. Zealots, and to some degree

---

[5] There are 43 total data points in Table 8 despite the fact that I only examined 40 legal cases. This is due to the fact that 3 cases nullified some clauses of an initiative and upheld others. This required double coding for those 3 cases. Also, one caveat should be made for California Proposition 215. It was coded as "upheld". In the case challenging Proposition 215 (medical marijuana), the court refused to overturn the measure, but indicated that federal law banning the use of medical marijuana essentially made the proposition moot.

amateurs, often have other goals, such as sending political messages, depleting the resources of opposition interest groups, or simply challenging the existing precedent of the court. When drafters pursue these types of goals, it is likely courts will find the legislation unconstitutional regardless of the body of existing legal signals from the courts.

How Initiative Activists Compound the Problem

At first glance, the data above suggests that courts bear a considerable amount of culpability for the high rate of ballot measure nullification. However, a closer examination of the strategies employed by ballot measure drafters suggests that they contribute to the phenomenon. It is true that the courts sometimes send unclear signals to ballot measure drafters. But initiative drafters compound the problem by adopting an "incremental" approach to creating legislation.

Given that courts tend to indicate what is not constitutional rather than what is constitutional, drafters tend to respond by taking small, incremental steps towards constitutionality. Interestingly, many ballot measure drafters do not draft their first measure to be clearly constitutional, and then draft other initiatives that "push the envelope" by taking incremental steps away from current precedent. Instead, they begin by drafting "radical" measures that clearly challenge existing precedent. If and when that measure is invalidated, the subsequent measures take small steps back towards what is constitutionally acceptable. When the steps are too small, they meet with additional nullifications. This is a common problem for drafters with "zealot" tendencies. These groups do not want to take large steps. As they see it, large moves that ensure constitutionality are large moves away from their policy goal.

One way to describe this dilemma is to create a spatial model. Figure 1 presents a simple, one dimensional, "Downsian" policy space model. In the model Point 1 represents the most preferred policy location. Movement towards 0 represents a loss in utility. Point A represents a "constitutional point". Anything to the right of Point A is unconstitutional. Anything to the left will be upheld by the courts.

Figure 1

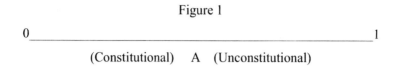

(Constitutional)   A   (Unconstitutional)

Obviously, all initiative drafters are confronted with an opportunity cost decision. In order to move their initiative to the left of Point A they must accept some utility loss by moving towards Point 0. Therefore, many initiative drafters inherently desire to move as little as possible past Point A. For example, Figure 2 below indicates such a situation. An initiative drafter would much rather be at Point B than Point C. Both measures are constitutional, but a measure at Point B achieves much more of the policy goal.

Figure 2

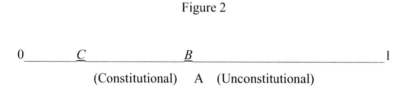

(Constitutional)   A   (Unconstitutional)

In many cases we see initiative groups take an incremental approach after their first experience with nullification. Figure 3 is descriptive of many term limits, campaign finance reform, and some of the more sophisticated pro-life campaigns. In each case, the initial attempt at change (point B) overreached and met with invalidation.

Figure 3

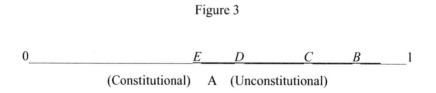

(Constitutional)   A   (Unconstitutional)

The subsequent campaigns marginally scaled back their goals in hopes of moving the measure to the constitutional side of Point A. Each subsequent attempt at reform/change moved their bills to Points C, D and in some cases, finally to Point E.

It doesn't necessarily need to be the same group that pursues the subsequent initiatives. Although professionals[40] are most likely to be repeat players, other less experienced ballot measure drafters learn from the successes and failures of others. Thus sometimes we will see three initiatives on the same topic pursued sequentially by three different groups. It is possible for an amateur[41] or zealot to pursue the first campaign, a professional to pursue the second campaign, and a lawyer to pursue the third campaign. However, each time they base their strategic legal decisions on the experience of the measure that came before them. It is common for all types of ballot measure drafters (except amateurs) to review recent attempts by other elites (working in the same content area) and identify where the courts found constitutional problems. For example, campaign finance reform advocates in California first looked at how other campaign reform initiatives fared in other federal districts before drafting their own initiative. The professional and lawyer drafters wanted to amend the language of their initiative to accommodate recent rulings (Interview # 25).

Interview data did not reveal any direct communication between the several groups. However, indirectly, the courts were acting as a communication mechanism for the disunited groups all pursuing campaign finance reform. Rulings against one measure were used by unassociated groups at later dates to draft more judicially defensible measures.

Consider the following examples of the incremental approach. Campaign finance measures had to keep increasing the donation limits before the courts would accept them. Term limits activists started by simply imposing term limits on federal office holders. After *Thornton*, they moved to "Scarlet Letter" bills. Scarlet letter bills placed statements such as "Disregarded Voter Intent on Term Limits" on the ballot next to members of Congress who did not vote for term limits. But the courts also invalidated those initiatives as well. Finally, term limits activists moved to pass bills that allowed for "voluntary declarations" that candidates could sign indicating they would support term limits. These measures the courts upheld. Anti-abortion activists learned to add exception clauses that released women from the restrictions of their initiative. An obvious pattern emerges. Ballot measure drafters do not jump from Point B to Point E. Instead, they incrementally move to Point E.[42] But again, it is important to realize how initiative drafters tend to differ from legislative drafters in this respect. Many anti-abortion advocates working with their respective legislatures take a different approach. These advocates start at a point they know is constitutionally acceptable, and then try to increase the number and scope of restrictions placed on abortion. Examples include parental notification, counseling requirements, and bans on late-term or partial birth abortions. This strategy allows advocates to add regulations until the courts say they have gone too far. But initiative drafters take an opposite approach, and begin far away from the constitutionally acceptable point and slowly "give in" to the law. As a result, they face nullification after nullification until they come far enough to satisfy the courts.

What makes this process more complicated for ballot measure drafters is that the most important information, Point A, is *neither known nor fixed.* As noted earlier, ballot measure drafters are quite open when they admit they have a difficult time interpreting the signals of the courts. They complain, with some justification, that courts move the location of Point A on a regular basis, or they fail to indicate where point A actually is. Instead, courts spend most of their time telling ballot measure drafters where Point A is not. For example, a 10th Circuit Court decision invalidating a Colorado campaign finance measure (Measure 15) rejected the "unreasonable twenty-four hour notice requirement" but went on to add "We cannot substitute our own judgment for that of a legislature as to a more appropriate and reasonable time frame."[43] In other words, twenty -four hours is too short, but we can't tell you what is not too short. Or, rejecting a scarlet letter initiative, the California Court asserted the language was "impermissibly coercive"[44] but failed to identify what type of language is permissive. Neither of these signals imparts enough information to initiative drafters to confidently fix future measures. As a result, the models in Figures 1-3 are not realistic. Instead, Figure 1-3 should look like Figure 4.

Figure 4

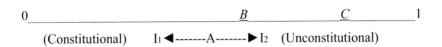

Consider an initiative drafter who is drafting a measure at Point B, or a drafter who initially drafted a measure at Point C but has since moved to Point B. In either case, the drafter sincerely does not know if her measure meets constitutional standards. Because Point A is either unidentified by the courts due to ambiguous rulings, or Point A is constantly moving because courts "move the target," ballot measure drafters have a difficult time deciding where to place their initiatives on the spectrum. As a result, drafters believing that the "constitutional point" is at I_2 construct an initiative at Point B, but then later find out that the "constitutional point" is actually at I_1.

Conclusion

Once again, the data show that institutions are integral players in the political process—at both the individual and aggregate level—and how those institutions are structured affects how individuals develop political strategies and how institutions interact with one another. The initiative process has its own set of rules, and those rules affect the measures' nullification rate. The fact that initiatives can be challenged on content and procedural grounds increases the chance of a court loss. Because initiatives cannot be amended after the signature collection process begins, drafters are prevented from making amendments to maintain an initiative's constitutionality. In addition, the fact that the initiative process takes place in a multi-institutional setting subjects initiatives to the discretion of other political actors. This discretion creates a "principal-agency" dilemma, allowing ideologically motivated or institutionally protective actors to defeat initiatives. And finally, it is clear that the nature of the court system imposes informational deficiencies upon initiative elites. Because these elites tend to pursue policies that have limited judicial histories, they find themselves writing on the *Tabula Rasa*. As such, they have limited guidance from the courts as to what language is or is not constitutional. Ultimately, the strategic and rational actions of sophisticated and savvy initiative elites are not enough to overcome the barriers created by the institutional structure of the initiative process. Despite the rational behavior of initiative elites, these barriers lead to high rates of judicial nullification.

---

[1] Briefly reviewing, I identified six different actors in the initiative process: zealots, amateurs, professionals, lawyers, politicians and victims.

[2] Initiatives may be altered, but if they are, all previously collected signatures, affirmed title, and ballot summary are void.

[3] Montana initiative drafters experienced a similar event in 1999. See *Marshall v. Cooney*, 975 P 2nd 325. In Oregon, the *ex post facto* concerns became so great, the legislature feared every initiative ever passed in Oregon would be suspect. They considered calling a special session of the Legislature to protect measures passed in the early 1980s. See "Special Session Unneeded," *The Register-Guard*, August 26, 2001. 3B.

[4] For example, in 1994 Congress passed the Unfunded Mandates Act, which required all new federal mandates to state governments to go through new bureaucratic procedures to be valid. If the courts went back and nullified all unfunded mandates passed prior to 1994 which did not follow those procedures, the number of nullifications would have been in the thousands.

[5] One procedural source of friction between the initiative process and the courts comes from the fact that there is a fine line between constitutional revision and constitutional amendment. Many state constitutions allow for the initiative process to amend the constitution, but not to revise it (Tolbert, Lowenstein and Donovan, 1998; Collins and Oesterle, 1994); a restriction not imposed on legislatures. Whenever there is a question about the difference, it falls to the courts to decide whether or not a ballot measure has stepped past the line of amendment and crossed into the arena of revision. As one can imagine, this is a very vague standard and is going to be subject to multiple interpretations not only among different courts but also among various initiative elites. For example, California's Supreme Court upheld Proposition 13 as an amendment to the state constitution, despite the fact it completely altered the way the government could finance itself. Yet the same court struck down Proposition 115 as a revision of the state constitution because it required the courts to adopt the federal courts' interpretation of civil rights laws. See *Amador Valley Joint Union High School District vs. State Brd of Equalization (1978) (149 Cal. Rptr. 239) and Raven vs. Deukmejian (1990) (276 Cal Rptr. 326).*

[6] Because of conference committees, amendments can even be offered after the final vote.

[7] In one case, the initiative drafters went so far as to lobby the public NOT to vote for their initiative. Proposition 225 (CA) was a "scarlet letter" term limit bill. After the bill had qualified for the ballot, other circuit courts had invalidated similar measures as "pejorative." The proponents of 225 took out ads in the voter guide asking voters to vote against their initiative.

[8] A Colorado subject had a similar experience. After drafting Amendment 16, a land use reform initiative, the voters of Colorado adopted a separate Amendment imposing a single subject rule on all initiatives. The drafter did not have the resources to begin his campaign anew, noting, "We'll just have to hope." The Colorado court did not reject his initiative.

[9] The fact that initiatives cannot be amended after signature gathering begins can also indirectly lead to initiatives failing. Consider the case of a Colorado initiative drafter who drafted and submitted a measure that would alter the way the state awarded public contracts. After the initiative was submitted, he began to expend what little resources he had to collect signatures. In the middle of the process, the Colorado Supreme Court accepted a challenge to the title of his initiative, and subsequently changed the title. This had the effect of making all the previously collected signatures invalid and ultimately resulted in the abandonment of the project. Cases like this highlight the fact that judicial nullification of initiatives is most likely higher than the 54% reported by Miller (2000). His data does not record cases in which judicial action leads to initiative rejection prior to Election Day.

[10] For example, Dave Frohnmayer (OR) and Bill Jones (CA) both ran for governor after serving as Attorney General or Secretary of State. This statement appears to challenge other statements about the nature of how actors behave once they have acquired institutional titles. This is not necessarily so. Peltason's classic work, *Fifty-Four Southern Justices*, suggests that southern judges put aside their personal beliefs in the face of the *Brown* decision. However, Peltason was studying unelected institutional actors. Attorneys general are elected and often seek other office. Therefore, it is more likely they will maintain a "political" outlook even after acquiring the title of Attorney General.

[11] As another example, Lupia et. al note that California's Proposition 184 "Three Strikes Law" was very unpopular in San Francisco. Their data show that district attorneys from that area of the state filed the fewest "three-strike" complaints. Their conclusion was that this was a directed effort to thwart the enactment of Proposition 184.

[12] Schuman had published a law review article claiming the entire system of direct democracy violated the Guarantee Clause of the Federal Constitution and the US Supreme Court should strike the system from state constitutions. See "Emerging Issues in State Constitutional Law," 67(3) *Temple Law Review* (Fall, 1994).

[13] This was the first of many moves that raised suspicions about the sincerity of the defense. Schuman had no trial experience. He was appointed to oversee the administration of some 200 lawyers working for the Attorney General's office. Therefore, when he chose himself to defend such a high profile case, despite his lack of any trial experience, it appeared to be an unorthodox move.

[14] Governor Kitzhaber was an open critic of Measure 7, and drafted an opinion piece that was published in the Oregon 2000 Voter Guide.

[15] Merritt notes that Kitzhaber's staff attorneys claimed the reason for the meeting was to discuss how Measure 7 would affect the budget. However, the notes from the meeting did not have any reference to budgets or spending. All the notes referred to legal challenges to Measure 7 that did not exist at the time of the meeting.

[16] These two acknowledgements are significant. In order for plaintiffs to prevail in a hearing seeking an injunction, they must show the court that a lack of immediate action will lead to irreparable harm, and that there is a strong likelihood that they will eventually win on the merits of the case.

[17] I identify Ron Prince by name in this section. Although Mr. Prince was an interview subject, and his anonymous comments appear throughout the book, the information provided in the following section, although discussed during our interview, also appears in public domain print.

[18] See *Children Who Want an Education v. Wilson*, Case No. 94-7570 MRP.

[19] See *League of United Latin American Citizens v. Wilson* at 908 F.Supp. 775 (9th Cir).

[20] See Chance, Amy. "Davis sends Prop. 187 to mediation" *Bee Capitol Bureau* (April 1, 1999).

[21]   See "Federal Judge Okays Settlement on California Proposition 187" VISALAW.COM accessed at H*www.visalaw.com/99oct/24oct99.html*H.

[22] See California Coalition for Immigration Reform, "The History of Proposition 187" Press Release (10/3/2002) accessed at H*http://ccir.net/references/187-history.html*H.

[23] Principal-agency theory defines principals as those who are endowed with authority. Agents are delegated a principal's authority to carry out a task desired by the principal. However, as most theorists note, agents have the ability to use the authority of the principal to pursue their own preferences.

[24] Truman once noted to an aide of the incoming President Eisenhower, "He'll sit there all day saying do this, do that, and nothing will happen. Poor Ike--it won't be a bit like the Army. He'll find it very frustrating."

[25] Kiewiet and McCubbins argue that principals can limit the independence of agents but the methods are costly. Examining the problem of agency loss in Congress they suggest four ways to prevent agency loss: contract design, expending resources to ensure that agents hold a similar preference as the principal, monitoring, or institutional checks. However, none of these options are available to initiative elites. Initiative elites cannot bind justices to contracts, and have little influence on who sits on the court. Some have tried monitoring, by highlighting instances when courts act contrary to the dictates of an initiative, but this has no noticeable effect on the behavior of justices. The only institutional check available is to amend the constitution, which of course runs right back into the original agency loss [to the courts] dilemma.

[26] The proposition attempted to remove apportionment responsibility from the legislature to the courts.

[27] Some examples include: Montana Revised Statutes 45-8-201, Tennessee Code Annotated 39-17-901, and Colorado Revised Statutes C.R.S. 18-7-101.

[28] My research indicates that some drafters are not concerned with judicial review. Interview data from some drafters indicates they employ the initiative process to send political messages, indirectly influence legislatures, or simply to consume the resources of opposition groups. However, for the purposes of this chapter I assume sincere motives on the part of drafters.

[29] Black's Law Dictionary defines a case of first impressions as a case that "presents an entirely novel question of law for the decision of the court, which cannot be governed by any existing precedent."

[30] Nowhere is this more obvious than when reading Justice Stevens' majority opinion in *Thornton*. Stevens, a prominent liberal on the court, drafted his opinion as a Scalia-like originalist. Because Stevens had no precedents to follow, he had to resort to the Federalist Papers and Constitutional Debates to formulate an argument. Stevens did try to find some precedent to follow. Citing *Powell v. McCormack* (1969), he noted that if the House could not refuse to sit duly elected members of Congress, per Constitutional qualifications, neither could states.

---

[31] In the 1993 case *Lloyd Corp v Whiffen* 315 Ore. 500; 849 P.2d 446 the court ruled, "We hold that persons seeking signatures on initiative petitions in the common areas of the Lloyd Center have a constitutional right to do so under Article IV, section 1, of the Oregon Constitution, subject to reasonable time, place, and manner restrictions. We further hold that three of the present restrictions, as adopted by plaintiff Lloyd Corporation (respondent on review) and approved by the trial court in this case, are unreasonable." In 2000, *Stranahan v. Fred Meyer* 331 Ore. 38; 11 P.3d 228 the court reversed itself noting, "For the reasons that follow, we now conclude that *Whiffen* does not state correctly the law of Oregon on that subject. We therefore reverse the decision of the Court of Appeals."

[32] Although Florida is not in my data set, the Florida courts provide an interesting example illustrative of this drafter's frustration. In 1994, the Florida court removed from the ballot a tax reduction measure, claiming that taxes and fees are different subjects.

[33] In a move that was eventually overturned by the Oregon Supreme Court, an Oregon District Court tried to add more teeth to the separate vote clause. In *Sager v. Keisling*, 167 Ore. App. 405 the court argued even if the language of the measure only affected one clause, but had the "effect of" altering more than one clause, the measure was in violation of the separate vote rule. This ruling was overturned in order to uphold Measure 16, the Doctor Assisted Suicide bill.

[34] At the state level, House members were limited to six years, Senators were limited to eight years, and the total anyone could serve in both chambers was 12 years. At the federal level, House members were limited to six years and Senators were limited to 12 years.

[35] See *Lehman, et. al v. Bradbury*, et. al at 333 Ore 231 (2002).

[36] Montana initiative drafters experienced a similar event in 1999. See *Marshall v. Cooney*, 975 P 2nd 325. In Oregon, the *ex post facto* concerns became so great, the legislature feared every initiative ever passed in Oregon would be suspect. They considered calling a special session of the Legislature to protect measures passed in the early 1980s. See "Special Session Unneeded," *The Register-Guard*, August 26, 2001. 3B.

[37] Colorado initiative drafters faced the same dilemma. In a release from the Colorado Department of Law, the Attorney General summarized Judge Sparr's ruling on Amendment 15. "Judge Sparr ruled that the limits in Sec 1-45-104(2) of the FCPA on individual personal and political committee aggregate contributions to a state office candidate were unconstitutional as being too low, although the state could indeed enact contribution limits that would pass constitutional scrutiny." (Press Release 8/13/99).

[38] "Scarlet letter" measures sought to place information next to a candidate's name indicating that he had failed to support a term limit measure in the past.

[39] There is no analysis of cases that provided "no future guidance". This was omitted for a variety of reasons. First, in some instances, no future initiatives were written on the same subject, resulting in an inability to draw any causal relationships. Second, there is the danger of double counting the results. If a legal decision failed to provide signaling for future initiatives and a subsequent initiative failed for that reason, it would be counted as a case of "no prior guidance." The data on "no future guidance" presented in Appendix B is simply to highlight the signaling deficiencies of the courts.

[40] A drafter is classified as a professional if they are repeat players with an institutional support system behind them: fundraising apparatus, polling firms, professional legal advisors, and professional campaign advisors.

[41] I classify a drafter as an amateur if they are first time ballot measure drafters with little knowledge of the initiative system, the legal norms of their policy area, and little knowledge of politics.

[42] Obviously, zealots reject the incremental approach. Any movement towards the "constitutional point" is seen as political and capitulating.

[43] See *Colorado Right to Life v. Buckley* at 236 F.3d 1174: 2000 US App.

[44] See *Bramburg v. Jones* at 20 Cal. 4th 1045; P.2d 1240

Chapter Six

Behavioral Causes of Judicial Nullification

There is much debate about institutions' impact upon individual behavior. In political science, two epistemological camps dominate. In one, theorists argue for the attitudinal theory, which states that individuals simply pursue political objectives based on policy and value preferences (Spaeth and Segal 1989, 1995, 1997; Prichart, 1961; Dahl, 1957). In contrast, other judicial and public choice theorists argue that individual decisions are mediated, encouraged, and refined based on the institutional environment in which the decisions are made (March and Olsen1989; Gillman and Clayton, 1999a, 1999b). The study of judicial nullification of ballot measures engages this debate. Chapter 5 clearly identified the institutional reasons that initiatives fail before the courts. However, the nature of the initiative process, especially the institutional "rules of the game," both attract and contribute to certain behaviors that also cause the judicial rejection of ballot measures. The purpose of Chapter 6 is to identify the behavioral causes of judicial nullification, but especially to identify how the institutional structure of the initiative process facilitates the behavioral causes of nullification.

The line between institutional causes and behavioral causes is not always clear. The behavioral causes of nullification are the result of individual decision making of initiative elites. To understand the high rates of judicial nullification, we must understand why initiative activists make the decisions they do. To outside observers, it often appears that initiative elites have made obvious mistakes and therefore, the reasons for nullification are clear and simple. However, a closer examination of the strategies of initiative elites, and a clearer understanding of their goals and how they pursue those goals, reveals a deeper understanding of the initiative process and why they so often fail.

Coalition Building and Ideological Purity

Scholars examining social movements have long studied the internal dynamics of organizations and movements. They offer a considerable body of research on why movements succeed or fail. Social scientists have examined how resource mobilization (Gamson, 1975; Freeman, 1983; Jenkins, 1983), identity creation (Pizzorno, 1978; Taylor and Whittier, 1992; Wilcox, Jelen and Leege, 1993), framing (Snow and Benford, 1988, 1992), the collective action problem (Olson, 1965), and of course, organizational schisms due to ideological heterogeneity (Roche and Sachs, 1969; Barkan, 1979; Downey, 1987), impact the success of a social movement. Common to most of these studies is the argument that ideological heterogeneity, which causes organizational dilemmas, is a prominent cause of social movement failure (Roche and Sachs, 1969; Barkan, 1979; Downey, 1987; Mansbridge, 1986; Gamson, 1990; McAdam, McCarthy, and Zald, 1996; Castells, 1997). Ideological heterogeneity exists when a mobilizing organization contains both passionate activists unwilling to compromise the "mission" of a movement, and, at the same time, members willing to compromise the "mission" in order to ensure the movement's success. This tension typically creates obstacles for a social movement. Most research shows that ideological heterogeneity causes factionalization within social movement organizations (SMOs), and eventually leads to a schism within organizations.

Yet, few scholars consider, let alone test, the impact of ideological heterogeneity on direct democracy campaigns' (DDCs) consistent failures.[1] Both direct democracy campaigns and social movements arise, mobilize, and destruct in similar fashion. Drawing from the extant social movements' literature, as well as 45 in-depth interviews with DDC leaders, it becomes clear that direct democracy campaigns function like miniature, or short-term, social movements. Because DDCs and social movements mobilize in similar fashion, they also implode in similar fashion. A key characteristic of both social movement failure and DDC failure is the presence of ideological heterogeneity.

Similarities between Direct Democracy Campaigns and Social Movements

Luther Gerlach (1999) describes social movements as segmentary, polycentric, and reticulate. DDCs can be described in similar terms. Consider each of Gerlach's characteristics. *Segmentary* denotes movements in which many diverse groups divide and fuse, proliferate and contract. Similarly, DDCs, in an attempt to garner a wide base of support, also bring together a variety of interests, individuals, and established groups. Sometimes, internal tensions cause DDC coalitions to divide. At other times, DDCs mobilize new activists, which cause the number of subgroups to proliferate. Over time, many of these new groups fuse to create larger groups, or, some groups cease to exist altogether.

Gerlach uses the term *polycentric* to describe social movements that have multiple, temporary, and sometimes competing centers of influence. Again, the diverse nature of direct democracy coalitions ensures that they also include many "leaders," all competing for influence over the campaigns' direction. Groups entering coalitions bring with them existing leaders. It is natural for these leaders to jockey for influence. Each leader brings a different level of commitment to the ideological purity of the mission. The polycentric nature of DDCs almost ensures factional competition. Furthermore, some of the coalitions created to pursue initiatives are temporary. Coalitions that did not previously exist are brought together solely to pursue a single initiative. After the campaign, lacking any *raison d' etre*, the coalition disperses.

Reticulate refers to a social movement with loose yet integrated and overlapping membership networks sharing general ideals. DDCs are also reticulate. Direct democracy coalitions comprise people with a shared general goal, but who are also members of other interest groups and coalitions. It is common for members of pro-life groups to also be members of anti-tax groups, or anti-affirmative action groups. Likewise, individuals who push education funding commonly belong to pro-health care groups or campaign finance reform networks. Interview data suggest that many direct democracy leaders know each other. Either they have worked on campaigns together, or they have utilized each others' resources. Partnerships arise when there is broad agreement about the general goals of the DDC. Different subgroups of a coalition may take the lead of different DDCs due to differing intensities about the movement's goal, but as long as other coalition members share the general goal of the DDC, they are willing to contribute.

To Gerlach's three characteristics of social movements, two more characteristics should be considered: outsider status and the collective action problem. Outsider status inheres in direct democracy campaigns. In fact, most direct democracy activists utilize the initiative process because they lack access to traditional political institutions. Even if activists are pursuing mainstream policy initiatives, they may not have the money, clout, or political standing to approach the legislature. A legislature has "gatekeepers" that the initiative system does not. There are infinite access points to direct democracy. In other cases, initiative activists pursue agendas outside mainstream politics such as doctor-assisted suicide or marijuana legalization. Again, even if voting majorities will support such policies, powerful groups or legislators can use minority vetoes prevalent in the legislative process to block such issues. Additionally, initiative activists sometimes seek to challenge established political institutions' autonomy by proposing term limits and campaign finance reform – both unpopular with sitting legislators. Because DDC activists lack access, some initiatives are designed to influence legislatures exogenously (Gerber,1998).

Once activists choose the grass-roots direct democracy route, they face collective action problems that inhere in all voluntary associations pursuing a public good (Olson, 1965). That is, lacking selective incentives, direct democracy campaigns experience difficulty mobilizing the voluntary cooperation of activists, potential fundraisers, and coalition partners upon which activists rely.

Ideological Heterogeneity in Social Movements Organizations

Social movements have been described as "clusters of organizations, overlapping networks, and individuals that share goals that are bound together by a collective identity (Whittier, 1997, p. 761)." Social movement organizations have also been described as organizations run by "bureaucrats" and "enthusiasts" (Roche and Sachs, 1969). "The bureaucrat is concerned primarily with the organizational facet of the social movement, with its stability, growth, and tactics. He seeks communication, not excommunications (p.208)." In contrast, "the enthusiast concerns himself primarily with what he deems to be the fundamental principles of the organization, the ideals and values which nourish the movement. No reconciler, he will concentrate on the advocacy of these principles at the risk of hard feelings and even of schism (p. 209)." Being an appeaser, the bureaucrat "is prepared to compromise in order to promote unity and cohesion within the organization and to broaden its external appeal (p.210)." The enthusiast, however, "full of confidence in the truth of his convictions, operates on the principle that if the people refuse to share his vision, so much the worse for them...Damn the electorate! Full speed ahead (p.210)"

Roche and Sachs identify three negative consequences that result from ideological heterogeneity. First, "[the enthusiast's] firm belief in the basic articles of his credo may lead him to be dogmatic and doctrinaire and *into unfortunate excesses* [my emphasis] (p.216)." Second, the enthusiast creates the "impression that the speaker considers himself pure and uncontaminated. Such homilies can arouse great resentment, and sometimes lead to...schism (p. 216)" And third, "With his fervor and sense of righteousness, he can easily become a prisoner of his own presuppositions (p.217)." Subsequent research shows that the ideological heterogeneity that Roche and Sachs describe has adversely impacted several social movements.

Ideological tensions negatively impacted the anti-nuclear movement of the late 1970s (Barkan, 1979; Downey, 1987). Barkan argues that SMOs often face the dilemma "between the need to win external support" and at the same time, appease "the ideological leanings of the membership base (p.20)." He notes, "protest leaders who employ moderate tactics to win a favorable press image and appeal to target officials may risk alienating movement activists (p.20)." Barkan credits ideological heterogeneity for weakening the effectiveness of the anti-nuclear group, War Resisters League (WRL).

Downey, studying the Clamshell Alliance of the same movement, drew very similar conclusions. He observed that the group was unable to navigate "irreconcilable political and personal differences" of its members, and "disagreements based on strong principles that people do not want to compromise..." led the Clamshell Alliance to "split into two groups in 1979, both of which disbanded by the end of 1981 (p.357)" Downey concludes that "ideology always plays a role in the process of resource mobilization undergone by voluntary social movement organizations." And, "not surprisingly, the tension proved to be irresolvable, even by a factional split (p. 371)."

More recent work supports the earlier research (Mansbridge, 1986; Gamson, 1990; McAdam, McCarthy, and Zald, 1996; Castells, 1997). Jane Mansbridge shows how ideological heterogeneity led to the failure of the Equal Rights Amendment (ERA) movement. While Phyllis Schafly crafted a unified message in her opposition to the ERA, the more decentralized, and ideologically diverse groups supporting the movement spoke with several, and at times, contradictory voices. The inability of the ERA movement to coordinate a coherent response to charges of co-ed bathrooms and a female military draft resulted in weakened support for the Amendment.

William Gamson's more empirical study reinforces Mansbridge's findings. His study of 53 "challenging groups" highlights three key points. First, few groups avoid factionalism because "it is the nature of the beast (p.99)." Second, mobilized groups that suffer factionalism are more likely to fail than those without it. His data shows that "less than one-fourth of the groups that experience it [factionalism] are successful, in contrast to 70 percent of those that escape it (p.101)." Given these two facts, Gamson concludes "centralization of power is a device for managing internal division (p.104)."

However, although ideological heterogeneity presents institutional dilemmas for SMOs, its presence does not guarantee social movement failure. Some SMOs survive ideological heterogeneity (Castells, 1997; Staggenborg, 1999; Halcli, 1999). In various works, they note that the women's movement (Castells, 1997, pp. 176-184; Staggenborg, 1999, pp. 110-114), the green movement (Castells, 1997, pp.110-121), and the gay rights movement (Halcli, 1999, pp.146-148) all have organizations that suffer from some degree of ideological heterogeneity. However, all three movements continue to move forward despite differing degrees of factionalism.

Research of NARAL's early history and subsequent internal schisms highlights the ability of some SMOs to adapt and therefore overcome ideological heterogeneity (Staggenborg, 1999). Staggenborg notes that between 1972 and 1974 NARAL modified its decision-making procedures and professionalized its staff to alleviate tensions between "longtime leaders and entrepreneurs of NARAL and the newer activists who objected to 'power being concentrated in the hands of a few men in New York.'"

ACT UP organizations in the early 1990s also suffered from ideological heterogeneity and suffered organizational schisms (Halcli, 1999). Halcli writes, "Usually a few members would leave the larger group to form a new organization devoted to treatment issues while the original chapter maintained a broader focus (p. 147)." However, these schisms did not lead to the direct abandonment of the gay rights movement. At times, schisms lead to "product differentiation" where subsets of a movement offer different services or concentrate on specialized agendas (Heinz, Paik, & Southworth, 2003). The specialization prevents subsets from competing for members and financial support. In fact, Halcli notes, "other members did not view the existence of divisions within the organization as an obstacle, but as a primary source of organizational strength....promoting innovation and commitment among membership (p.147)."[2]

The environmental movement perseveres despite extreme ideological heterogeneity. There are mainstream organizations such as the Sierra Club, Audubon Society and the Wilderness Society. There are extremist groups such as

Earth First!   There are groups in-between, such as the National Resources Defense Fund and the Environmental Defense Fund. Yet, Castells observes,

> "Collective action, politics and discourses grouped under the name of environmentalism are so diverse as to challenge the idea of a movement. And yet it is precisely this cacophony of theory and practice that characterized environmentalism as a new form of decentralized, multiform, network-oriented, pervasive social movement (p. 112)."

Castells' description of the environmental movement highlights how ideological tensions within a movement can be overcome if the movement has time to adapt to internal factionalism.

Some social movement theorists go so far as to suggest that ideological heterogeneity actually contributes to social movement success. Herbert Haines (1988) observes that the presence of extremist groups leads to greater support for moderate wings of a social movement. In his study of radicals during the civil rights movement, he found that funding increased for moderate groups as radical groups threatened to undermine the movement. McAdam, McCarthy and Zald (1996) also suggest that the presence of extremists in social movements is not always damaging to the movement. Citing other research, they note, social movements "appear to benefit from the presence of a 'radical' wing (p.14)." Winfred Poster (1995) notes that ideological heterogeneity may have benefited the women's movement of the 1960s. She hints that radical wings of a coalition may influence moderate wings (or event the state) to adopt more radical policies. However, Kim Voss (1996) argues that "the radical flank effect is not always positive (p.235)." Her analysis of the collapse of the Knights of Labor suggests that the Knight's strategy "which drew upon the ideology of working-class republicanism, did not work, and it led to internal schisms that rent apart the organization (p. 255)." Like research on the impact of ideological heterogeneity in general, the research on radical flank effects appears mixed.

Given the competing case studies, it appears that ideological heterogeneity poses a problem for SMOs, but not an insurmountable problem. The challenge for social movement groups is to develop mechanisms that mediate the destructive nature of ideological heterogeneity. If they can, the group survives, if they cannot, the group factionalizes and loses influence.

Fortunately for some social movements, the process of developing mechanisms to mediate ideological heterogeneity can occur over time. Because social movements do not have an identifiable watershed event that makes or breaks the movement, they can slowly adapt to internal factionalization. As Castells, Staggenborg, and Halcli show, the women's movement, green movement, and gay rights movement engage in a variety of arenas, pursue many differentiated goals, and have some successes and some failures. Although each of these movements suffered some degree of ideological heterogeneity, the lack of a temporal end point allowed the movements to adapt to internal dissensions. In contrast, Mansbridge's study focuses on a unique social movement that required a one-time electoral success (passage of the ERA). The ERA had to have a punctuated success during specific state referenda. Whereas time never runs out on the women's movement, the clock ran out on the ERA.

The temporal variable may shed light on why some SMOs survive ideological heterogeneity and others do not. Similarly, the temporal differences between long run social movements and short run DDCs may also explain why internal schisms are a "more poisonous pill" to DDCs. Unlike most social movements, DDCs must have a decisive, one-time, electoral victory to be successful.

Direct Democracy and Ideological Heterogeneity

When Mansbridge studied the ERA movement, she concluded that all political movements are faced with "a basic tension between reaching out and reaching in." She notes, "To change the world, a movement must include as many people as possible. But to attract devoted activists, a movement must often promote a sense of exclusivity" (p. 178). Her study highlighted the fact that many coalitions face a tension between activists who want "doctrinal purity," and those who want to "get the amendment ratified." Mansbridge argues that the pro-ERA movement was beset by many activists who "preferred being right to winning," while other activists "in the name of getting the Amendment ratified found themselves opposing friends who took a 'purer' ideological line (p.76)." Her conclusion was that social movements can either develop ideologically homogeneous groups or heterogeneous groups, but homogeneous groups have an advantage in the political process. Her model provides insight into the study of direct democracy. In some ways, each initiative campaign is a miniature social movement. Many of Mansbridge's observations, as well as other social movement theorists, are applicable to the initiative process.[3] Groups using the initiative process to promote social and political change face the same tensions as groups involved in the ERA or other social movements.

There is an absence of literature examining ideological heterogeneity in DDCs. Early studies such as Magelby (1984) and Cronin (1989) consider the process and evaluate the quality of legislation that direct democracy produces. Later studies such as Bolwer and Donovan (1998) and Dubois and Feeney (1998) scrutinize voters' ability to navigate considerable information costs associated with direct democracy. More recent studies (Gerber, 1998; Broder, 2000; Ellis, 2002) look at the impact of money. However, there is no literature that examines the internal dynamics of coalition formation. Ellis (2002) notes that initiatives "belong to the few who write the measures, not to the many who vote (p.79)." However, his research ignores the internal dissent that occurs between the "few who write the measures."

Internal dissent occurs because initiative campaigns attract all types of activists, and each activist has a unique level of commitment to the "mission" of the movement. Some members act like zealots, jealously guarding and advocating the ideology of the campaign. Other members act like lawyers[4] and tend to put practical politics above ideology. Lawyers seek compromise. Zealots seek confrontation. Direct democracy coalitions typically bring together both types of activists. The heterogeneous composition of the coalition often results in organizational tensions. Zealots desire an ideologically pure initiative. Lawyers desire an initiative that will be accepted by the voters and upheld by the courts.

Rarely are the two criteria compatible. More often than not, ideological tensions cause the coalition to fracture.

When direct democracy coalitions fracture, two separate groups typically emerge. One group adopts an ideologically pure stance. The other group focuses on practical politics. In other cases, coalitions do not fracture, but shrink and become more homogeneous. Heterogeneous coalitions become more homogeneous either through the ejection of some members or a voluntary exodus. The new, more homogeneous coalitions either retain most of the zealots or most of the lawyers. Homogeneous coalitions represented by the more ideologically committed members tend to be more radical in their politics. Figure 2 shows the two ways that splintering heterogeneous coalitions result in either one or two ideologically purer coalitions. This process is explained in detail in the subsequent section.

Figure 2: Homogenizing Initiative Coalitions

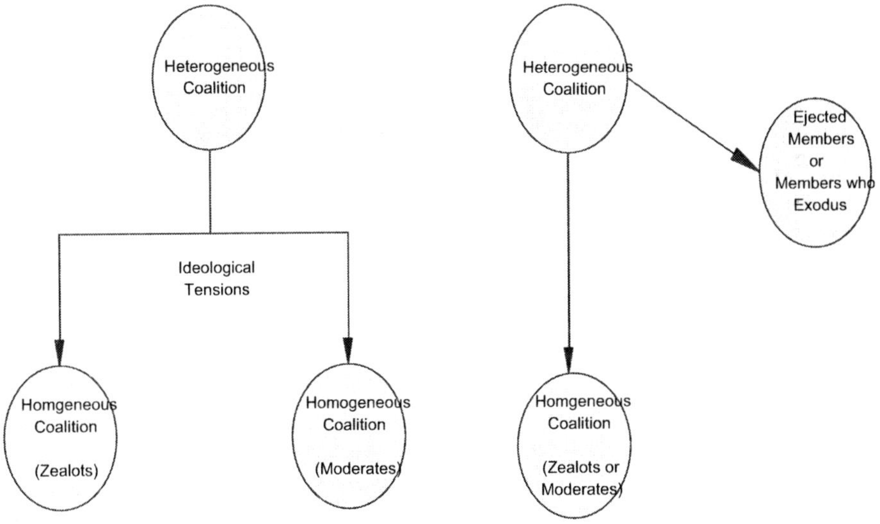

Even DDCs that have a narrow political focus suffer from ideological heterogeneity. It is often assumed that because a group is pursuing a narrow goal, the members of the groups have a homogeneous view of the issue. Such is not the case. Even groups that have a narrow focus suffer from dissention caused by differing levels of commitment to the mission of the initiative. For example, a group of Libertarians pushing tax cuts may all agree that tax cuts are essential. However, there may be considerable disagreement over the extent of the tax cuts.

As a result of the process outlined above, three types of groups engage in the initiative process. The first type is a "heterogeneous" group. A heterogeneous group contains individuals who hold all types of attitudes with respect to ideological purity. As noted earlier, some initiative activists are zealots, unwilling to compromise principle in order to achieve political victory. In contrast, lawyers and other moderates focus on ensuring the legality and political viability of an initiative, and are more willing to compromise their ideology. A heterogeneous group contains both types of activists. The fundamental tension for most heterogeneous groups is finding a balance between the two factions in order to prevent the coalition from factionalizing to the point of disbanding. Consider the following comments from members of heterogeneous groups:

> In 2000 we pushed a campaign reform initiative that also placed limits on contributions to initiatives. We thought that would be fair since we were trying to limit other politicians. But it split our group. Then when some people only wanted to limit corporate contributions and others wanted it to go to zero, all hell broke loose. We never got on the ballot. So, this year we had to compromise about the $100 limits. I [the zealot] didn't want them in, but Dan [the lawyer] did. We essentially agreed to disagree. It may be a problem. If the $100 limits get us, I hope that severability will save us (Interview # 86).

Another activist in a heterogeneous group:

> In the end, we had to draft two separate bills. We couldn't come to an agreement on how to deal with marijuana. We all agreed hemp should be legalized, but only some of the more edgy people wanted to legalize marijuana, too. It was that or we would have spent the whole time fighting each other (Interview #97).

The second type of initiative group is the "homogeneous-zealot" group. This group contains mostly zealots. As a result, the group rarely argues about doctrinal purity. Most of the members agree that the principle of their cause trumps political and judicial reality. The homogeneous-zealot group is typically created when a heterogeneous group fails to maintain its coalition. Most of the zealots are either ejected, or choose to leave a broader coalition that contains more moderate, compromising members. The zealots then proceed to form their own group. In some circumstances, a charismatic leader will attract individuals with similar political views and create, from the ground up, a homogeneous-zealot group. Regardless of how homogeneous-zealot groups form, the following comments illustrate their internal mechanics:

> In 1990 we spent a good part of the year trying to get all the "life" people to the table. But the Right to Life people were impossible to work with. It's impossible to get all these people to agree on anything. The result was a waste of my time and we accomplished nothing. We never have invited them back since…when it comes to coalitions we are the 82nd Airborne of the life movement. There's dissent among life groups, but not within ours (Interview # 91).

Or, consider these comments from an anti-tax activist:

> In '88 we had a guy that gave us $25,000 but he wanted us to put in a clause he really wanted. But I didn't want it, and I convinced the group it was a bad idea. He threatened to walk. We did him one better. We gave him his $25,000 back, and told him to go. I needed to make it clear, I was calling the shots…we [his initiative group] may be working within a democracy, but we aren't a democracy (Interview # 93).

In these two examples it is clear that maintaining doctrinal purity is more important to the activists than the money or support of powerful, yet "dissenting" interest groups. No accommodation was made to compromise. Through a process of self-selection or ejection, groups increased their homogeneity.

The third type of initiative group is the "homogeneous-moderate" group. These groups form and exist for the same reasons homogeneous-zealot groups exist. They form by either ejecting the more radical elements from their group, leaving only moderates, or they choose to leave a group they feel is dominated by zealots. Most of the members believe that enacting some legislation, even if it deviates from what they consider ideal, is better than losing at the ballot box or in court.   These groups come to be dominated by politicians, lawyers, and professional direct democracy consultants.

An example of a homogeneous-moderate group is the coalition behind a doctor-assisted suicide initiative. Doctor-assisted suicide is an issue that naturally attracts passionate and disparate individuals. The co-leader of this group made it clear that his primary focus was to "tear the issue away from the radicals."

> The Hemlock Society was involved with our movement at the beginning. But they wanted to include language about euthanasia. We knew that wouldn't fly with the voters or the courts. I had to be very clear that this measure was not about euthanasia. They eventually got the picture and left us alone. In general I work with very pragmatic people, but sometimes you have to tear an issue away from the radicals. That's what we did with Measure 16. The radicals [the Hemlock Society] had the issue, and we tore it away from them (Interview # 84).

The advocate of an open adoption measure expressed similar concerns:

> I started this process alone. But I eventually got together with Bastard Nation. They were a lot more radical than I. But they had resources and a website. We used the Internet to collect a lot of the signatures. But eventually, I had to distance myself from them (Interview # 80).

These comments illustrate that the process of homogenizing the homogeneous-moderate group is the same as for the homogeneous-zealot group. However, instead of ejecting the moderates, these groups eject the radicals.

The three groups identified usually form in a specific temporal sequence. Heterogeneous groups form first. These initial groups tend to cast a wide net in hopes of finding supporters, activists, and funding. As a result, individuals with all types of attitudes towards the importance of ideological purity are thrown together. The combination is usually untenable.[5] Thus, most heterogeneous coalitions are short-lived.

One reason heterogeneous groups implode is because leaders do not have control over selective benefits which help hold coalitions together. Members of loosely associated groups will be "free riders" unless the group's leadership can offer its members "selective benefits" (Olson, 1965). Selective benefits can be anything from membership benefits, magazines, financial discounts, and so on. Olson notes that without control over selective benefits, leaders of groups had little chance of directing the behavior of its members. The same is true for leaders of initiative coalitions; they cannot threaten members with the loss of benefits. Again, Mansbridge's comments on the ERA movement are enlightening:

> The ERA was a public good that had to be promoted or defeated by voluntary activity. Because neither passing nor defeating the ERA promised any immediate tangible benefits to activists, both sides recruited people by appealing to principle...because activists were volunteers, they were not subject to much organizational control. Even when an organization wanted to rein in activists for pragmatic reasons, it had few good ways of doing so (p.118).

In initiative coalitions, disgruntled members can threaten to withdraw support and funding. And because the heterogeneous group does not hold a monopoly over access to the initiative system, the "exit" option becomes more enticing than the "loyalty" or "voice" options.[6] From the standpoint of an *adamant* initiative activist, exiting an existing coalition to create a new one may be as enticing as using one's "voice" to alter an existing coalition, which requires fighting with other, equally passionate members who hold different world views.

Of course, staying in an existing coalition has advantages. An individual may have influence over the agenda of a powerful, existing political group. Fundraising networks may already be established. Affiliation with a certain group may lend an individual a level of credibility or prestige. However, for passionate initiative activists, these benefits may not be enough to outweigh the attraction of having complete control over a group's agenda or the content of an initiative. Many direct democracy activists prefer to have complete content control over a smaller group than to compromise within a larger, more politically powerful group.

Ideological heterogeneity also causes a coalition to schism because only the moderates have an incentive to compromise. Expected utility theory illustrates why this is so.[7] For a zealot, the utility of passing a scaled-back initiative is zero. Therefore, there is no incentive for them to compromise. If an ideologically pure initiative passes and is subsequently struck down by the courts, the utility is also zero (unless they have secondary goals).[8] But for the zealot, the utility for the first option is a guaranteed zero. In the second case, there is always the possibility that a sympathetic or political judge will allow the initiative despite constitutional defects. No matter how small that probability, it still results in an expected utility greater than zero.[9]

The incentive structures for the moderates are different. In a heterogeneous group, it is the zealots who bring most of the energy and motivation. They are willing to pound the pavement to get signatures. They are the ones willing to raise money, write letters to the editor, and do the footwork. In many cases, the moderates in the group cannot get their measure on the ballot without the zealots to do the work.[10] If the moderates push the zealots too hard, the zealots will exit. This leaves the moderates with two possibilities. Either the measure will be constitutional, but will never make the ballot or pass the voters. Or, the measure will have some unconstitutional clauses, but will have the chance that it passes the voters. Of these two options, the first option results in a guaranteed utility of zero. The second option leaves open the possibility of a sympathetic or political judge. But no matter how slim that possibility is, the expected utility is still greater than zero. The end result is that moderates, in a heterogeneous group, are more willing to compromise than zealots. For example, here is what one drafter experienced.

> Author: Your measure was drafted after California had taken a stricter stance on the single subject rule in *Senate v. Jones*.
> Drafter: Yes.
> Author: And yet your measure had four separate clauses. What was your thinking on this?
> Drafter: I warned them. I said this might be a problem for us.
> Author: Warned who?
> Drafter: The people backing us. The ones with all the money.
> Author: So you went to them and said, "The measure as it stands now is unconstitutional"?
> Drafter: Not those exact words, but basically yes.
> Author: And their response?
> Drafter: They told me their polling indicated more support for the four clause initiative. It became clear to me, we went with the four clauses, or we had no money (Interview # 20).

This dialogue shows that the drafters of the initiative and the financial supporters of the initiative can have different strategies. The drafter clearly feels it is better to pursue a scaled-back initiative that will not run into legal troubles, even if the scaled-back initiative is less likely to pass. The financial supporters of the initiative want the measure to pass the electorate, even if it means flirting with unconstitutionality. The zealots in this case were the financial supporters. The polling data suggested the scaled-back measure would pass, just with a lower margin for error. The financial supporters were willing to almost guarantee invalidation in order to get all four clauses into the bill. In the end, the drafter was correct. The measure was nullified on single subject grounds. As a result, the drafter chose not to work with the same financial supporters in future initiative campaigns.

Given this outcome, it is foreseeable that moderate members begin to see the futility of maintaining broad-based coalitions. Eventually, through a process of self-selection, new homogeneous groups form. Either through exit or through ejection, most of the moderates end up in one group, and a majority of zealots end up in another group. Thus, we see a process dominated by two types of initiative groups: the homogenous-zealot group and the homogeneous-moderate group.[11]

Table 9 identifies the distribution of activists and coalitions in the data set. Table 9 also identifies how often those coalitions were successful in placing a measure on the ballot. In total, 45 activists representing 28 coalitions placed 49 initiatives on the ballot. The 11 heterogeneous coalitions placed 17 measures on the ballot, more than any other group. They failed to get their measure on the ballot 5 times. Homogeneous-moderate coalitions placed fewer measures on the ballot, for a total of 12, but never failed to garner ballot access. Homogeneous-zealot groups placed 14 measures on the ballot, but suffered a significantly higher rate of access failure; 13 of their measures were never made the ballot. Individuals who were not part of any coalition were the smallest part of the data set. They were able to place 6 measures on the ballot while failing 5 times.

The People vs. The Courts

Table 9: Types and Frequency of Initiative Coalitions

Type of Coalition	Frequency[6]			
	Activists	**Coalitions**	**# of Initiatives Placed on Ballot**	**# of Failed Attempts to Make Ballot**
Heterogeneous Coalition	18 (40%)	11 (39%)	17	5
Homogeneous-Moderate	11 (24%)	8 (29%)	12	0
Homogeneous-Zealot	11 (24%)	9 (32%)	14	13
Subjects not in any Coalition[7]	5 (11%)	N/A	6	5
Totals	45	28	49	23

It is argued that ideological heterogeneity adversely impacts DDCs in each of the three initiative stages. Ideological heterogeneity consumes resources and time during the drafting stage, thus preventing DDCs from getting their measure on the ballot. Second, ideological heterogeneity facilitates the adoption of more radical, and therefore, less mainstream provisions in ballot measures. The result is less political support and a greater likelihood of electoral defeat. Third, the adoption of more radical provisions in ballot measures also increases the likelihood that courts will invalidate such measures. Simply put, coalitional schisms that result from ideological heterogeneity contribute to direct democracy campaigns' failures for two primary reasons. Factionalization within groups wastes time and resources, preventing measures from making it to the ballot. Or, zealot influences within groups result in legislation that is beyond the median voter. Legislation beyond the median voter is either unpopular or unconstitutional. The first leads to electoral defeat, the latter to judicial nullification.

---

[6] Sometimes, more than one activist was interviewed from the same coalition. Therefore, the frequency of activists is higher than the frequency of coalitions. In addition, coalitions were classified according to the nature of the coalition *at the time of the interview.* However, many Homogeneous-Moderate and Homogeneous-Zealot coalitions were at one time part of earlier Heterogeneous groups.

[7] This type of activists might be referred to as a "lone wolf". They do not form or join coalitions, but act on their own.

Table 10: Success and Failure Rates by Coalition Type[8]

Type of Coalition	Electoral Defeat	Judicial Nullification	Passed and Upheld or no Court Challenge	Totals
Heterogeneous Coalition	3 (18%)	10 (59%)	4 (24%)	17
Homogeneous-Moderate	2 (17%)	3 (25%)	7 (58%)	12
Homogeneous-Zealot	4 (29%)	6 (43%)	4 (29%)	14
Subjects not in any Coalition	2 (33%)	1 (17%)	3 (50%)	6
Totals	11	20	18	49

Table 10 examines only those measures that garnered ballot access and identifies how successful the various coalitions were at seeing their initiatives implemented as policy. The data tell an interesting story. Homogeneous-moderate coalitions fared far better than heterogeneous and homogeneous-zealot coalitions. Homogeneous-moderate coalitions attempted 12 initiatives. A majority, 7 initiatives, navigated all the electoral and legal hurdles to become law. Only 2 initiatives proposed by homogeneous-moderate coalitions lost at the ballot box, and only 3 were invalidated by the courts.

Comparatively, homogeneous-zealot coalitions were less successful. Of the 14 measures in which these coalitions gained ballot access, 4 lost at the ballot box and an additional 6 were rejected by the courts. Only 4 initiatives were eventually enacted as law.

Heterogeneous coalitions were less successful than homogeneous-zealot coalitions. Although heterogeneous coalitions had greater success getting ballot access, only 4 initiatives were eventually enacted as law. 3 initiatives suffered electoral defeat and an additional 10 suffered judicial nullification. As Table 10 indicates, heterogeneous coalitions were successful only 24% of the time; the lowest percentage rate of any coalition type.

---

[8] Table 10 computes percentages based on a denominator that counts only measures that garnered ballot access. Computing electoral success requires that one divide the number of success by the number of electoral opportunities. By including measures that were never voted upon in the denominator would distort the electoral success percentages.

Combining data regarding failed attempts to make the ballot from Table 9 with the data from Table 10 examining electoral and judicial failure rates further buttresses the claim that homogeneous-moderate groups enjoy the greatest DDC success rates. Because none of the homogeneous-moderate coalitions from the data set failed to make the ballot, including such numbers does not affect their overall success rate of 58%. However, homogenous-zealot coalitions failed to make the ballot 13 times, decreasing their overall success rate to 4 out of 27 attempts, or 15%. Heterogeneous groups failed to make the ballot 5 times decreasing their overall success rate to 4 out of 22 attempts, or 18%.

The sections below offer some qualitative data to help explain the quantitative results from Tables 9 and 10.

Ideological heterogeneity frustrates ballot access

Coalitions often organize to draft legislation but in-fighting consumes time and resources to the point that no version of the measure makes it to the ballot. A coalition pursuing a campaign finance reform measure illustrates.

> Author: What kept your measure off the ballot?
> Drafter: We spent so much time fighting among ourselves. The pragmatists wanted basic limits on corporate contributions. The purists wanted to go all the way to zero. And they wanted to regulate contributions to initiative campaigns.
> Author: But you knew limits of zero would doom your initiative.
> Drafter: Yes, we knew, and that's what split our group in two.
> Author: What happened after your group split in two?
> Drafter: That year, neither of us got a measure on the ballot.

Once coalitions split into separate groups, it becomes very difficult to raise enough money, and maintain enough activists to make the ballot. Direct democracy advocates typically meet to draft legislation before they begin to raise money, collect signatures, and publicly campaign. However, when the first step (drafting) takes an inordinate amount of time, the other stages are neglected. A lack of signatures makes the measure ineligible for the ballot. A lack of money and campaigning impacts the likelihood of electoral success. An earlier interview segment buttresses this conclusion.

> In the end, we had to draft two separate bills. We couldn't come to an agreement on how to deal with marijuana. We all agreed hemp should be legalized, but only some of the more edgy people wanted to legalize marijuana, too. It was that or we would have spent the whole time fighting each other (Interview #97).

However, the group did not have the resources to pursue two separate initiatives on the same ballot. The end result was that neither measure made the ballot.

Comments about factionalization from the leader of a pro-life DDC further support the hypothesis that ideological heterogeneity frustrates ballot access.

> In 1990 we spent a good part of the year trying to get all the "life" people to the table. But the Right to Life people were impossible to work with. It's impossible to get all these people to agree on anything. The result was a waste of my time and we accomplished nothing. We never have invited them back since…when it comes to coalitions we are the 82nd Airborne of the life movement. There's dissent among life groups, but not within ours (Interview # 91).

In the above scenario, multiple pro-life activists sought to combine resources to push an initiative. However, in-fighting over mission purity led to a complete and permanent dissolution of the coalition. The project was a "waste of time" in that no measure was produced as a result of their collaboration.

Ideological heterogeneity produces bills that are defeated at the polls

Even measures that qualify for the ballot can be defeated due to coalitional factionalization. As noted earlier, zealots either leave heterogeneous coalitions to form homogeneous-zealot groups, or, because zealots lack an incentive to compromise they exert considerable influence on heterogeneous groups. Regardless, both actions can result in legislation that is beyond the preferences of the median voter. Consequently, groups seeking to limit homosexual rights, abortion rights, and labor rights or groups attempting to legalize hemp or reform the campaign system often lose. These types of coalitions naturally attract zealots and the zealots push the content of the bill to policy extremes that result in defeat by the electorate. The dialogue below illustrates how an anti-abortion group factionalized around the issue of including a "health exception."

Author: Why did you split from [your state's] Right to Life?
Drafter: They wanted a clause out. It was the emergency circumstances clause. The way I had it written, judges could waive notification [to a parent] if it was a medical emergency.
Author: And you weren't willing to pull it?
Drafter: That's what kept the bill legal. You asked me earlier if I read previous case law. And I told you I did. I knew if we didn't allow for the exceptions, we would lose [in the courts].
Author: Did you try to explain that to them?
Drafter: Of course. But it was no use. These guys think they can overturn *Roe.* But we in the pro-life movement have to accept reality. The Court [US Supreme Court] had its chance with *Casey.* We had six conservatives on the court then and they still upheld it. They're [zealot members of the coalition] beating their heads against the wall because they won't accept *Roe.*

This activist is clearly not a zealot. He is willing to compromise in order to gain some incremental restriction on abortion. And it is clear he does not believe that any initiative will ultimately result in the repeal of *Roe.* However, his willingness to compromise alienated the more ardent opponents of abortion.   The dialogue below, from a member of Right to Life, and also a member of the same drafting coalition, illustrates.

[Activist above] was too political. We were not going to accept anything from him that accepts or reinforces *Roe v. Wade* **in any way** [speaker's emphasis].   If we introduce proposals that conform to *Roe*, we are essentially accepting that case as morally correct. We might as well give up the fight if we do that (Interview # 53).

In the above case, "too political" meant the identified actor was willing to compromise in order to increase the likelihood of electoral success and avoid judicial invalidation. The tensions between the two groups lead to a schism in which the more militant group pursued their own initiative. However, during the campaign, the more moderate groups refused to endorse the measure, or contribute resources towards its passage. The initiative pursued by the homogeneous-zealot group was defeated at the polls.[12]

In the above case, the moderates withdrew their support contributing to the measure's defeat. In other cases, the zealots withdraw their support. A California campaign finance reform coalition illustrates. In the late 1990s, a wide coalition of reform activists created a coalition to limit the influence of money in California politics. However, the more moderate members of the coalition insisted on "watering down" the measure to appease powerful political influences. The move caused tensions within the coalition. One leader described the problem.

> Ron basically got into bed with the Republicans. He gave away the house. By the time they were done compromising we felt we couldn't support the bill any longer. I'm not saying our lack of support killed the measure. But, we did withdraw our support—politically and financially (Interview # 23).

The California case illustrates that ideological heterogeneity, especially tensions surrounding mission purity, can lead to the withdrawal of either zealots or moderates. Regardless, the impact is similar. A loss of campaign resources can adversely impact the likelihood of electoral success.

Ideological heterogeneity produces bills that are challenged in court

Even measures that qualify for the ballot *and* achieve electoral victory, can *still* fail due to coalitional factionalization. Direct democracy legislation is constrained by constitutional norms. Successful initiatives are challenged in court 50% of the time. In turn, the courts invalidate 54% of challenged initiatives (Miller, 2000). One reason ballot measures are nullified by courts so frequently is because homogeneous-zealots groups ignore constitutional mandates, or zealots within heterogeneous groups lobby for the inclusion of unconstitutional provisions within a measure. The examples below illustrate.

In 1995-96, Public Interest Research Groups (PIRGs) from both Colorado and California were involved in campaign finance reform initiatives.[13] In both cases a coalition of zealots, lawyers, and professional direct democracy advocates came together to draft the legislation. Internal debates concerning statutory language revealed tensions over what limits should be imposed on contributions. In California, members of Common Cause and other non-profit advocacy groups wanted "safe" higher limits (Interview #24).[14] Members of PIRG, acting like zealots, wanted limits of $100. They threatened to withdraw their support for the measure if limits were higher than $100. Although this demand was not met, it had the effect of leading to a compromise that kept limits lower than what the lawyers felt were constitutional (Interview # 23). In the end, PIRG members did withdraw from the coalition and drafted their own Proposition 212, which failed to garner electoral victory. Unfortunately for the other half of the coalition, the pre-withdrawal compromise appeasing the PIRG demands eventually led to the judicial invalidation of the successful Proposition 208.[15] In the end, ideological heterogeneity destroyed both movements. One member's comments are enlightening,

> Drafter: After our research, and other feedback, we raised our limits to $1,000 and we made restrictions based on election cycles, not fiscal years, and we changed the way we regulated lobbyists.
>
> Author: But you still had your initiative nullified because the limits you established were too low.
>
> Drafter: Yep.
>
> Author: Why not play it safe and pick limits you knew would be upheld?
>
> Drafter: Well, the PIRGs were pushing really low limits. They have this "dripping faucet" approach to campaign finance reform. They want to keep going at it until the courts change. They had had one small victory in the past with small limits, so they were convinced if we just kept coming back with the same thing, eventually the courts would give in.
>
> Author: Why not ignore them?
>
> Drafter: Eventually we did. But by that time, the bill was pretty much established, we had already started collecting signatures, and it was too late to change. When we started ignoring them, they left to draft their own version (Prop 212). Their express purpose was to overturn *Buckley*.[16]

A very similar story plays itself out in Colorado. There, PIRG members again acted like zealots. Although they did not withdraw from the coalition, they did push for $100 limits. And again, those very low limits led to the courts rejecting Amendment 15. As one member noted,

> These guys [PIRGs] didn't know when to quit. Time after time, low limits are being struck down by the courts, and they keep going at it like it never happened. I'm there trying to explain it, citing case law, and I might as well have been speaking a foreign language. All they could say was, "they have $100 limits in other states." Of course, in a lot of those states, the limits were being challenged, but the decision hadn't come down yet (Interview # 46).

Another member noted,

We had a hard time convincing the PIRG people $100 limits wouldn't be upheld. But they were pretty adamant. They would threaten to walk. They would assure us that $100 limits could be upheld. They'd tell us they had been implemented in other states and localities. They were talking about Vermont and Cincinnati. On an ideological level we agreed with them. Everybody wanted low limits, but some of us were just awake to the reality of the situation. One hundred dollar limits is probably not going to make it. But again, they were pretty adamant (Interview # 47).

The frustration of the lawyers in the coalition is apparent. It is clear they felt they had a winning issue, but the fixation of the PIRGs on past obscure victories was sabotaging the process. In the end, the lawyers in the group were correct; Amendment 15 was invalidated by the courts.[17] For many heterogeneous coalitions, courts serve to displace conflict. When factions within a coalition cannot compromise, they rely on the courts to settle the issue. By saying "let the courts decide" heterogeneous coalitions can move beyond coalitional gridlock and start collecting signatures and engaging in campaign activities. However, such a strategy simply delays the impact of ideological heterogeneity.

Ideological Heterogeneity is More Destructive to DDCs

Much of the social movement literature describes how ideological heterogeneity leads to factionalized social movement organizations. As the data from Tables 10 and 11 indicate, because DDCs exist in the same environment as social movements—segmentary, polycentric, and reticulate—DDCs also suffer from the social movement dilemma. However, where social movements can often persevere by factionalizing into separate groups which all pursue the same agenda with different intensity, means, and methods, DDCs need to acquire a one-time electoral victory to be successful. Therefore, ideological schisms and factionalism become more problematic for DDCs.

The key variable is time. Electoral cycles impose deadlines upon DDCs but not upon social movements. Freed from a time constraint, social movements have the ability to adapt. When faced with ideological heterogeneity, social movement organizations can sometimes develop new institutional decision-making processes or fracture into multiple, but more homogeneous groups that continue to pursue the general goals of the movement. For example, there have been many political events promoted by the environmental movement,[18] but none of these events have been a "make or break" moment for the movement. For DDCs, most elections are a one-time, "make or break" event for the mini-movement.

The temporal limitations of DDCs may also explain why DDCs do not benefit from radical flank effects. Haines (1984, 1988) argues that radical flank effects can benefit a movement by increasing support for moderate, and therefore, more politically mainstream groups. However, radical flanks effects are a *long run process*. Before radical flank effects "kick in" there must be differentiation of groups, competition between differentiated groups, and then a mobilization of moderate support. DDCs do not have the luxury of such a time consuming process. By the time DDC groups differentiate, Election Day has come and gone.

The narratives of social movement activists differ from those of direct democracy activists. Direct democracy activists continually note how ideological heterogeneity "runs out the clock" on their movements. In some cases, time wasted on ideological heterogeneity prevents ballot access:

> Then when some people only wanted to limit corporate contributions and others wanted it to go to zero, all hell broke loose. We never got on the ballot. (Interview # 86)

> But the Right to Life people were impossible to work with. It's impossible to get all these people to agree on anything. The result was a waste of my time and we accomplished nothing. (Interview # 91)

In other cases, time constraints limit the ability of DDCs to adapt. Signature collection must start early in the process, and once the first signature is collected, the content of the measure cannot change. If polling or legal decisions indicate that the content of the measure should change, activists must weigh the benefits of a better bill versus the costs of starting the signature collection process anew.

> But by that time, the bill was pretty much established, we had already started collecting signatures, and it was too late to change. (Interview # 25).

> The Court's decision came down in the middle of our new campaign. We had already drafted the measure and collected thousands of signatures. If we changed the bill that late in the process, we would have had to start all over. We never would have made the ballot. So, we crossed our fingers and hoped for the best (Interview # 100).

The obvious conclusion when comparing the effects of ideological heterogeneity on social movements organizations and DDCs is that heterogeneity is more destructive to the latter. Whereas some social movements can adjust to ideological tensions, DDCs run out of time or resources because an established election date presents an abrupt end to their ability to adapt.

Despite the tensions caused by ideological heterogeneity, Table 11 indicates that heterogeneous coalitions were able to pass 4 initiatives which subsequently survived judicial challenge. Therefore, the data suggests that ideological heterogeneity is not insurmountable. Case studies that deviate from the predicted outcome merit further scrutiny. My research suggests that heterogeneous DDC coalitions can overcome ideological heterogeneity if they move quickly to homogenize their coalition or limit the size of their coalition.

Again, time becomes the most important factor. The four DDCs that overcame ideological heterogeneity identified and mediated ideological tensions early in the campaign's life cycle. Leaders of successful heterogeneous DDCs responded to ideological heterogeneity by ejecting zealots early or limiting the size of the leadership cadre. Some DDC leaders did both. Consider the following comment from a successful heterogeneous campaign leader that illustrates both strategies,

> When we came together to push state level term limits we had Reform Party members, Libertarian Party members, and Republicans. Some members were more loyal to their party than to the term limits movement. Terry and I saw early that we were going to have some problems about the content of the measure. Therefore, early in the drafting process we limited the drafting committee to just a handful of people. We invited supporters from all over the state, but we kept the drafting committee small enough to avoid internal dissension (Interview # 40).

To varying degrees, each of the successful heterogeneous DDCs adopted a similar philosophy. Ejecting zealots early, or at least denying them a significant role in the strategic decisions of the campaign, served to limit the impact of ideological heterogeneity upon the movement. The easiest way to limit the impact of zealots in a DDC is to create drafting committees that contain only a few of the more moderate members of the coalition.

Behavioral Pathologies of Homogeneous-Zealot Coalitions

The remainder of this chapter addresses destructive behaviors that are predominately employed by homogeneous-zealot coalitions. There are three basic trends among homogeneous-zealot groups that lead to judicial nullification. First, these groups suffer from the Iron Law of Oligarchy.[19] Small subsets of the coalition gain an inordinate amount of control, and shift the focus of the group to more radical goals. Typically, a charismatic or egotistical leader comes to dominate homogeneous-zealot groups. As the groups turn inward, they develop characteristics more like a sect than a grassroots movement. Secondly, homogeneous-zealot groups come to view themselves as "outsiders." As outsiders, they adopt strategies that are characteristic of political groups who do not believe they can win. Frustrated by their inability to win, they use other political tools the initiative process puts at their disposal. These include such tactics as using the initiative process to send political messages, or to deplete the resources of opposition groups. And third, players in the initiative process do not accumulate secondary benefits from passing legislation. Unlike elected legislators who get better committee assignments, increase the probability of reelection, or receive other "perks" of office, when initiative activists pass legislation, they do not "earn" these benefits. As citizen legislators, they remain citizens even after a political victory. The end result is that homogeneous-zealot groups come to be dominated by small groups of uncompromising, crusade oriented activists, who have behavioral or strategic characteristics that ensure failure.

The Initiative Process and the Iron Law of Oligarchy

Once again, Mansbridge's insights into the ERA movement provide guidance to understanding leadership in the initiative process. When discussing leaders of the various ERA movement groups she writes,

> In organizations that have chosen ideological exclusivity as a means for building community, leaders are likely to be even more radical than their followers, for the leaders now serve not as intermediaries and ambassadors to the outside world but as moral exemplars whose function is inspiration. While traditional organizational theory predicts that leaders will grow more conservative than the rank-and-file, both Ellie Smeal of NOW and Phyllis Schlafly of STOP ERA—although undoubtedly less radical than some of their more active volunteers—were almost certainly further apart in their views than were the majority of people who gave time or money to their respective movements.

In the same manner, leaders of homogeneous-zealot groups tend to be further apart from the majority of people who support the goals of their initiative. The reason the iron law of oligarchy is more influential in the initiative process (or social movements) than in the legislative process, is that legislatures have institutional restraints upon the oligarchy and the initiative process does not. All legislatures delegate decision-making power to committees, speakers, whips, and majority leaders. However, despite the delegation, the discretion of these groups or individuals is limited by structural rules, such as discharge petitions, majority rules, and parliamentary procedure. However, initiative oligarchies are not restricted by institutional procedures to counter oligarchic tendencies.

In addition, the reason oligarchies develop in initiative coalitions is partly understood by comparing the way initiative elites and legislators acclimate themselves to politics. Political actors who come to prominence in the initiative process have very different experiences, and sometimes different motivations, from political actors who do so through the legislative process. The unique experiences they face can influence personal and political behaviors. Political actors who are socialized in an institutional setting learn to rely on the institution for guidance. Political actors who are socialized in an individualistic and isolated setting, such as the initiative process, tend to rely on themselves or close friends.

Consider freshman legislators who come to office as "backbenchers." They spend much of their first term learning the institutional process of the legislature or Congress (Hibbing, 1991). They are immediately surrounded by paid staffers, all of whom have expertise in specific aspects of the legislative process (Krehbiel, 1991). In addition, most legislative institutions have legal councils built into the legislative process. In essence, like any other institution, corporate or political, new members are socialized into the culture of the process.

In addition, the relative permanence of staffers in Washington and state legislatures, along with the rise in career politicians, creates an institutional memory (Davidson and Oleszek, 1977). Simple mistakes are caught by staffers early on. Experienced committee members can assist new legislators. New legislation is subjected to peer review of both supportive and hostile experts. In the end, new legislators can't get their bills to the floor until they have passed through several filters.

Almost none of this is true for initiative drafters. They come to power in a completely different political culture. Other than the *Initiative and Referendum Institute* in Washington D.C., there is no single organization that brings together disparate initiative elites.[20] The peer review process of initiatives is ad hoc at best. Other than professionals who have participated for a lengthy time, most initiative drafters must wander through the legal rules of the initiative process without any institutional support, and therefore, almost no institutional memory. Lacking institutional support, they turn to themselves or to a close group of associates. Unfortunately, the initiative process requires a sophisticated understanding of the law. Those initiative groups that turn to themselves tend to draft initiatives that courts reject.

In the process of interviewing all the subjects for this study, it became clear that members of homogeneous-zealot groups have "behavioral pathologies" that lead to ballot measure nullification. Simply put, homogeneous-zealot groups acclimatize themselves to politics in the initiative process, and not the legislative process. They tend to isolate themselves from outside advice, and they learn "political habits" that are self-destructive. This is most likely to occur with zealots or amateurs who fail and become frustrated with the process.

Of course, what is "self-destructive" and what constitutes "pathologies" is in the eye of the beholder. These behaviors are self-destructive if the primary motivation of initiative elites is to pass legislation. Initially, most initiative drafters do have sincere motivations to enact legislation. However, over time, the lack of institutional supports and the existence of institutional barriers frustrate elites, and cause them to adopt other strategies that do not include actually implementing legislation. Eventually, they come to use the initiative system to frustrate other political actors, rather than to implement their own legislation. Once the goal of implementing legislation has been taken off the table, other uses of the initiative process, specifically drafting arguably unconstitutional legislation, can be seen as rational. Even unconstitutional initiatives attract political attention, send political messages to established political elites, and deplete the resources of opposition political groups. These strategies are discussed in detail later in the chapter.

The Charismatic and Egotistical Leader

In Chapter 4 it was argued that higher rates of nullification cannot be completely explained by the amateurism of initiative drafters because many initiative elites are sophisticated political actors. However, amateurism can *contribute* to the level of nullification. Not all initiative drafters are amateurs, but some are. The porous nature of the initiative process allows amateurs to gain access. Amateurs tend to make simple and obvious mistakes. Whenever a system exists where optometrists draft campaign finance legislation, wedding photographers draft criminal penalty legislation, pastors draft abortion regulations, or accountants draft land use regulations, legal technicalities are bound to be overlooked. There were many examples of amateur drafters making simple mistakes, due to a lack of political experience and the lack of an institutional structure to provide guidance. Consider the following anecdotal list: individuals drafting law before reviewing Lexis-Nexis to see what the existing case law proscribes; individuals believing that passage of an initiative automatically makes their bill constitutional; refusing to adopt changes suggested by the State's Legal Council or Attorney General's office; failing to understand the difference between a constitutional amendment and a statutory bill; and writing a bill on the same day it must be certified by the state (in the Secretary of State's office, no less).

There is nothing new about the argument that ballot measures are nullified due to the amateur status of the drafters. However, what is overlooked in the literature is that the relatively easy access to the initiative system promotes egoism. In a legislative arena compromise becomes essential (Davidson and Oleszek, 1998). Even the most strong-willed legislator must modify her bill to ensure passage. No matter how much power a legislator achieves in one house, that power is completely independent of power structures in the other house, or other branches of government. But more importantly, frustrated or adamant legislators cannot "take their business elsewhere" by moving to a different legislature.

The initiative process does not require compromise. Once an initiative leader has taken a poll that shows a majority of the public supports his bill, there is no political reason to compromise. Other branches of government cannot obstruct the initiative nor can interest groups get access to powerful committee chairpersons to bottle up the measure. As Madison feared, in direct democracy, the power of the majority is unstoppable. Many initiative drafters are aware of this, and it affects their psychology. Once they see the poll numbers, they begin to see themselves as "speaking for the people." In some respects, initiative elites come to believe that they are leading the people, that they personify the power of the people, and therefore, they do not need to compromise or should not compromise. As noted in Chapter 4, many professional initiative drafters go from obscurity to become prominent political figures overnight. As they get caught up in the media that surrounds them, they become almost addicted to the attention. But more significantly, they see themselves as deserving of the attention.

The development of ego becomes an important force when it is coupled with the easy access to the initiative system. Most drafters do not work in isolation. They are members of coalitions. Coalitions, by their very nature, require compromise. However, within the initiative system there are infinite points of access. If initiative elites do not like the compromise, they can always leave the coalition and draft a new initiative.[21] In the legislative arena, because there is only one point of access, this is not possible. Legislators who disapprove of how their bill is being restructured cannot go to the "other legislature."

What we see in the initiative process is that coalitions have the ability to be a moderating force, causing drafters to think about the legality of initiatives.[22] However, the ease with which disgruntled elites can leave the coalition and still access the initiative process encourages egoism. This is because the ability to "exit" creates very homogeneous groups. People who agree with the existing coalition stay; those who do not, leave. Over time, coalitions form that have very similar worldviews. But, through a process of natural self-selection, all the radical elements get into one group. Most of the radical groups are led by an egotistical leader. Everyone who surrounds the leader has one point of view. There is no dissent. These elites adopt an attitude of dismay when anyone outside their organization disagrees with them. When these attitudes are coupled with supportive poll numbers, the megalomania grows.

Even professional activists such as the Washington initiative group, Permanent Offense, are subject to this failing. Permanent Offense successfully passed I-695, a measure that limited car-licensing fees to $30 and required a public vote on all future tax increases. The Washington courts rejected the initiative on the grounds it violated the single subject rule. Permanent Offense returned the next year with a similar initiative, I-722, termed the "son of I-695." The initiative was again passed, and again nullified by the courts. On their third attempt, they changed tactics, and simply tried to reduce taxes. They used an existing tax statute but changed one word. They changed "106%" to "101%," having the effect of limiting tax increases to 1% of the previous year's assessed value. The bill passed and was never challenged in court. After their victory, the group returned with two new initiatives, I-267 and I-776, both of which made multiple changes to the Washington statutes, ranging from transportation issues to taxation issues.[23] Just focusing on the drafting of I-747, it seems as if the group had learned to navigate the initiative process in a way to avoid judicial nullification, yet also achieve some of their policy goals. Yet, after examining I-267 and I-776, it appeared as if Permanent Offense had failed to learn anything from their past experiences with I-695 and I-722. The most obvious question was, why did they return to a twice-failed strategy? An interview with one of the members of Permanent Offense offers some insight.

> Author: Why are you dealing with so many issues in both I-776 and I-267?
>
> Drafter (angrily): What do you mean?
>
> Author: Well, you deal with some transportation issues, some taxation issues, and it appears, some physical infrastructure issues.
>
> Drafter: They are all "rationally tied" to one subject—transportation. There is no problem.
>
> Author: Isn't that what you argued with I-695 and I-722?
>
> Drafter: We're polling at over 60% on this.
>
> Author: I see. But will that help you with the courts?
>
> Drafter: They have been looking for someone to challenge I-747 and no one will do it. The courts can't touch it.
>
> Author: However, you only changed one word of an existing statute in that measure. Aren't the new initiatives a lot different?
>
> Drafter: They're still "rationally tied" to one subject—transportation.

It became apparent that this line of questioning would lead in circles. But the response about polling numbers is interesting. When asked about the legality of the measure, the response was to point to public support, as if that deflected any need to meet constitutional precedent. The respondent is also focused on his past success. His rationale seems to be, if I-747 wasn't challenged, then he had finally convinced state officials he was right and they were wrong. It appears he has lost sight of the fact that the only reason the measure was not challenged is because it changed only one word of an existing statute.

After leaving the issue to move on to other topics, the interview later returned to the issue of the apparent violations of the single subject rule. In doing so, it became clearer how ego was pushing his decisions.

Drafter: I researched this topic. In fact, I was the one who came up with the idea for car tabs. I was also the one who wanted to change I-722. I told [...] that it must be changed, but they didn't listen. Now what I want to do is make it mandatory to teach the Washington Constitution in all high schools. Did you know that it is supposed to be required to teach our constitution to students? Well, they don't. I discovered that law and now I want to make sure it's enforced. I called the state superintendent's offices and asked him, how are you implementing this law? He didn't have anything for me.

Author: I see. But how is that going to help you with I-776 and I-267?

Drafter: You're not getting it. All of my bills are constitutional; it's just that no one knows the Constitution well enough to realize it. The courts get away with stopping our initiatives because no one knows what they are doing is wrong. That's why I'm going to make everyone learn the Constitution.

Author: Have you already started collecting signatures?

Drafter: No, some people in the group don't want to pursue this issue.

Author: Who's against it?

Drafter: Doesn't matter because I'm going to do it anyway. If they want to help, great. If not, I can do it myself.

This segment of the interview highlights two important issues. First, some initiative drafters get caught up in their success. They begin to see themselves as having a monopoly on the truth. And second, if others do not see their truth, they are not required to compromise. The infinite entrance points of the initiative process allow them to exit existing coalitions and pursue their measures alone or with a new group. What is interesting about this interview is that it is not unique. The first-person language and egotistical tone were common to many of the interviews. This example simply shows the extreme to which it can be carried. Having faced defeat at the hands of the court twice, his solution is to change the way the entire state views the constitution, rather than scale back the content of his measures, as he did with I-747.

The Bunker Mentality

Initiative elites who are members of homogeneous-zealot groups often envision themselves leading a political crusade. They view themselves as challenging the system, facing down powerful special interests, angry elected officials, and a skeptical media. This attitude is intensified when elites surround themselves with likeminded people, as noted in the previous section. The result is that they develop a "bunker mentality." This mentality manifests itself as an attitude that the initiative drafter is fighting a lonely battle against the world. To the elite, the masses are behind them, but the "powers that be" are not. One manifestation of the bunker mentality is a very low level of trust of people outside their homogeneous group. Therefore, some elites tend to withdraw into defensive strategies that do not serve them well. Specific strategic decisions that develop as a result of the bunker mentality are the refusal to subject initiatives to outside peer review, to ignore state-mandated peer review, and the tendency to stick with a process that was successful in the past, but is currently leading to failure.

Many initiative elites will not subject their initiatives to outside peer review. They will only circulate the measure to people who are part of their organization, hold an equivalent worldview, or belong to other organizations that hold the same worldview. The reasons vary. Some elites feel that by showing their initiative to others they will be "tipping their hand to the enemy" (Interview # 91). Others don't want to hear negative feedback, especially if it means scaling back the scope of their initiative. And still others don't trust the feedback they receive. Consider the following interviews.

> Author: Can you explain how you vetted your measures?
> Drafters: It's a multi-step process. I start with an idea and get a rough draft conceptually on paper. Then I pass it out to about 10-20 people, but no lawyers.
> Author: Why no lawyers?
> Drafter: Well, not at first. But basically, you give it to twenty lawyers and you're going to get twenty opinions. Most of them telling you what you can't do. But after we get a draft we like, we do hand it out to a few lawyers.
> Author: What lawyers?
> Drafter: People we know. People we have worked with before.
> Author: What about people who might not agree with what you're trying to do? What about lawyers who work for the "opposition"?
> Drafter: No. I did that once, but it is basically tipping your hand to the enemy. The less they know about what we are doing the better.

Not all initiative drafters who suffer from the bunker mentality are as distrustful of lawyers. But, as the following interviews show, many elites resist giving their bills to anyone but a favorable audience. For example, in Oregon, labor unions are backing an initiative to ban payment of signature gatherers on a per-signature basis. Courts have rejected this type of bill in the past.[24] One has upheld it.[25] Thus, in response to questions about the legality of the measure, they respond that a similar measure has been upheld one other place one time, and therefore their measure might withstand judicial scrutiny. This is a risky strategy. Rather than using lawyers to anticipate anything that could go wrong, they are using lawyers to provide hope for the possibility of success. As one drafter put it, "Lawyers are so negative. They just say 'no' and tell you why it won't work. I would rather give it to a lawyer who understands what I am trying to do" (Interview # 53). In the course of the research I began to refer to this attitude as the "lawyer as lifeline" approach. Consider another example.

> Author: Can you explain how you vetted your measures?
> Drafter: We sent it out to all the national organizations. They let us use their in-house counsel.
> Author: What about other organizations? What about "opposition" organizations?
> Drafter: They're just going to tell you it's unconstitutional.
> Author: Well, they might be right. The case law seems pretty clear here.
> Drafter: Our guys went through all the state law decisions. They found places where it had been upheld.
> Author: But weren't those decisions overturned at the federal level?
> Drafter: Yes, but you have to use what you can find. These are the best decisions in our favor.

Again, what we see is a reliance on lawyers to indicate what is possible rather that what is probable.[26] The drafter above was not interested in using a lawyer to sincerely critique the initiative. Instead, he was using legal advice more as a mental life raft to keep his measure afloat. This attitude was common among pro-life and campaign finance activists. Anytime a decision came down that might cast some doubt on existing precedent, or offer a new twist, they would grasp at it.

Again, the Washington group Permanent Offense provides a telling example. In 2001, the state court ruled,

> I -722 necessarily required the voters who supported one subject of the initiative to vote for an unrelated subject they might or might not have supported. For example, a person who desired systemic changes to future property tax assessments but did not want to fiscally burden cities with the refunding of 1999 tax increases was required to vote for both measures or neither. Similarly, a person who did not own a home or was otherwise unconcerned with changing methods for assessing property taxes but did desire refund of other fees was required to go for both measures or neither.

In 2002, the group advertised on its Website that I -776 would implement four changes. It would repeal a series of excise taxes, impose a $30 maximum for licensed tabs, repeal a $15 fee for different counties, and required that all new taxes be subject to a public vote. But clearly anticipating that someone would question whether this initiative met the single subject requirements, they added one last paragraph, which read,

> The single subject of I-776 is limiting government-imposed charges on motor vehicles. Our attorney Jim Johnson drafted I-776 and thoroughly researched the ramifications of the taxing fee repealers (sic) contained in it and we all agree that I-776 is legal and constitutional. Remember, Jim Johnson drafted I-747 which took effect in December without a single legal challenge.

The use of a lawyer here is more to assure the voting public that the initiative is constitutional, than to actually ensure it is constitutional; which it clearly is not. In this case, the initiative was "vetted" by the four leaders of Permanent Offense and their lawyer. The support of their lawyers is more a public relations strategy than a legal strategy. In this case, the bunker mentality manifests itself in the form of over-reliance on one attorney who won one legal battle. For Permanent Offense, the fact that they think the measure is constitutional, and their lawyer who drafted it agrees, is enough to serve their purposes. No attempt was made to vet the initiative to outside counsel.

There were also respondents who simply ignored feedback from the attorney general or their state's legal council. In states like Colorado and Montana, initiatives are required to go through a process of pre-election review.

In other states, it is optional. In some cases, drafters who had received feedback from a state legal official simply refused to alter their initiative accordingly. Again, the bunker mentality got in the way of success. For many elites, the attorney general or legal council is seen as an extension of the forces they are opposing. Their advice is viewed with suspicion and sometimes contempt. A clear example of this mentality is expressed by the following,

> I know these guys have a job to do. But so do I, and we're not on the same team. Of course they say it's unconstitutional. But just because they say it is doesn't make it so…they just don't want to see my initiative on the ballot. Or, they want to rein me in as much as possible. You have to remember, attorney generals [sic] are elected too (Interview # 22).

In the example above, the measure was defeated by the voters and never faced judicial scrutiny. But the attitude expressed sheds light on the way some initiative proponents view the sincerity of state officials. Given this apparent distrust, some elites reject some of the most qualified advice they receive.

Another example of the bunker mentality is the tendency of initiative elites to stick with one strategy that has worked in the past, but is no longer effective. They may receive updated advice, but they chose to ignore it, insisting that what has worked in the past will work again. This is most noticeable with respect to drafters' attitudes towards the courts. At one time, the courts were more accommodating towards initiatives. Unless an initiative was blatantly unconstitutional, many state (elected) courts looked the other way.[27] Some scholars call this the "crocodile in the bathtub" syndrome (Uelman, 1997), meaning elected courts are afraid of overturning popularly elected measures for fear of reprisals during retention elections. However, recent rulings by state courts suggest the courts are no longer as accommodating towards initiatives. This is important because some initiative drafters have been involved in the initiative process for a long time. The courts upheld their bills back when the courts were less restrictive. But since then the courts have become more suspicious of ballot measures. What leads to problems for these long-time participants is that a drafter remembers that he won in a particular way before, and sees no need to change. But, the legal environment has changed and he is no longer getting by the courts. When asked about clauses in their initiatives that might lead to judicial problems, common responses were "I did that in '78 and there was no problem" (Interview # 20), or "When I passed Measure [...], the courts didn't do anything" (Interview #17), or "We won with Measure [...]" (Interview # 9).

An interesting insight is that many of these interview subjects were associated with Proposition 13 in some way. They had either worked on the measure or knew the people who did. When asked how they initially became involved in the initiative process, a common response was, "I knew Howard Jarvis," or, "I was friends with Paul Gann," or "I helped with Prop 13 back in California." This indicates that the success of Proposition 13, and the subsequent upholding of the very lengthy and complicated initiative by the courts, created an attitude in some long-time participants of the initiative system that political popularity trumps strict adherence to procedural requirements. It helps explain why these respondents have had less success in the initiative process in more recent years. It may be that the courts themselves have contributed to their need for increased participation in the initiative system today. By sending signals in the past that initiatives would be lightly scrutinized, they have encouraged veteran drafters to pay minimal attention to legalities in their more recent initiatives.

A concrete example of drafters sticking with the same failed strategy because it worked once in the past can be found in the way Public Interest Research Groups (PIRGs) approach campaign finance reform. For campaign finance reform, the major legal hurdle is adopting contribution limits that do not violate the First Amendment's freedom of speech clause.[28] Almost every time a campaign finance initiative was nullified, the judge made a decision based on the excessive contribution limits. At first glance, this appears to be an issue that initiative drafters could easily circumvent. A second initiative in the next election cycle with higher limits seems a logical response. However, although some advocates have grudgingly increased their contribution limits in subsequent initiatives, the reason for continued judicial rejection of these initiatives is contribution limits remain too low.[29]

Enacting Legislation is Not a Short Run Goal

Whenever political scientists examine the strategies individuals use, whether it is in the context of game theory, attitudinal models, or institutional models, certain assumptions about behavior are adopted (Muller, 1996). In most cases, these assumptions relate to the goals of the actor. For example, when we examine prisoner's dilemma games, we assume "rationality," and conclude that all actors are seeking to maximize their rewards. In attitudinal and institutional models of judicial behavior we assume that actors are trying to pursue personal policy preferences through opinion drafting, granting or denying *certiorari*, or voting strategically on the bench (Rohde and Spaeth, 1976; Segal and Spaeth, 1993). However, these models only have predictive power because, in general, if the assumptions about goal seeking are correct. In contrast, if the original assumptions are incorrect, then the observed outcomes of participants in a game, or in real life, may not make sense.[30]

In terms of the initiative process, empirical evidence highlights a high level of judicial nullification. Thus, initial assumptions are that either the behavior of the initiative elites is unsophisticated, or judges must be applying an unfair standard to initiatives. However, in rare cases there is an alternate explanation. For some zealots, successfully enacting legislation is not always the primary goal. In fact, in some cases, initiative elites want their initiatives to be challenged, or even overturned, in court. Given that permanent policy creation is not a goal of some players in the initiative system, it makes perfect sense that many initiatives do not become permanent policy. Only by understanding the true nature of these initiative elites' goals can one understand the strategic decisions and "mistakes" they make.

Initiative elites may have goals other than creating policy that withstands judicial scrutiny for three reasons. In some cases, initiative elites openly disagree with current legal precedent. Therefore, they purposefully draft legislation that is unconstitutional to "get their foot in the legal door" (Interview # 43). By having an initiative challenged, they can make a case before the courts that their approach to this policy should be adopted over existing law. Second, many initiative drafters just want to "send a political message" (Interview # 94). Initiatives attract attention from media, established state political elites, and the federal government. Because the initiative system offers access to groups that may not have access to traditional political institutions, these "fringe" groups use the initiative process to air their views and pressure more moderate legislators. And last, initiatives can be about resource attrition. Ballot measures are expensive to pass and to oppose. In many cases, initiative elites draft measures that are clearly unconstitutional but very threatening to powerful interest groups. These powerful groups, fearing that there is a slim chance the initiative will be upheld, dump considerable resources into opposing the initiative. Some initiative activists know this and continue to pursue these types of initiatives, in hopes of weakening an interest group they oppose. Each of these three strategies is examined below.

Challenging Existing Law

Chapter 3 identified initiative participants whom are zealots. The key characteristic of zealots is that they are unwilling to compromise their values in order to produce a ballot measure that will withstand judicial scrutiny. It is the zealots who most often adopt the strategy of drafting initiatives for the purpose of challenging existing precedent. Nagle (1997) comments,

> But sometimes initiatives knowingly present constitutional questions. The voters approving Colorado's Amendment 2 and California's Civil Rights Initiative were well-informed of the constitutional dangers of their actions. The whole point of California's most recent defeated campaign finance proposal was to challenge *Buckley v Valeo*.

For the zealot, scaling back an initiative to meet constitutional restrictions is capitulation; true victory can only be achieved by overturning existing law. Given this strategy, it is not surprising that many initiatives written with this goal in mind meet with nullification.

Of the many initiative zealots who used initiatives to challenge existing law, two groups best exemplify this strategy. Both campaign reform advocates and anti-abortion advocates seek to overturn landmark federal case law. For campaign reform advocates, the 1976 case *Buckley v. Valeho* is seen as the major obstacle preventing election reform. For anti-abortion advocates, *Roe v. Wade* still stands out as their major impediment. Therefore, it has been the goal of many initiative drafters to use ballot measures as a vehicle to overturn these cases.

An examination of campaign finance reform initiatives and their advocates in California, Colorado and Oregon reveals similarities in their strategies. Consider the following three dialogues.

> Author: What reason did the judge give for striking down your initiative?
> CO Drafter: Our limits were too low.
> Author: Why did you pick the contribution limits you did?
> CO Drafter: The PIRGs were very influential. They wanted $100 limits.
> Author: Were you or they aware of *Buckley*? Did you consider *Buckley* when drafting?
> CO Drafter: Yes, we looked at *Buckley*, but we were right.
> Author: What do you mean, "we were right"?
> CO Drafter: I mean we were right and *Buckley* is wrong. $100 limits should be upheld. Money is not speech.
> Author: But you knew your bill would be challenged?
> CO Drafter: We were pretty sure. But other states were challenging *Buckley*. Some were succeeding. We needed a vehicle for challenge here in Colorado. It's not like the courts were going to come to us and say they changed their mind.

It is clear that the Colorado activist is interested in pursuing a policy outcome. However, it is equally clear that he is aware that his initiative, as it was written, runs afoul of constitutional mandates of the time. But, rather than modify the bill, he prefers to challenge the status quo. It is the hope of many elites who adopt this strategy that they will find a court more sympathetic to their cause. In this specific case, the drafter feels he has a chance of overturning *Buckley*. He is interested in the possibility that the court may offer a new precedent interpreting *Buckley*, which would permit lower limits. Or, in the case of a lower court loss, he hopes that he can appeal to a higher court, possibly the Supreme Court, and there establish a new precedent that either overturns *Buckley*, or at least allows for more flexibility with contribution limits. The interview with an initiative elite involved in drafting California's Proposition 208 reveals a similar attitude.

> Author: Did you examine previous case law before you drafted your initiative?
> CA Drafter: Yes. I had access to a lot of "think tank" literature.

Author: What changes did you make to your original bill as a result of that literature?

CA Drafter: After our research, and other feedback, we raised our limits to $1,000 and we made restrictions based on election cycles, not fiscal years, and we changed the way we regulated lobbyists.

Author: But you still had your initiative nullified because the limits you established were too low.

CA Drafter: Yep.

Author: Why not play it safe and pick limits you knew would be upheld?

CA Drafter: Well, the PIRGs were pushing really low limits. They have this "dripping faucet" approach to campaign finance reform. They want to keep going at it until the courts change. They had had one small victory in the past with small limits, so they were convinced if we just kept coming back with the same thing, eventually the courts would give in.

Author: Why not ignore them?

CA Drafter: Eventually we did. But by that time, the bill was pretty much established, we had already started collecting signatures, and it was too late to change. When we started ignoring them, they left to draft their own version (Prop 212). Their express purpose was to overturn *Buckley*.

In the case below, the initiative was never challenged in court because it failed to make the ballot. However, the same attitudes and goals that led the above two drafters to have their initiatives struck down by the courts are still evident.

Author: What kept your measure off the ballot?

OR Drafter: We spent so much time fighting among ourselves. The pragmatists wanted basic limits on corporate contributions. The purists wanted to go all the way to zero. And they wanted to regulate contributions to initiative campaigns.

Author: But you knew limits of zero would doom your initiative.

OR Drafter: Yes, we knew, and that's what split our group in two.

Author: So why did you continue to expend time and resources on a bill you knew was unconstitutional?

OR Drafter: For one, we know that if the courts keep striking down campaign finance laws they are going to lose credibility. In the long run that helps us. If the courts do lose credibility, they will eventually have to get it back by supporting one of our laws. We are coming back in 2002.

Author: So you didn't care if the bill was unconstitutional?

OR Drafter: Not really (speaking only for himself, not the coalition).

The examples above show a consistent attitude towards the courts. These drafters knew their initiatives were unconstitutional. However, the interviews establish that drafting a sustainable initiative was not their primary goal. However, in the above case, we see a slight difference in the strategy. The previous two cases were clearly attacks on existing precedent. In the last case above, it is evident that initiative elites were challenging precedent, but also concerned with wearing down the courts, embarrassing the courts, or providing an opportunity for the courts to "change their mind." This is a "political," rather than legal, strategy. The last group feels that initiatives provide public pressure on the courts, and that continual public pressure may force the courts to "appease" the demands of the people who are seeking lower limits.

An Oregon anti-abortion activist put it more succinctly. "I don't pay for these initiatives. And I get nothing out of them either. I hope they do take me to court (Interview # 94)."

Sending a Political Message

Some ballot measures create a high level of salience with the public.[31] Millions of dollars are spent in the media advocating or opposing initiatives (Gerber, 2001; Zisk, 1987). As a result, even if initiative elites cannot achieve a policy victory through the passage of an initiative, they can still impact the political agenda. Initiative elites have the power to shape what people are voting about, even if they cannot completely determine how they vote. By setting the agenda, initiative elites gain power within the political environment simply by putting an issue before the public. When an initiative passes with 60% of the vote, even if the courts find it unconstitutional, legislative representatives still take note of the fact that the policy was endorsed by a large segment of the voting population. Therefore, an initiative can serve as a very public vote of confidence for a policy even if the courts reject it. Subsequently, initiative activists can use the vote as leverage when engaging in the legislative arena.

Research revealed six policy areas where initiative elites used initiatives as a tool to send a political message. In the areas of taxation, abortion, Indian gaming, judicial behavior, legalizing marijuana, and urban growth, initiative elites have used ballot measures to influence their state legislature, the federal

government, or simply to raise public awareness of an issue. Initiative drafters
are aware that an initiative that is narrowly defeated, or passed but nullified,
encourages legislatures to enact a more "moderate" version of the measure, or to
refer a more moderate measure to the people in the form of a referendum. Like
the initiative elites who use the process to challenge existing law, initiative elites
who seek to send a political message rarely care whether their ballot measures are
constitutional.

Consider the case of an initiative activist who drafted a bill requiring
judges to take a new oath promising to interpret the state constitution through the
original intent of the framers. Clearly, this bill has many legal problems. One on
level, it would be impossible to enforce. Judges would have to apply to law to
themselves; and who besides judges would determine if a decision was an
originalism decision? On a legal level, such a restriction would probably violate
the separation of powers doctrine. Therefore, the obvious question remains—why
would an activist expend resources on such a project? The drafter's responses
highlight why.

> Author: So do you have any belief this bill would be upheld by the
> courts?
> Drafter: Of course not.
> Author: Then why all the effort?
> Drafter: First of all, if the judges strike it down then I can just use that
> against them. Second, I can educate the people. People are going
> to ask, why this measure is on the ballot? They are going to ask
> why we need a new oath. The answers to these questions will start
> a dialogue. But mostly, it will pressure the legislature. If this
> passes, legislators are going to say, "Hey, people are pretty upset
> about this. We better do something."

This interview makes a good first example because it exhibits three different
motivations in terms of sending a political message. He wants to scare the judges,
speak to the people, and get the legislature to take up his cause. However, it is
clear from his first answer that even the drafter has no belief the bill is legal.

In a more subtle case, an anti-tax activist reveals he is more interested in
speaking to his state's legislature than passing a defendable measure. In this case,

the activists had submitted the same initiative three times. Although the focus of the questions was the single subject rule, his answers provide a different insight.

> Author: You have submitted the same bill three times. However, since you first submitted it, the courts have adopted a stricter interpretation of the single subject rule. Don't you feel you need to alter the bill to meet the new standards?
>
> Drafter: Probably, I must confess I didn't stay up on that ruling. But I know what you're talking about. The thing is, even if it does pass, it's hard to make the legislature do what it doesn't want to do.
>
> Author: I'm not sure I understand.
>
> Drafter: If they want to raise money, they can raise money notwithstanding my initiative. They would just do it in other ways. But, every time my initiative gets a lot of votes, it reminds those guys that we don't like taxes.
>
> Author: Do you think you have been successful?
>
> Drafter: Hell, yes. The Republicans adopted my initiative word for word in their platform. When that happened, I quit running the initiative.

Often, the public comments of legislators or other political figures encourage this approach to initiative politics. By admitting they are affected by initiatives, even when they are defeated at the polls or overturned in court, state actors motivate initiative drafters to use measures as a tool of indirect pressure. After Oregon's Measure 7 was invalidated in court, Oregon's House Minority Leader noted, "Certainly we have to address people's concerns when 53% of them vote for it."[32] About the same measure, the Oregon House Speaker argued that even though the measure had been rejected by the courts, "we need to at least have a discussion of how we [the Legislature] would implement the law."[33] In a Washington case, the tax limitation measure I-722 was overturned in court, but the King County Executive admitted to limiting tax increases that year. "We held back because the voters have been telling us that they want us to cut back,"[34] he said. In a similar fashion, the Washington Legislature voted to limit car tabs to $30 soon after an initiative enacting the same limit was overturned in court.[35]

Initiative elites are aware of the press they receive. They often use such press to bolster their fundraising efforts or to make arguments in favor of their initiatives. They often argue that voters should pass their initiative even if it is unconstitutional, because it will have indirect pressure on the legislature.

Another interesting example came from two groups of Indian activists who wanted to provide Las Vegas-style casinos on Indian reservations. They came from two different states, but it is clear they had similar goals and strategies.

> We fully expect a challenge. Probably in the legislature and the courts. But we have two things going for us. Originally the legislature didn't was to pass a lottery either. But after it passed via an initiative they backed off. Probably because it passed big. Second, our courts are more sensitive to politics. We just voted one out last year. If we win big, I don't think they will want to be the ones to say "no" (Interview #61).

A different Indian gaming activist put it a little differently, but the approach is clearly similar.

> What started this all going was the governor. He abandoned the laissez-fare attitude that the state had always had towards Indian gaming. So we put out our initiative. The first time we ran it, it passed with 63% of the vote. That was more than the governor got. But it wasn't a constitutional amendment...so we lost in the [state] Supreme Court. However, it did get Governor [...] to the table. He met with us and made some new campaign promises. In 2000 we came back, but this time with a constitutional amendment. It's currently being challenged by the Feds, but Governor [...] has agreed not to have the state challenge it (Interview # 10).

In a more blatant case of indirect pressure, an activist in Colorado drafted a very strict anti-growth initiative. He admitted the bill had many legal problems, especially with contract and property law. However, he noted, "My main goal was just to bluff the legislature." Although that measure was defeated because of a technicality in the title hearing, he returned in 2000 with an even more radical bill. "I wanted the legislature to see the writing on the wall. If they didn't do something, I would. Of course I drafted this very radical bill. Don't think it would have survived very long. But it sure put fear into the legislature."

Some activists simply want an issue to stay on the minds of the public. They don't believe that their bill will pressure the legislature in the short run, but feel that voters will eventually pressure the legislature if the issue stays salient. Tax, abortion, and marijuana activists commonly adopt this strategy.

Some anti-abortion and marijuana activists take the attitude that they are in for a long fight. Simply by keeping abortion or the legalization of marijuana on the radar screen, they feel they are slowly winning the battle.[36] Because they have little confidence that the courts will uphold their bill, very little effort is placed on ensuring constitutionality. Talking with an abortion activist who had yet to have an initiative upheld by the courts, I questioned why he was still involved in the initiative process and why he had not modified his ballot measures to meet constitutional standards. He replied, "We are in this for the long run. We need to raise public awareness before we have a chance to change the law" (Interview # 97). His comments are almost identical to the following marijuana activist:

> We are getting an incredible amount of attention because of this [ballot measure legalizing the sale of marijuana]. I've been interviewed by all the major media outlets. The federal government is watching us. They know the war on drugs is a sham. When we pass this initiative, they're going to know that we know, too. Eventually, Congress is going to have to admit failure or keep coming into all the states that pass these measures and continue the pattern of repression (Interview # 101).

Tax activists exercise the strategy of using a ballot measure to send a powerful political message, but they use the strategy to prevent the passage of legislation, rather than supporting it. When voters pass ballot measures that cut taxes, and do so by a large margin, legislatures are reminded of the public opposition to taxes. Tim Eyman, an anti-tax activist, has successfully passed two tax limitation measures in his state.[37] The court nullified both measures. However, he is currently submitting essentially the same initiative for the third time. The following email correspondence reveals why he is pursuing a seemingly futile strategy.

> When political judges vetoed voter-approved Initiative 695, politicians frantically embraced the $30 tabs during that election year. [The governor] said, "Despite the court's ruling, we have no intention of returning to the old system of high license tab fees." $30 license tab fees are here to stay...Initiative 695 helps politicians keep their promises. Passing Initiative 695 also sends politicians a message: don't increase taxes and fees unless you ask voters' permission first.

If the past is any indication of how the courts will rule on the current initiative, it is likely that it is headed for nullification. However, that does not mean the initiative drafter will view the campaign as a failure. For this drafter, success has been attained simply by sending the legislature the message that he is watching what they do.

When initiative drafters have goals other than immediately implementing policy, they spend fewer resources ensuring an initiative is constitutional. My data indicates initiative elites have tangential goals, such as influencing state and federal government, or simply maintaining the salience of a particular issue.

Resource Attrition

As Gerber and Garrett (2001) show, initiative campaigns are expensive. They are expensive to back, and expensive to oppose. And initiative drafters know that ballot measures overturned in court are no less expensive to oppose. As a result, some activists use the initiative process to deplete the resources of interest groups they oppose.

A common tactic is to draft a measure that would have serious consequences for a specific group. For example, Lloyd Marbet spent much of the 1970s and early 1980s attempting to shut down the Trojan nuclear power plant in Oregon.[38] For Marbet the stakes were high. But for the employees, owners and interested parties of the power plant, the stakes were "life or death." If any initiative seeking to shut down the power plant passed and was upheld, they would lose everything. Having such high stakes means that relying on the courts to step in becomes a very risky strategy. Half of challenged initiatives are struck by the courts. But that also means that half are upheld. Given the stakes, many threatened groups choose to fight initiatives in the political arena as well as the legal arena. In doing so, they get two chances to defeat a threatening initiative, but at the same time, they are playing into the hands of some initiative activists.[39]

Two groups attract the ire of initiative drafters more than any other group—the government, and teachers' unions. The government is the focus of term limit initiatives, tax cut initiatives, campaign reform initiatives, and more. But teachers' unions place a close second when it comes to angering initiative elites. The most probable reason is that education budgets make up a large part of state budgets, and education lobby money is very influential in state politics.

Thus, many of the people I spoke with saw teacher's unions as "partners in crime" with the government. To many ballot measure activists, teacher's unions provide the money to help government officials to stay in power, and in turn unions receive the bulk of state funds and political influence.

Because the cost of defeating initiatives is so high, initiative elites can win even when they lose. This is especially true when challenging the power of unions.[40] The political power of unions comes from two resources—voters and money. Ballot measures can't deter voting, but they can consume money. Nowhere was this clearer than when I met with an activist who had repeatedly run the same initiative every two years, yet had never seen his initiative enacted as policy.

> Author: You keep running this initiative and you keep losing. Why?
> Drafter: Why am I running it or why am I losing?
> Author: Well, both.
> Drafter: You know, get my message out. Hope one time I win.
> Author: Since this interview is anonymous, let me ask you plainly: is resource attrition one of your goals?
> Drafter: Absolutely! Every dollar they spend on me...one less dollar they spend on lobbying, complaining, asking [the legislature]for more money.

Another drafter, who was also focusing on teacher's unions, admitted he had the goal of resource attrition, but as more of a secondary goal. His comments are representative of the attitudes of many of the initiative elites.

> Look, I see where this question is going. Would I say it to the newspapers? No. But since this is off the record; do I want my initiative to pass? You bet. Do I want my initiative to be upheld by the courts? You bet. But do I know I am sucking their coffers dry. You bet. Does that bother me? Not one bit. I'll keep drafting the initiative as long as my financial supporters are behind me and I can get the signatures. Eating away at the resources is not always my primary goal, but it's up there (Interview # 92).

In the cases where resource attrition is a goal, whether primary or secondary, elites prefer not to admit it openly. Although many drafters eventually admitted their desire to use up the financial resources of groups they opposed, such information was only forthcoming after I reminded the interviewee of the confidential nature of the process.[41] Their reluctance to reveal this information was analogous to a poker player who does not want to reveal he is bluffing. It is important to drafters that their opponents believe they are sincerely seeking a policy change. Otherwise, their initiatives would attract less opposition and therefore deplete fewer resources. Furthermore, initiative elites who adopt this strategy are usually professionals. Professionals have the structural support and the financial ability to run initiatives repeatedly.[42] Therefore, there is less incentive to draft constitutionally defendable measures. On one level, they don't care if the measure is constitutional. But on a second level, they know they will have another chance to pass the initiative in subsequent elections.

The culmination of all the above interviews leads to one clear conclusion. Ballot measure drafters in homogeneous-zealot groups are not always seeking to immediately pass new law. They have other strategic goals, such as challenging existing legal precedents, sending political messages to the state or federal government, or depleting the resources of opposition interests groups. Given these goals, it should not be surprising that many ballot measures do not meet constitutional standards. In some cases, it would be wasteful to expend resources ensuring constitutionality, and in other cases, meeting constitutional standards would actually prevent the initiative drafter from meeting her primary goal. In the three cases I have identified, it is far more important for a measure to pass than to be upheld. Failed initiatives do not get challenged in court. If an initiative losses badly in the election, the next time the drafter returns to the political arena, he will not elicit the "fear" he wants. In turn, if his opponents are not afraid, they will not expend significant resources to defeat him. And lastly, if an initiative loses at the ballot the political message sent will not be very powerful. Given these incentives, it is understandable why ensuring constitutionality is not the top priority.

The Initiative Process and Secondary Benefits

When it comes to the initiative process and secondary benefits, there aren't any. Secondary benefits are perks that are gained by successfully passing legislation and staying in office. Mayhew (1974) shows that the primary motivation of members of Congress is to get re-elected. He concedes that members of Congress have normative policy goals, but shows that implementing them is not the ultimate arbitrator of their decision-making. The trappings of office such as prestige, travel, and other perks make re-election their foremost motivation. Therefore, it is understandable that members of Congress are willing to compromise. It is absolutely essential that they do so, or they would never pass any legislation. Without passing legislation, they would appear ineffective to their constituents. As Davidson and Oleszek (1998) note in their discussion of congressional strategies, "the lesson is that compromise is inevitable in crafting laws; those who are unwilling to give ground are bound to be disappointed."

In the initiative process, few, if any, secondary benefits for passing legislation are passed on to the drafter. Because initiative drafters don't run for office, re-election is never a consideration. The state does not provide salary, offices, or official titles to citizen legislators.[43] Initiative drafters who pass more ballot measures don't get better committee assignments, promoted to higher office, or attain leadership positions within the legislature. This fact alters the incentives for drafters of ballot measures. Whereas a member of a legislature might accept a scaled-back version of their bill in order to announce a legislative accomplishment to their constituents, initiative drafters feel no such pressure. As one interview subject noted, "I don't get anything if this passes, why should I compromise" (Interview #94)? To many initiative elites, especially those involved with homogeneous-zealot groups, the only benefit for success in the initiative process is seeing their values implemented into law. Therefore, compromise becomes doubly defeating. They abdicate their values, but receive nothing substantive in return for abdication.[44]

An illustrative comment comes from an activist working with a group on term limits. After the courts had repealed their initiative, they returned with a new initiative. One decision they had to make was whether or not to backdate the term limits so that legislators who had already served eight years would not be eligible for another eight years. In the end they decided to make the term limits retroactive despite concerns it would violate the *ex post facto* clause of the Constitution. When asked why, part of his response was,

> We have no vested interest in the process. Win or lose, we're in the same boat. This is strictly a public service so we can have a true citizen legislature as the Founders envisioned. We might as well try this version first. If the courts strike us down, we can always come back with a version without the retroactivity. We expect a challenge either way. So if this fails, all we're out is two years of the same old thing [current legislators in office] (Interview # 81).

What is clear from the above comment is that there is very little incentive for the drafter to try the more conservative bill. He doesn't see anything in it for himself. It might be that if a term limits bill without the retroactivity passed, and he received some secondary benefit because the bill passed, there would be more incentive to compromise. But because no secondary benefits entice him ("Win or lose, we're in the same boat"), he has no incentive to reduce his policy demands.

Conclusion

This chapter focused on the behavioral reasons for the judicial nullification of ballot measures. I argue that ballot measure coalitions go through a predictable life cycle. In the initial stages, the net is cast wide to bring together as many activists and supporters as possible. However, these initial heterogeneous coalitions are not sustainable, because tensions develop regarding "doctrinal purity." As a result, more homogeneous groups develop—moderates in one group, and zealots in another group. It is the zealot groups that face higher rates of nullification, because they suffer from three problems. Following the Iron Law of Oligarchy, zealot groups are led by charismatic and egotistical leaders who radicalize the group. They feel like outsiders, and develop a "bunker mentality," insulating themselves from moderating influences. Once this happens, these groups have very little chance of passing constitutional legislation. Understanding this, they begin to pursue secondary goals, such as resource attrition or sending political messages. And finally, given that no secondary benefits accrue to the drafters for passing legislation, they are even less likely to compromise for personal gain.

---

[1] The data set for this book is limited to initiatives. It does not include referenda, which pass approximately 70% of the time, or recalls. Initiatives pass less than 50% of the time and an additional 25% of those are invalidated by courts. If one also includes all the initiatives that never make it to the ballot, "consistent failures" is an accurate term.

[2] Halcli does concede that ACT UP membership fell by the late 1990s, but attributes the decrease in activity to "activist burnout" and because ACT UP meetings lost their political chick as the "in place to be."

[3] In fact, many states held referenda with respect to adopting the Equal Rights Amendment.

[4] I will use the terms "zealot" and "lawyer" for the remainder of the chapter. I chose the term lawyer because most direct democracy advocates who exhibited this type of behavior were either lawyers or politicians.

[5] For example, one Oregon coalition pursuing campaign finance reform eventually split into two factions: one part of the coalition wanted to pursue a limited campaign finance reform measure, the other half eventually decided they wanted a measure to abolish capitalism! After which, it become clear to the three initial, and moderate leaders that a more homogeneous group of moderates would be needed to realistically pursue their initiative.

[6] In one of the seminal works in political science, Hirschman (1970) argues that unsatisfied individuals of either nations or smaller groups are faced with basically two options—to "exit" the group or to "voice" one's opposition. However, when the "exit" option is not available, as it is not in many cases, there is a tendency for an increase in the intensity of the "voice" option. For example, since most abortion activists do not consider leaving the US a realistic option, they are very vocal about their opposition to abortion. In contrast, many historians argue America avoided internal strife during the early 1800s because an open frontier provided an easy "exit" option. For an empirical defense of Hirschman's theory, see Orbell and Uno (1972).

[7] In the 1950s von Neumann and Morgenstern established "expected utility theory." The notion was based on the idea that individuals made decisions based on two criteria—the utility and probability of success. If the "expected utility" were greater than the "expected costs," an action would be taken. For example, people would pay .25 at a 50/50 probability of earning a dollar. The costs are known at .25 and the expected utility is (.5) x $1.00 which is .5. Because .5 is greater than .25, the action would be taken.

[8] Many respondents in my research indicated they were pursuing "symbolic goals," attempting to pressure the legislature, or simply trying to expend the resources of opposition groups.

[9] Mathematically, we get the following. If the utility of passing a scaled back bill is zero, then the costs of passing the bill or compromising on the bill, *no matter how small*, are always going to be greater than zero. However, even if the probability of a judge upholding an unconstitutional bill is incredibly small (1%), the expected utility is still positive and therefore greater than zero, which is the utility of a compromise bill.

[10] In such cases, Homogeneous-Moderate groups will pay outside professionals to collect signatures to avoid this problem. However, moderates still have trouble raising funds. In general, political supporters willing to donate money to the campaign are more zealot-like, and are less willing to donate money for moderate initiatives.

[11] Of course, new initiative groups are always forming. These new groups tend to be heterogeneous groups. But the life cycle of an initiative group leads them to transform from a heterogeneous group to one or both of the homogeneous groups.

[12] These groups also suffer from the Iron Law of Oligarchy. Small subsets of the coalition gain an inordinate amount of control, and shift the focus of the group to more radical goals. Typically, a charismatic or egotistical leader comes to dominate homogeneous-zealot groups. As the groups turn inward, they develop characteristics more like a sect than a grassroots movement. Secondly, homogeneous-zealot groups come to view themselves as "outsiders". As outsiders, they adopt strategies that are characteristic of political groups who do not believe they can win. Knowing this, they use other political tools the initiative process puts at their disposal. These include such tactics as using the initiative process to send political messages, or to deplete the resources of opposition groups. The end result is that homogeneous-zealot groups come to be dominated by small groups of uncompromising, crusade oriented activists.

[13] In California, Proposition 208, and in Colorado, Amendment 15.

[14] By "safe," the advocates meant they wanted higher limits would not be invalidated by the courts.

[15] See *California Pro-Life Action Council, et al v. Scully, et al.* 164 F 3d. 1189 (1999).

[16] *Buckley v. Valeo* at 424 US 1 (1976) is the landmark case establishing campaign spending as free speech.

[17] See *Citizens for Responsible Government State PAC v. Davidson* at 236 F.3d 1174 (2000 US APP).

[18] The Wild Scenic Rivers Act (1968), The Clean Water Act (1972), The Clean Air Act of 1990.

[19] Robert Michels (1915) argued that the formal organizations eventually develop ruling oligarchies. Organizations, originally idealistic and democratic, eventually come to be dominated by a small, self-serving group of people who achieve positions of power and responsibility. This can occur in large organizations because it becomes physically impossible for everyone to get together every time a decision has to be made. Consequently, a small group is given the responsibility of making decisions. Michels argued that members of the oligarchy would become enthralled with their elite positions and more inclined to make decisions that protect their power, rather than represent the will of the group. Despite any protestations and promises that they would not become like all the rest, those placed in positions of responsibility and power often come to believe that they too are indispensable, and more knowledgeable than those they serve. As time goes on, they become further removed from the rank and file.

[20] The Initiative and Referendum Institute acts as a clearinghouse for all the rules and regulations that exist for initiative drafters in each state. They are attempting to provide the function of 'institutional memory' for scattered initiative elites.

[21] A prominent drafter, Don McIntire, notes, "Politics is the art of compromise. That's a form of art I don't care too much for." See Beggs, Charles. "Initiative leader plans more measures," *The Register-Guard*, October 4, 1999. 5B.

[22] This is the case in heterogeneous-moderate groups. In fact, the exact opposite can occur, when coalitions homogenize themselves.

[23] In I-776 Sec 3 limits vehicle tabs to $30, Sec 4 repeals six existing tax laws, and Sec 5 restricts future bond sales. I-267 Sec 1 requires sales taxes to be deposited in the motor vehicle fund, Sec 2 redirects the way taxes should be spent in the transportation department, Sec 3

develops a new auditing system for the state, and Sec 5 implements the creation of new carpool lanes.

[24] *See On Our Terms 97 PAC v. State of Maine* at 2000 US Dist Lexis 11937.

[25] *I&R Institute v Jaeger* at 241 F.3d 614.

[26] In these circumstances, the lawyer is not an equal participant in the coalition. He or she is simply a hired employee. Therefore, we do not see the typical tensions that develop when a lawyer, as described in Chapter 4, is part of a coalition with amateurs or zealots.

[27] When Proposition 13 passed with 65% of the vote, it made extensive changes to the California Constitution, but the court rejected challenges that the measure revised the constitution, arguing the provisions were "reasonably germane."

[28] See *Buckley v. Valeo* at 424 U.S. 1, the seminal case in this matter.

[29] See *Carver v. Nixon* 72 F.3d 633; 1995 U.S. App. Invalidated Missouri Proposition A which contained $100 limits, *Citizens for Jobs v Fair Political Practices Commission* at 16 Cal. 3d 671, *SEIU v. FPPC* at 955 F.2d 1312 (9th Cir), and *Van Natta v Keisling* at 324 Ore. 514.

[30] For example, consider two actors engaged in a prisoner's dilemma game where one or both players do not have the goal of winning the most points or avoiding the most losses. It would be nearly impossible to predict an equilibrium outcome. To an outside observer who has made assumptions about the goals of the players, a Nash equilibrium would be obvious, while at the same time, the fact that the players were not adopting the Nash equilibrium would be unexplainable to the observer.

[31] For example, Proposition 187 led to extensive public protests and still resonates in California politics eight years after its passage. See "Simon's harsh words on immigration may haunt campaign," *San Francisco Chronicle*, April 20 (2002) pp. A1. Also, The Oregon Elections Division records that in the six-year period between 1993 and 1999, the second highest voter turnout was for Oregon's vote on doctor-assisted suicide.

[32] See "Land –use system challenged," *The Oregonian*, January 1, 2001. A8

[33] See Beggs, Charles. "Lawmakers differ on need to change Measure 7 rules," *The Oregonian*

[34] Waters, Dane (2001). *I&R Update* Vol. 4, No. 4.

[35] See Cook, Rebecca. "Son of 695 takes first steps toward ballot," *The Idaho Statesman*,

[36] In Ukiah, California activists promoted and passed Measure G allowing residents to legally grow marijuana. The petitioners admitted they had no belief the measure would supercede state and federal law or be upheld by the courts, but argued it would be an important first step in challenging the thinking that makes using marijuana a criminal offense. See Nieves, Evelyn. "County makes effort toward legalizing marijuana-growing," *The Oregonian*, October 1, 2000. A21.

[37] He passed I-695 and I-722 (the son of I-695). Both were struck down as violating the single subject rule.

[38] Marbet was the chief petitioner for Measure 14 (1988), Measure 4 (1990) and Measure 5 (1992).

[39] In a similar example, one respondent had run an initiative dramatically increasing the cigarette tax in his state. The tobacco companies spent a significant amount of resources defeating the initiative. He wanted to continually run the initiative every election cycle just to impose costs on the cigarette industry. However, the coalition he put together to support the initiative would not support his efforts.

[40] Ronald Buel writes, "They [initiative backers] don't win many. But they do cause their target opponents to spend millions to defend against their measures. The AFL-CIO and other unions drag millions of union dollars into Oregon to beat back Sizemore every time. This prevents Oregon unions from spending their political money to elect candidates or on some proactive initiative they might prefer."

[41] Some activists are more open about this strategy. Bill Sizemore comments, "All the money public employee unions spend fighting these two measures is money that will not be available to fight our [other] measure." See "Unions save for ballot battles," *The Register-Guard.* January 16, 2000. A5.

[42] Although none of my interview subjects who were professionals admitted it, it is very possible that nullification provides job security. Most professionals receive funding from outside sources. As long as the issue is still around, there is still a need for an initiative activist to tackle the issue. As long as that need exists, they will continue to get funding for their organizations. Therefore, indirectly, there is some incentive to draft bills that do not meet constitutional standards. It ensures a project for the next election cycle.

[43] This point becomes very clear when one visits the offices of initiative drafters. Not once did I meet an initiative activist whose office or headquarters could be considered plush. In most cases, they had small one- or two-room offices with scattered second-hand furniture. And the locations of these offices ranged from out of the way strip malls to warehouse districts.

[44] This is not the case for many homogeneous-moderate groups who are seeking to achieve a specific policy that benefits their coalition. For instance, many of the Native American groups who were using the initiative process to legalize gambling were more than willing to compromise. The reason is that there was a huge secondary benefit to passing the legislation— millions of dollars in gambling revenue.

Chapter Seven

Challenging the Courts: Initiative Drafters Fight Back

Between 1960 and 1998, the people of Oregon, Colorado, and California passed 127 citizen-sponsored state ballot measures. More than half of those ballot measures were challenged in court. In all, state and federal courts invalidated 33 of them. Many of the invalidated ballot measures were highly popular and salient. In Oregon, the state Supreme Court invalidated a very popular term limit initiative.[1] In Washington, the state Supreme Court invalidated an admired tax limitation measure.[2] And in California, the courts invalidated a popular, but divisive, immigration limitation provision.[3] In each case the state Supreme Courts had their supporters and opponents. But an undeniable side effect of such high profile decisions is to drag courts into the firestorm of political debate. Richard Ellis' recent book, *Democratic Delusions: The Initiative Process in America* reflects on judges' tendency to invalidate ballot measures. What is clear to Ellis is that the courts are invalidating measures for political, rather than legal reasons. He notes, "groups [come] to court with political grievances dressed up in constitutional garb, and the judges [are] generally willing to provide redress (p.22)." The problem, Ellis suggests, is that when courts hide political decisions behind the veil of constitutional decisions, the courts lose legitimacy. Furthermore, even moderately educated observers know when the courts are "pulling a fast one." When the courts appear to be political, they invite a political response; and initiative drafters are becoming all too willing to provide such response.

With increasing frequency, state courts are being called upon to nullify popular direct democracy initiatives. Courts are the logical battleground for individuals who opposed successful initiatives. Direct democracy is a purely majoritarian system. 51% of the voters mandate the law regardless of the intensity of opposition from the other 49%. However, in the courtroom, the playing field is leveled. Courts are an institution relatively immune to majoritarian influences. In court, one plaintiff can prevail against 10 million voters. However, when one litigant prevails against millions of voters, there are bound to be repercussions. In a nation with a history of majority rule, voters are apt to react forcefully to such a powerful minority veto.

The purpose of this chapter is to examine how judicial nullification of popular and salient ballot measures will affect the politicization of state judicial elections. It would be unrealistic to assume that initiative drafters, who contribute a significant amount of time, resources, and personal commitment towards the passage of those initiatives, will sit idly by while courts invalidate their measures. Initiative drafters are politically sophisticated actors who have considerable political resources at their disposal. In most states, even judges must stand for election or retention. Initiative drafters are becoming well aware of that fact, and in doing so, are seeing an opening. Direct democracy activists are beginning to ask: If judges are vulnerable to electoral defeat, then why not use our political skills to retaliate against judges who invalidate our measures?

There are many ways to attack a sitting state judge. Some are more effective than others. The approach most commonly used by initiative activists is to increasingly bear the costs of challenging sitting state judges; primarily, by assuming the "information costs"[4] associated with electoral politics. State justices are relatively insulated from electoral reprisal because voters rarely have enough information about judicial candidates (incumbents and challengers) to hold them responsible for actions contrary to their political preferences. It is known that voters will not actively seek information about judicial candidates. Therefore, most citizens vote blindly in judicial elections, most typically selecting the incumbent candidate. However, initiative activists are beginning to bear the cost of informing voters in state judicial elections. If voters won't go out and get information about judges, initiative activists are going to provide it for them. Since these activists providing the information have a political cross to bear, the information is going to be less than flattering. In the face of damaging information, judges are going to feel compelled to respond. This means commercials, campaigning, and the fund raising necessary to carry out these events. All this points to the coming politicization of state judicial races.

Recent political events have encouraged scholars to take an increasing interest in state judicial elections. For example, sitting members of Congress are becoming involved in state Supreme Court elections,[5] unpopular tort liability decisions have moved state Supreme Courts to center stage,[6] and more often, sitting justices are facing electoral competition.[7] As a result, campaign spending in judicial elections is rising, as are the use of campaign advertisements.[8] All of this is occurring as the United States Supreme Court has invalidated state measures limiting state judicial candidates from raising and spending campaign money.[9]

All of these events have led social scientists to examine the conditions that lead to judicial electoral challenges (Bonneau and Hall, 2003). The usual suspects have been identified: the type of institutional mechanism for electing and retaining judges (Brace and Hall, 1995), the salience of issues courts were required to rule upon (Hall, 1992), and the amount of money and interest group participation in the election (Dubois, 1986). However, completely ignored in these empirical studies is the role of direct democracy activists seeking to retaliate against judges who have invalidated state ballot measures. The omission is glaring given that we know, *ipso facto*, that any successful ballot measure has garnered the support of at least 50% of the voting public. Therefore, any judge or court which invalidates such a measure is, by definition, acting contrary to the majority will of the public. It seems logical that these types of rulings will attract the ire of not only voters, but especially the activist(s) who spent considerable time and money to ensure the passage of the ballot measure. However, judges only need to fear electoral reprisal if the voting public has enough information to connect the judge/court to the invalidation of the popular initiative. Typically, this is not the case (Lorvich and Sheldon, 1984; Baum, 1987). However, direct democracy activists are increasingly willing to provide such information to the voters.

Initiative elites are becoming increasingly willing to challenge the courts' tendency to invalidate their ballot measures. Frustration over repeated judicial nullifications is leading towards open hostility to the courts. As a result, many of the initiative drafters are engaged in ongoing projects aimed at unseating sitting justices.

Because of the significant time lag between judicial elections,[10] the work of angry initiative drafters may not "bear fruit" for some time. However, it is likely that states with the initiative process will experience increased political activity in the arena of judicial politics over the next ten years.

Democratic or Republican Government?

For many, it is unclear whether the high rates of judicial invalidation represent a story of institutional success or failure.. From one perspective, the fact that initiatives are nullified so often is a sign that America's Madisonian system is working exactly as it was designed to function. From another perspective, high rates of nullification raise the specter of Platonic judges acting as a supra-legislature, wielding an indiscriminate scythe against the majority's will. As with most dilemmas in American politics, the answer probably lies somewhere in between the two extremes. The high rate of judicial nullification of ballot measures brings with it the defense of minority rights so critical to Madison's vision of what a republican form of government should entail. At the same time, when judges are drawn into political debates, and are called upon to mediate challenges to popularly elected initiatives, there is a risk of politicizing the courts.

The framers of the American political system were wary of purely democratic forms of government. Madison's fear of factions is clearly indicated in the *Federalist Papers* and the constitutional debates. The framers' reliance on minority vetoes to protect minority interests from the overwhelming power of majority factions is evident. Some of the safeguards developed include the system of checks and balances, presidential vetoes, judicial review, filibusters, committees, and a host of other parliamentary procedures. However, the reality of the initiative process is that none of these minority checks exist except judicial review. Therefore, as the institution solely responsible for insuring that initiatives do not violate minority rights, the court's scrutiny can be expected and even welcomed. From this perspective, judicial nullification is a story of success. It highlights the fact that despite the development of a new political institution, with rules that run to the democratic extreme, Madison's system of institutional checks still prevails and protects.

However, the data also suggest a story of failure, or at least a story of potential danger. As initiative challenges draw judges and courts into political battles more frequently, the political insulation so vital to the courts may be eroded. Former California Supreme Court Justice Joseph Grodin observes, "It is one thing for a court to tell a legislature that a statute it has adopted is unconstitutional; to tell that to the people of a state who have indicated their direct support for the measure through the ballot is another" (quoted in Ulmen, 1977, p. 1135). When one judge is required to overrule the wishes of two million voters, it is unlikely that the public will respond by applauding the integrity of the system of checks and balances. The rejection is felt personally, and reacted to personally.

Not just the voters react to judicial nullifications. The individuals who drafted the measure are also likely to feel the sting of judicial action. However, unlike the public in general, many initiative drafters have access to well-financed political organizations that can mobilize machines for fundraising and voter outreach. Professor Uelmen notes, "The initiative crocodile can be labeled the angriest because the promoters of the initiative measures tend to take personal pride in their handiwork, and take personal offense when a court messes with it (p.1148)." Along with this "personal offense" sometimes comes the desire to respond politically.[11] Theories of institutional interaction make it clear that encroachments upon an institution's autonomy are typically resisted. The danger alluded to earlier becomes the way in which initiative activists choose to respond to judicial invalidation of their measures.

An initiative proponent can do very little to respond to federal courts that invalidate his measures. Federal judges are appointed for life and are relatively insulated from political pressures.[12] The same cannot be said for state courts. Most states have some form of democratic retention or elections for justices. Because state courts are institutionally different, and more subject to political influences, initiative elites are focusing their ire there.

The Insecurity of State Courts

Melinda Hall (1992) notes that 38 states utilize some form of popular control of judges. In these states, judges face either partisan elections, nonpartisan elections, or retention elections. As Julian Eule (1994) notes, 21 of the 23 states that permit popular initiatives hold their judges accountable through a form of democratic election.[13] Much of Hall's (1987, 1992, 2001) research, both independently and in collaboration with Paul Brace (1988, 1992), demonstrates that state supreme courts are more susceptible to political pressures. The overwhelming consensus of research suggests that state courts are more influenced by politics because sitting judges must face the voters from time to time (Richardson and Vines, 1970; Jaros and Canon, 1971; Hall, 1987). More specifically, the literature indicates state judges are most likely to be influenced when dealing with high salience issues such as death penalty cases, abortion law, and popular initiatives (Hall, 1992; Uelmen, 1997; Brace and Langer2002).

Uelmen (1997) and Eule (1994) argue that initiatives present an especially difficult problem for state judges. Together, they highlight some anecdotal cases where judges invalidated popular initiatives and were subsequently defeated at the next election.[14] Their concern is that judges may decide not to reject unconstitutional measures for fear of losing their seats. The evidence does not lend credence to their fear. Over half of all initiatives challenged in court are rejected by the courts, including highly popular term limit, campaign finance, and anti-crime statutes. Despite the evidence that suggests judges should be afraid of nullifying popular initiatives, the fact is they appear not to be afraid of doing so. This is most likely due to the fact that voters have very little information when it comes to judicial elections (Baum, 1987). Even in competitive judicial elections, the incumbent almost always wins (Hall, 2001).

Given the empirical evidence, what Uelmen and Eule should fear is an informed voting public. It is only when judges vote contrary to the ideology of the public and the public is aware of those votes that judges face electoral defeat.[15] As long as voters forget that a particular judge has nullified a popular initiative, the courts will remain politically insulated. This is not unlikely given that most judges only face retention elections every ten years (Hall, 1992). Therefore, fears of a politicized state court will only occur if some political actor decides to bear the costs of informing voters about the judges and their records.

Initiative elites are becoming increasingly willing to bear those costs. Frustration over repeated judicial nullifications is leading to open hostility to the courts among initiative activists. When these activists were questioned about the difficulties of lawmaking within direct democracy, the most common response focused on the inability to avoid judicial interference. As a result, many of the initiative drafters revealed ongoing projects aimed at unseating sitting justices.

Challenging the Courts: Four Case Studies

State judges are insulated from electoral reprisal because voters rarely have enough information about judicial candidates to hold them accountable for decisions contrary to the voter's preference. Only in rare cases, in which the media plays a significant role in 'educating' voters about a particular judge or a particular ruling, do judges face credible electoral consequences.[16] In other words, voters are unwilling to bear the information costs associated with judicial elections. Therefore, one relatively simple and cost effective way for initiative activists to challenge judges and courts is to bear those information costs for the voters. If voters are made aware of judicial decisions that are contrary to their political preferences, it is more likely they will have enough information to vote their preferences in judicial elections.

Initiative activists have found four ways in which to bear information costs in judicial elections. First, activists can gather information about a particular judge, her controversial decisions, any popular initiatives that were invalidated, and release that information to the media, or through grass roots newsletters. Or, they can release that information to the campaigns of judicial challengers.

Second, disgruntled activists can find and support qualified candidates to run against sitting judges when their term is up. Typically, most coalitions created to draft ballot measures include at least one lawyer, usually more. Such individuals are easily convinced to run against judges who invalidated their measure. Because they were intimately involved in the ballot measure campaign, contributing lawyers feel an intense bitterness when their measure is overturned. But, unlike other members of the coalition, lawyers are qualified to serve as judges. The nexus of anger, qualifications, and a well financed initiative coalition to financially support the candidacy makes it appealing for them to run.

Table 11: Types and Rates of Challenges to Judicial Autonomy

		All Respondents	Only Respondents who Suffered Judicial Nullification	Only Respondents who Suffered State Court Judicial Nullification
# of Respondents		45	38	28
# of Activists who Assumed Information Cost for Voters*		13 (29%)	12 (32%)	12 (43%)
	Media Campaigns	3 (7%)	3 (8%)	3 (11%)
	Electoral Campaigns	5 (11%)	5 (13%)	5 (18%)
	Institutional Changes*	2 (4%)	1 (3%)	1 (4%)
	Symbolic Measures	3 (7%)	3 (8%)	3 (11%)

* Only one activists chose to challenge judicial autonomy even though he had never experienced judicial nullification.

Third, changing the way judges are elected can serve to lessen the need for information costs in judicial elections. Some direct democracy activists are attempting to make it easier for voters to remove judges, or to select judges that share the voter's ideology. For example, appointment and election of judicial candidates based on geographical region increases the likelihood that a candidate will represent the political values of a specific area. With this "reform," voters are provided with informational cues about a judge's ideology. Voters can more easily assume that a judge from a rural area will have "rural values" and judges from urban areas of the state will have "urban values." Other activists have pursued the inclusion of a "None of the Above" option in judicial elections. With this option, voters who have no information about specific candidates can still "retaliate" against sitting justices.

Fourth, symbolic measures raise awareness of issues, especially issues that reflect poorly on the courts. Many direct democracy activists assume that judges are not held accountable for unpopular decisions because the public at large has little information about how judges work. Therefore, they engage in symbolic protests that attract media attention or forces electoral action. For example, an Oregon activist proposed an initiative to change the state judicial oath. He accepted the fact that the measure would not likely pass, and if it did, the courts would invalidate it. However, the press coverage the measure would attract was a sufficient reason to run the initiative.

Assuming Information Costs through Media Campaigns

"If they strike down Measure 7, it's war. We're going to go after the judge with everything we've got. We found out he let a child molester go on a technicality. We're going to use that against him [in the next election]." These comments were offered prior to the Oregon Court's ruling by an activist closely tied to the effort behind Measure 7. Measure 7 was a controversial property rights measure that passed in Oregon with 51% of the vote, but was overturned by lower court judge Paul Lipscomb and eventually found unconstitutional by the Oregon Supreme Court. The initiative activist quoted above has had a number of his ballot measures invalidated, Measure 7 being the most recent. Although many of the initiatives he worked on have been upheld, the courts invalidated two initiatives about which he cared passionately. In addition, he has lost many lower court decisions, such as title hearings and signature-gathering lawsuits. His response was to start compiling "opposition research" on sitting judges.[17] At the time of my interview, this activist was in the process of identifying a select number of judges who were responsible for invalidating prominent initiatives. His goal was to create a "dossier" for each judge, highlighting decisions that the public might find controversial. The information will be used to run television commercials and to release to the press at the appropriate times. It is interesting to note that the initiative proponent was not singularly focusing on cases where ballot measures where overturned, but instead focusing on any decision that might paint the judge in an unfavorable light.

This strategy is clearly designed to increase the political costs to judges for nullifying ballot measures. The drafter identified here is aware that judges are typically re-elected because voters have very little information about candidates. He is also aware that voters will not bear the costs of finding that information. To remedy the situation, this activist is assuming the costs for the voter, but for his own purposes.[18] His ultimate goal is to strip from the courts the traditional insulation judges have in political disputes. He concludes, "I don't want an independent judiciary, I want an accountable judiciary."

Similarly, disgruntled direct democracy activists can bear information costs by directly running media commercials for judicial candidates. In 1999, the Oregon Supreme Court invalidated Measure 40, a measure that altered many aspects of the criminal procedure process. As a response to this decision, attorney Greg Byrne ran for a position on the Oregon Supreme Court. To assist the campaign, Crime Victims United, a prominent backer of Measure 40, paid for, and ran campaign commercials for candidate Byrne. Although the approach is different, the goal is the same. Crime Victims United sought to assume some of the information cost associated with judicial elections. However, in this case, the method is to run advertisements providing positive information for a favored candidate, rather than disseminating negative information for a disfavored candidate.

Both examples above illustrate that direct democracy activists inherently understand what could be termed the "Law of Judicial Elections"—judges need only fear counter-majoritarian rulings if the public is aware of the ruling and can associate the ruling to a particular judge or court. The data suggests that direct democracy activists are willing to bear the costs to make such connections.

Assuming Information Costs through Electoral Campaign

In 1994, the team of Bill Sizemore and Bob Tiernan, an Oregon state legislator, succeeded in passing Measure 8. The measure repealed the mandatory "pick provision" for state employees. Because the teachers' union is so powerful in Oregon state politics, they were able to get the state legislature to guarantee them a yearly 8% return on their retirement funds. If the market provided an 8% return or higher, the teachers kept the money. Yet, if the return was less than 8%, state tax revenue had to make up the difference. Not surprisingly, a variety of state employee unions filed suit claiming the measure violated the Contracts Clause of the US Constitution. The Oregon Court, relying on a novel new "fundamental fairness" doctrine that is found neither in the Oregon Constitution nor Oregon statues, ruled the measure unconstitutional. The Court divided 4-3 and the dissenting justices offered a blistering critique of the majority's clearly political decision. In response to the decision, Bob Tiernan, the measure's supporter, elected to run for the State Supreme Court. Although he eventually lost his bid for a seat on the Court, since 1994, several other initiative activists have followed Tiernan's approach. It is becoming quite common for disaffected initiative drafters to run for judicial offices.

In 2000, Oregon voters narrowly passed Measure 7, a property rights measure that would require the state to compensate landowners if regulations decreased the value of their property. The measure was backed by Larry George, and long time initiative activist Bill Sizemore. Shortly after the election, a coalition of environmental groups filed suit to have the measure overturned.

Eventually, the Oregon Supreme Court did overturn the measure on highly dubious constitutional grounds. The court argued that because the measure exempted strip clubs from the land-use compensation provisions, the measure also altered the "freedom of expression" clause in the Oregon Constitution, making it invalid under the separate vote rule! The drafters of Measure 7 included the exemption for strip clubs because they wanted to maintain the state's power to re-zone districts with strip clubs without having to commit state funds to strip club owners. Under the Court's logic, the backers of Measure 7 would have needed to run a completely separate Constitutional Initiative exempting strip clubs from the rest of the provisions in Measure 7. In truth, the Court was simply looking for a reason to invalidate a law they did not like. The strip club loophole allowed them the opportunity.

The measure's backers were justifiably irate at the Court's blatant judicial manipulation. However, the judicial politics of this case did not end with the Supreme Court's decision.   David Schuman, the lead Oregon state attorney assigned to defend Measure 7, was appointed to the Oregon Court of Appeals soon after his failure to successfully defend the measure.   A day after his appointment, Robert Swift, a supporter of Measure 7, filed a complaint with the Oregon State Bar arguing that Schuman purposely lost the case as a *quid pro quo* with Gov. Kitzhaber for the Appeals seat.[19]

In response to the judicial treatment of Measure 7, David Hunnicutt, the principal attorney involved in the drafting of the measure, ran for Schuman's Oregon Appeals Court seat in the following election. His campaign message promised Oregon voters he would be a "judge who followed the law, not wrote the law." Mr. Hunnicutt lost the election with 41% of the vote. However, Charles Beggs noted, "The court race was high-spending by usual standards. Schuman raised more than $200,000, mostly from lawyers; and a family farm group with ties to OIA [Oregonians in Action] garnered $165,000 to help Hunnicutt." Furthermore, the Money in Politics Research Project noted that independent expenditures, a rarity in judicial elections, were a relevant factor in the judicial race, noting, "The Oregon Family Farm Association PAC spent

$128,000 on independently produced radio ads attacking Schuman and supporting David Hunnicutt through May 12th. During the same period the Oregon League of Conservation Voters spent $36,500 for mailings opposing Hunnicutt. Adding the campaign contributions plus independent expenditures reveals $138,000 raised to support Hunnicutt and $225,500 raised by Schuman's allies." Although Hunnicutt lost his bid to unseat Judge Schuman, he clearly succeeded in firing a "shot across the bow" in judicial politics. The message was simple: if you strike our measures down, you will face electoral competition. For judges, who are accustomed to running unopposed, this is quite a change from politics as usual.

The strategy of running candidates to unseat judges who have invalidated popular initiatives is gaining popularity among initiative elites. The case of Montana's CI-75 illustrates this approach. In 1999, the Montana Supreme Court invalidated CI-75, a constitutional amendment that would have required public approval of all tax increases.[20] The chief sponsor, Ron Natelson, was particularly upset with the court. In response to the court's decision, Natelson launched a statewide campaign to change the makeup of Montana's highest court. He focused his particular attention on Justice Leaphart, who was up for re-election just three years after the *Marshall* case. Natelson characterized the court in this way: "This court is what we call an outlier. Their direction is dramatically different than a traditional court. I've never seen anything like it in my 30 years in the law business, except maybe the California Supreme Court in the 1970s."[21] The chairman of Natelson's anti-tax organization was more critical, referring to the justices as "seven black-robed terrorists" who had "overturned the wishes of 176,000 voters."[22]

Natelson's sentiments were echoed by the many state legislators who had supported CI-75. Representative Orr commented, "The court is out of control. It's time for a revolt at the ballot box." Calling for a new constitutional convention, another representative noted, "The Montana Supreme Court is a bunch of ultra-liberal supreme dictators."[23]

Sensing a change in the political environment, Natelson embarked on a statewide campaign to encourage lawyers to run for positions on the state

Supreme Court. In particular, Natelson drafted an ex-teaching assistant, Bob Eddleman, to run for the seat held by Justice Leaphart.[24] In addition to drafting candidates, Natelson put forth a five-point judicial reform plan, which called for partisan elections in all judicial races. A Natelson critic and colleague called the plan "politicizing [the courts] to the hilt" and claimed that it would result in a loss of judicial independence.[25]

However, an independent court is not seen as a positive by many initiative proponents. Having succeeded in the very populous arena of direct democracy, they are often angered by what they see as elitist courts subverting the "will of the people." Initiative drafters are coming to realize that despite the rarity of truly competitive judicial campaigns, justices do indeed have to survive in a democratic system. From the perspective of the initiative proponent, the problem stems from the fact that judges usually run unopposed. The natural strategic response is to find qualified candidates to run against judges who have invalidated their measures.

Eliminating the Need for Information Costs through Institutional Change

The two preceding cases offer examples of initiative activists concentrating their efforts on the electoral aspects of the courts. Either by assuming information costs or promoting opposition candidates, their goal is to increase the political costs to judges of ballot measure nullification. In the following cases, the initiative elites adopt a different strategy. Rather than participating in judicial elections, they seek to alter the judicial institution by changing the rules of the game.

Don McIntire is a successful initiative proponent in Oregon. He was the chief sponsor of Measure 5, a tax reform measure that acted as a catalyst for other tax rollback measures. Although he has never had one of his measures invalidated by the courts, he is a strong advocate of the system in general and feels the courts have become too activist when it comes to nullifying initiatives. In response, he drafted and qualified for the 2002 Oregon ballot Measures 21 and 22.[26] Measure 21 requires

> In all elections for the position of judge, "None of the Above" shall be listed on the ballot as an official candidate in addition to all other candidates…when more votes are cast for the "None of the Above" candidate than for any other, special elections will be held in May and November, until the position is filled. (ORS 251.215)

McIntire explains the rationale for his new initiative in these terms.

> We don't really vote for judges, we simply rubber stamp lone candidates. In most elections for judge, voters know that virtually every seat will list but one candidate. That's why people don't pay attention to the judges. Judges have a tremendous impact on our society, and to many Oregonians, not always for the better. Now, the voters will have a significant, democratic method of getting the attention of those who wear the black robes.[27]

Gregg Clapper, the co-chief petitioner, makes clear that Measure 21 is a direct response to the way judges have invalidated numerous initiatives. In the Official 2002 General Election Voters' Pamphlet, he notes:

> If you get angry when some judge invents a reason to throw out a voter approved amendment like Ballot Measure 7, or when another judge reaches into the Constitution and yanks out the Term Limits amendment, approved overwhelmingly by Oregon voters ten years earlier, Ballot Measure 21 will provide you with a powerful way to effect a return of common sense to our sometimes autocratic and elitist judges.[28]

One of the proponents of Measure 7 made a similar argument. He comments,

> Maybe your issues about some judges [*sic*] decisions aren't the same as mine. Perhaps you don't care that some of our judges have gone overboard to frustrate the death penalty, or thrown out Measure 7 or Term Limits, or that they let the murdering Dayton Rodges off the hook on a technicality…use the ballot box as a means of making believers out of some of our "untouchable" judges.[29]

It is clear that Mr. McIntire and his supporters also understand that information costs and the lack of challengers affect judicial elections. However, their response to judges who invalidate ballot measures is different from the first two examples. The "solution" provided in Measure 21 is a one-step answer. Initiative elites who become involved in judicial elections engage in a continual process. They must continue to find and finance qualified candidates. Or, they must continually gather information about judicial candidates and then disseminate that information to the voters. However, Measure 21 seeks to alter the system of electing judges and therefore create a permanent response.

The proponents of Measure 21 apparently feel that individuals become upset when judges invalidate measures,[30] but the power of incumbency is too strong to overcome. Therefore, people continue to re-elect the same judges. By offering a "None of the Above" option, voters can vote against a judge they dislike without having to vote for a judge about whom they have no information. Based on the written arguments in the Voters' Pamphlet, the indirect goal of the measure's proponents is likely to make judges conscious of the "None of the Above" option. As one proponent suggested, "It also challenges the [judicial] candidate to earn the vote of his/her constituents."[31]

Although McIntire and Clapper contributed a great deal of time and effort to the campaign to pass Measures 21 and 22, they did not provide the financial backing. The financial backing came from Loren Parks, an Oregon businessman. Parks had been one of the major backers of Measure 40, the victims' rights bill that was overwhelmingly passed by Oregon voters but subsequently invalidated by the Oregon Supreme Court's creative reading of the Oregon Constitution in the famous *Armatta* decision. The *Armatta* decision was the Court ruling that created the Oregon separate vote rule out of thin air. Measures 21 and 22 provided Parks with an avenue for payback. Parks contributed $124, 605 dollars to get Measure 21 on the ballot and an additional $133, 848 to get Measure 22 on the ballot. After securing both spots on the ballot, Parks contributed an additional $600,000 to the "Yes on 21 and 22" campaign. In all, Parks provided 99% of the total funding for both measures.

Measures 21 and 22 both failed. However, had they passed, the measures would have contributed to the politicization of the courts. They would have required sitting justices to raise money, campaign, and consider the effects of their rulings on the attitudes of the voting public. Despite the twin losses, there is nothing to prevent the measures from being submitted again.

Assuming Information Costs through Symbolic Measures

Some initiative elites respond to judicial activism with purely symbolic measures. These measures are more designed to catalyze public opinion than to directly impact the court system. Two examples of this strategy are exemplified by Oregon's Lon Mabon and Washington's Monte Benham. In both cases, the activists are seeking to highlight their assertion that judges are ignoring their state constitutions when invalidating initiatives. Most initiative proponents who experience judicial nullification argue that courts have misapplied constitutional principles or created entirely new constitutional principles. In response, both men have drafted, and are currently seeking to qualify, measures that would have little impact on judicial behavior in the short run, but would raise the level of public debate about the interpretive power of justices.

Mr. Mabon, whose office is decorated with a prominent poster declaring, "Judges are NOT above the Law!" is currently pursuing a judicial oath initiative. The measure would alter the oath Oregon judges currently swear when assuming office. The new oath Mr. Mabon is proposing reads,

> Notwithstanding any other provision of this constitution every judge of Oregon law, before entering upon the duties of his office, shall publicly take and subscribe, and transmit to the Secretary of State, the following oath:

> I, _____, do solemnly swear or affirm that I will support and defend the national constitution of United States of America (1789), and the constitution of the Union state of Oregon (1859). And when discharging the duties of this office I will give allegiance to no other like jurisdiction, whether foreign or domestic. I will faithfully and impartially, in a manner free of all bias, discharge the duties of the judge of said state, according to the best of my ability. I further swear or affirm that I will honor and maintain the separation of powers doctrine *and I will not use my official duties to create law from the bench; as an interpreter of the law I will not substitute my opinion or preference, or that of any social faction, for the will of the people* [my emphasis], but shall adhere strictly to the intent of the framers, both of the law and of the constitution. Where such intent cannot be discerned, I will defer to the legislative branch to provide it. I will not accept any other office, except judicial offices, during the term for which I have been elected or appointed.

In the italicized material above, Mr. Mabon expresses his desire for a court that will defer to the "will of the people," which could readily be interpreted as the will of the people passing initiatives. The text suggests that Mabon feels courts have abused their discretion when ruling on challenged initiatives. However, Mabon was also very realistic when discussing the likelihood his initiative would be enforced or have any immediate effect on judicial behavior. Mabon understands that the oath has no enforcement mechanisms other than the judges themselves. Regardless, he is pursuing the initiative because he believes it will promote a dialogue about the behavior of judges. Given that many judicial decisions take place with very little publicity or scrutiny, Mabon feels that the initiative would force people to discuss the behavior of judges. In doing so, judges would in turn become aware that voters were focusing their attention upon them.

Monte Benham of Washington has a similar strategy to challenge the autonomy of the courts. Mr. Benham is convinced that the reason Washington judges can manipulate the state constitution for political purposes is because voters are completely unaware judges engage in such behavior. However, what is different about Mr. Benham's approach is that he feels judges have such leeway because Washington citizens don't know or understand their own constitution. He argues that judges in his state can write new constitutional law because the voters don't know that it is new, or "contrary" to the existing document.

In response, Mr. Benham is pursuing Initiative-285 titled, "Teach the Children," which requires the teaching of the state constitution in all high schools. His expressed purpose for drafting the measure is to teach Washington residents "the constitutional powers of the initiative drafters." He concludes that if residents know about their own constitution they will not let judges "get away with what they do to our initiatives." Indirectly, Benham is pursuing the same strategy as those elites who want to bear the information costs in judicial contests for voters. The earlier examples focused on how elites want to disseminate information about the behavior of judges. Benham wants to disseminate information about the limits of judicial powers, in the hopes that information will be used against "renegade" judges.

Conclusion

All of the case studies above highlight one principle: Initiative elites who become frustrated with the courts are seeking to use the initiative system to restrict the power and discretion of judges. Although each case illustrated a unique way of pursuing that goal, each policy will have the same effect. The strategies noted will all lead to a greater politicization of state courts.

As a caveat, it should be noted that not all policies will have the same impact. Initiative drafters suffer from a principal-agency dilemma when trying to force the courts to adopt certain behaviors.[32] As such, measures implementing a "none of the above" option or requiring a new judicial oath will most likely meet with judicial invalidation. These measures will briefly provide media coverage of issues concerning judicial behavior, and may indirectly make judges think about "the crocodile in the bathtub," but little else. Most of the time, these types of symbolic measures are pursued by zealots. Frustrated zealots often turn towards symbolic measures to make a political point. However, in some cases, professionals will also pursue symbolic measures. Having institutional assets to support them, an occasional symbolic measure is not necessarily considered a waste of resources. In essence, professionals benefit from an economy of scale in the initiative process and are able to pursue many initiatives at the same time. Professionals are also repeat players. As such, even a symbolic measure that is electorally defeated or judicially invalidated can affect future campaigns. Symbolic measures are a way for professionals to "fire a shot across the bow." Even a defeated "None of the Above" measure may have the effect of influencing a judge the next time he has a challenged measure on the docket.

In contrast, initiative elites becoming involved in judicial elections, either directly by drafting candidates or indirectly by providing "opposition research," will potentially have a large impact on the courts. These types of behaviors will require sitting judges to raise money, campaign, and engage in other political activities to stay in office. Given that the US Supreme Court recently ruled that judges cannot be barred from raising money and campaigning in judicial elections[33], there is already an institutional setting ripe for more contested judicial elections. The result may be a more political court and less confidence in the impartiality of the courts.[34]

In the end, this will be the price to be paid if the courts remain the only institution to maintain Madison's system of minority protections. Polls suggest public support for direct democracy, as a general principle, remains very high.[35] Therefore, it is very unlikely we will experience a state-sponsored rollback of the initiative system. Initiative drafters will continue to place measures on the ballot. Voters will continue to pass a large percentage of these measures.[36] And, if courts are continually required to invalidate over half of all challenged initiatives, initiative elites will react to protect the autonomy of their institution. In order to protect their institution, they will be forced to attack others, primarily the courts.

As the title of this chapter indicates, the attack will come in the form of politicizing the courts. However, to understand the impetus for the reaction to the courts, the mindset of initiative activists also needs to be understood. What a political pundit may call "politicizing" the courts, initiative activists call "democratizing" the courts. Most of the cases presented in this book illustrate ways in which initiative activists are trying to make the courts more democratic. They are finding new judicial candidates, they are trying to alter the ways in which judges are elected, and they are engaging in judicial campaigns in the same way they would legislative campaigns.

Given the culture of initiative activists, this approach makes perfect sense. The initiative process attracts people who are attracted to direct democracy. Initiative fights take place in a social narrative that pits the will of the people against established and isolated political elites. Of course, it is going to be those who function in the most democratic of institutions that react most viscerally to the most autocratic of institutions, judicial review. Being democratic activists, it should not be surprising that initiative activists adopt the old Populist mantra, "the cure for the ills of democracy is more democracy." The attack on the courts should be viewed from this perspective. Initiative activists are simply trying to fix a "broken" system by bringing more democracy to the courts. Most revealing of this attitude is the earlier comment, "I don't want an independent judiciary, I want an accountable judiciary" (Interview # 92).

What will make future battles over the independence of state courts interesting is to see how far the voting public will support initiative attempts to democratize the institution. Unhappiness with insulated courts is not a new phenomenon in American politics. Early Supreme Court justices were impeached by the Jefferson administration. The most famous case occurred when President Roosevelt tried to pack the Supreme Court with friendly judges after much of his New Deal legislation was invalidated. Congressman Gerald Ford spent much of his time in the House trying to impeach Supreme Court Justice Douglas. However, in each of these cases, Congress stepped back from the precipice of politicizing the courts. Jefferson's Congress refused to remove Justice Chase on purely political motives. The New Deal Congress balked at Roosevelt's power move. And Ford's work never got out of committee. In the past, leveler heads prevailed, and the courts' independence was maintained. One must wonder, however, if state ballot measures will attract the same type of political reflection and protect the state courts in the same manner.

Given this relatively bleak prediction about the future of direct democracy, one might question whether such an outcome is inevitable or avoidable. It is possible that the spiral of frustration initiative elites feel can be mediated. However, institutional reforms would be necessary.

Two institutional changes may serve to limit the number of judicial invalidations, and in turn, limit the level of frustration felt by initiative activists. Courts could institute a process of pre-election judicial review. Or, constitutions could be amended to require the use of the Legislature's Legal Counsel to "fix" measures before they are placed on the ballot. In some limited instances, both of these reforms have been used.

In rare cases, courts will act on an initiative before it comes to the ballot. California's Proposition 24 was rejected before it ever came to be voted upon. In a few instances, the Oklahoma Supreme Court will reject measures before they are submitted to the people. However, in general, most courts prefer not to rule on initiatives before they have become law (Collins and Osterle, 1995; Arrow, 1992). Courts tend to view these types of actions as "advisory" and outside the role of the courts (Radcliffe, 1994). Despite resistance, the use of pre-election judicial review would prevent clearly unconstitutional initiatives from ever making the ballot and thus gaining salience with the public or wasting the resources of initiative activists. If measures are rejected before elites spend millions of dollars gathering signatures, waging a political campaign, and feeling the elation of election-day victory, the resentment may be far less than when they are rejected after elections.

The state of Colorado requires that every ballot measure be submitted to the Legislative Counsel where a group of trained lawyers examines it for constitutional and legal defects. However, Colorado is one of only a few states to do so. If all states required such a procedure, legal mistakes could be fixed prior to the commitment of significant resources by initiative elites. Again, if mistakes are caught before elites commit resources, their frustration from judicial review may be much less than when invalidation occurs later in the process.

Indirectly, one way to limit the number of invalidations is to limit the number of challenges. The reason initiatives are challenged so often is that the courts are the only minority veto in the process. In the legislative process, passionately interested groups have an opportunity to amend or block legislation before it becomes law. The initiative process offers no such opportunity. Therefore, angry initiative opponents often use the courts as a way of fighting initiative-implemented policy because they have no other vehicle. If direct democracy was altered to allow for minority vetoes, the process would produce less polarizing initiatives. Less polarizing initiatives would be challenged less often.

However, there is a fine line between "fixing" the initiative process and creating a parallel legislative process. Each time the initiative process is changed to make it more like the legislative process, direct democracy loses some of it *reson d'etat*. The reason direct democracy has no minority vetoes is because similar vetoes in the legislative process have historically been used to prevent publicly desired legislation from being enacted. In the legislative process, small but influential interest groups, have the power to pigeonhole legislation. The essential component of reforming direct democracy is to create a system that does not engender the animosity of initiative elites because of continual judicial review, but at the same time, preserves the essence of the institution.

---

[1] Oregon Measure 3 was invalidated by Lehman v. Bradbury, 37 P3d 989 (Or 2002).

[2] Washington Initiative I-695 was invalidated by *HAmalgamated Transit Union Local 587 v. State*H, 142 Wn.2d 183; 11 P.3d 762; (Wash 2000).

[3] California Proposition 187 was invalidated by LULAC, et al. v. Wilson, et al., 908 F.Supp. 755, 763-764 (Cal 1995).

[4] *See generally* ANTHONY DOWNS, AN ECONOMIC THEORY OF DEMOCRACY 207-238 (Harper Row, 1957) in which he explains that voters must acquire information about candidates and the collection of that information poses cost to the voter. He argues that if the costs of collecting information is greater than the benefits of having the information, the rational voter will choose to remain ignorant.

[5] Justice at Stake Campaign, *Eyes on Justice* (Oct. 24, 2002), *available at* H*http://faircourts.org/files/EyesonJusticeforOct24.pdf*H.

[6] Id.

[7] Id.

[8] Deborah Goldberg & Craig Holman, *The New Politics of Judicial Election*, 2002 BRENNEN CENTER ON JUSTICE 7-11.

[9] Republican Party of Minn. V. White 247 F.3d 854 *aff'd* 536 U.S. 765 (2002)

[10] State judges typically face retention or re-election only once every ten years.

[11] Vitiello and Glendon (1998) note that elected officials also become upset with courts when initiatives are invalidated, as they refer with "almost religious fervor about the court's frustration of the will of the people."

[12] Despite this, some initiative activists have attempted to repeal lifetime tenure for federal judges. See HRJ Res. 77, 105th Congress—A proposal to give federal judges a ten-year term with the possibility of reappointment upon re-approval of the Senate.

[13] All of the states from which data was collected have some form of democratic election for their judges.

[14] For example, Justice Lanphier (NE) was removed from office one year after invalidating Nebraska's popular term limit initiative.

---

[15] It is for this reason that Hall and Brace study retention elections with respect to abortion and the death penalty. Typically, voters have more information about how courts voted on these two highly salient issues than other issues.

[16] A classic example would be the voter's removal of Rose Bird, Joseph Grodin and Cruz Reynoso from the California Supreme Court in 1986.

[17] The term "opposition research" has been used by professional campaigners for years as a colloquial term for "digging up dirt on a candidate."

[18] DONALD WHITMAN, THE MYTH OF AMERICAN DEMOCRACY (University of Chicago Press, 1995), argues this type of behavior is expected because those who have the most to gain from disseminating the information will bear the costs of collecting the information. It is for this reason, he argues, that democracy is actually a very efficient form of government.

[19] See, Bill Merritt, *Measuring up to the Bar*, Willamette Week Online (April 29, 2002) *at http://www. orcities.org /currentissues/M7/m7ns166.pdf*

[20] See *Marshall v. Conney* 975 P 2d 325 (Mont. 1999)

[21] "Law Professor Challenges the Court," *The Spokesman-Review* (April 2, 2002). It is relevant that Natelson refers to this court. This court was also the subject of much controversy and three of its members were eventually recalled by the voters.

[22] Montana Human Rights Network. Helena, MT (April 24, 2000) Press Release.

[23] Cathy Sienger. "Has the high court gone too far?" *Queen City New Service* (Jan 22, 1999).

[24] At the time of writing, this election has not taken place (Nov 2002).

[25] Cathy Sienger. "Has the high court gone too far?" *Queen City New Service* (Jan 22, 1999).

[26] On the same Oregon ballot was a second measure altering the way judges are elected. Measure 22 would require that Supreme Court justices be elected from districts, rather than appointed, and re-elected in all state elections. The declared purpose of the measure is to ensure that judges are elected from all regions of the state. However, many supporters of the measure are initiative activists who have experienced judicial nullification (Dan Meeks—Measure 9 and Larry George—Measure 7).

[27] Oregon Secretary of State's Office, "Official 2002 General Election Voters' Pamphlet" pp.29.

[28] Oregon Secretary of State's Office, "Official 2002 General Election Voters' Pamphlet" pp.31.

[29] Oregon Secretary of State's Office, "Official 2002 General Election Voters' Pamphlet" pp.31.

[30] As of publication, there is no polling data to support this assumption.

[31] Oregon Secretary of State's Office, "Official 2002 General Election Voters' Pamphlet" pp.32.

[32] Principal-agency theory defines principals as those who are endowed with authority. Agents are delegated a principal's authority to carry out a task desired by the principal. However, as most theorists note, agents have the ability to use the authority of the principal to pursue their own preferences. Kiewiet and McCubbins argue that principals can limit the independence of agents but the methods are costly. Examining the problem of agency loss in Congress they suggest four ways to prevent agency loss: contract design, expending resources to ensure that agents hold a similar preference as the principal, monitoring, or institutional checks. However, none of these options are available to initiative elites. Initiative elites cannot bind justices to contracts, and have little influence on who sits on the court. Some have tried monitoring, by highlighting instances when courts act contrary to the dictates of an initiative, but this has no noticeable effect on the behavior of justices. The only institutional check available is to amend the constitution, which of course runs right back into the original agency loss [to the courts] dilemma.

[33] Republican Party of Minn. V. White 247 F.3d 854 *aff'd* 536 U.S. 765 (2002)

[34] An American Bar Association poll suggests 75% of citizens express concern about the impartiality of judges who raise money for political campaigns. See "Politics, Money Erode US Trust in Judiciary" *The New York Times*, August 12, 2002.

[35] The 2000 *Portrait of America* poll reported that respondents in all fifty states registered greater than 50% support for the initiative process. In most cases, support levels were greater than 60%.

[36] Waters, Dane (2003) notes that 48% of all state ballot measures are passed by the voters.

Chapter Eight

The Courts and the People: A Cyclical Relationship

Robert Dahl once described the American political system as a "polyarchy." The term polyarchy describes a political system in which there are multiple points of access. His description of the American political system still holds true today. Both individuals and groups interested in affecting public policy have a variety of entrance points when it comes to state governments. Legislatures, city councils, planning and zoning commissions, school boards, the courts, elections, and of course, the initiative and referendum process, all afford such an opportunity. E. E. Schattschneider, in his classic *The Semi-Sovereign People*, argued that political actors will shift their resources and attention to the political venues that afford them the greatest likelihood of success. Taken together, Dahl and Schattschneider suggest that when an interested individual or group is denied access to one institutional entry point, they will naturally shift their attention to an alternative access point. Their take on American politics is an apt description of how the initiative and referendum process has been used in the past four decades. Like all eras, in the past few decades a broad range of political actors, from neophyte to professional politician, have sought to challenge the status quo. But, having had the door to traditional political institutions shut in their face, they have eventually made their way to the initiative and referendum process. Having been denied access to legislatures, they have become refugees of direct democracy.

But the initiative process and the legislative process are not the same, and as such, we should not expect the political battles that ensue to be the same. As political actors became more adept at utilizing the initiative process, an entirely new host of political issues, controversies, power struggles, and legal wrangling arose. A good part of these conflicts have been played out in state and federal courts. Initiative elites have sought to implement creative policies, radical policies, and policies that threaten mainstream political actors and interest groups. In response, the courts, more than any other traditional institution of government, have been called upon to rein in the expanding use of direct democracy.

The focus of this book has been to analyze and interpret the decades-long intra-institutional battle that has taken place between the initiative process and the court system. As noted many times, initiatives suffer a significantly higher rate of judicial nullification than do legislative acts. There are multiple reasons for this phenomenon. To fully understand why initiatives are so often invalidated by the courts, the institutional and behavioral hurdles that exist both within the initiative process itself, and its relationship with other institutions, need to be understood. From an institutional perspective, the "rules of the game" and the intra-institutional relationship between the initiative process and other powerful actors such as the legislature, the courts, and the executive branch are important. Hostile courts, executives, and attorney generals can all present barriers to direct democracy activists.

Concurrently, the institutional structure of the initiative process attracts certain behavioral pathologies that contribute to the high levels of judicial invalidation. The fact that there are infinite access points to the initiative process promotes egoism and discourages compromise. The fact that the initiative process relies on coalition building predisposes it to the problems associated with the iron law of oligarchy, allowing zealots to dominate the agenda. Zealots in turn become frustrated and eventually adopt strategies that are self-destructive. They sometimes resign themselves to using the initiative process as a form of political protest, rather than as a way to implement legislation.

To further understand the relationship between the courts and direct democracy, it is helpful to step back and look at the broader picture to see how the relationship between initiative elites and the courts is a historical relationship, as well as a legal one. Although not specifically highlighted earlier, it is clear that this historical relationship between the courts and the initiative process is cyclical in nature.

Initiative Elites and Courts: A Historically Competitive Relationship

Originally, the courts treated the initiative process with a benign neglect, giving them the benefit of the doubt. Courts went out of their way to uphold initiatives, choosing to defer to the "will of the people" when it came to direct democracy. Lengthy initiatives that clearly covered multiple subjects (such as Proposition 13 in California) were upheld despite being constitutionally suspect. Simply put, the level of judicial scrutiny of initiatives was relatively low, or as Ken Miller says, the courts adopted an "accommodationist" approach to initiatives. In this environment, initiative elites pursued statutory initiatives because the signature requirements were lower and consequently, the costs were lower. However, a variety of events disrupted this equilibrium. First, success bred further success. As other disaffected or marginalized individuals and groups observed the success of Proposition 13 (and other initiatives), they were encouraged to utilize the initiative process in the same manner. This resulted in the initiative explosion that occurred in the 1980s and 1990s. Term limits were passed, new laws were enacted, taxes were cut, and spending was mandated. Legislators, governors, and judges, fearing that they were losing control of the political agenda, the ability to control fiscal resources, and in some case losing control of criminal procedure, began to react. Legislators understood statutory initiatives could be eliminated or amended by a simple majority vote in the legislature. Governors came to understand they could frustrate the enforcement of most initiatives. And the courts realized that a robust interpretation of the single subject rule gave them much more latitude when it came to invalidating initiative statutes. Responding to the flood of initiatives, the courts began to adopt, as Ken Miller notes, a "watchdog" approach to direct democracy. Essentially, the level of judicial scrutiny changed as initiative elites began to use the initiative process to do more and to do it more often.

Not to be outdone, initiative elites reacted accordingly. Abandoning their effort to draft statutory initiatives, these elites increasingly began to draft constitutional amendments. Despite the fact that constitutional amendments have higher signature requirements and, therefore, higher costs, to initiative elites it was worth it. Constitutional amendments were insulated from legislative meddling, and more importantly, were more immune from adverse court rulings. For a short time it appeared as if initiative elites had taken the upper hand in this intra-institutional conflict. The victory, however, was short-lived. Courts began to develop innovative new ways to strike down initiatives. In some cases they created entirely new judicial doctrines, such as the separate vote requirement. In other cases, they simply ignored their own state constitutions. With the courts taking a more activist approach to direct democracy, the pendulum swung once again. The courts have put initiative elites in a legal catch-22. If they draft statutory initiatives, the legislature can overturn their legislation. If they pass constitutional amendments, the courts can swing the "separate vote" hammer.

The Oregon Supreme Court decision, *Armatta v. Kitzhaber* (1998) and California Supreme Court decision, *Senate v Jones* (1998), serve as watershed events in the relationship between the courts and initiative elites. Prior to *Jones*, it was rare for courts to use the single subject rule to invalidate state ballot measures. However, the *Jones* case was part warning shot and part announcement from the California Court. The decision announced that the long dormant single subject rule would be revived with the implicit warning that it would be used at the Court's discretion.

The Oregon Court's *Armatta* decision, however, announced the Court's open hostility towards direct democracy. The *Armatta* decision created a much more restrictive standard than the single subject rule by requiring that separate initiatives must be submitted if more than one clause of the constitution was altered—even if all the altered clauses dealt with the same subject. The majority opinion in *Armatta* noted the "separate-vote" requirement imposed a "narrower requirement" than the single-subject rule.

The *Armatta* decision was the Oregon Court's way of signaling to initiative drafters that the "accomodationist" period of direct democracy judicial review was over. In its place was the new "watch dog" approach. The *Armatta* decision looms even larger because other states adopted its standard of review. Within a few years, the Washington, California, and Montana State Supreme Courts had referenced or adopted *Armatta* as binding precedent.

The relevance of *Armatta* was not lost upon initiative drafters. The Court had clearly signaled that initiatives would be treated in a more hostile judicial manner. However, for initiative elites, the impact of *Armatta* went beyond a simple, one-time adverse legal decision. Initiative drafters viewed *Armatta* as abrupt, without precedent, and political in nature. Many initiative activists viewed the arbitrary nature of the *Armatta* decision as the Court's way of announcing that political considerations, especially normative considerations, would play a significant role in deciding whether an initiative would be upheld or invalidated. In the eyes of initiative activists, once the courts had declared themselves "political actors" rather than impartial "judicial actors," a political response became appropriate. It is only after *Armatta* and subsequent decisions based on *Armatta*, that we see initiative elites actively pursuing an "anti-court" agenda. In many ways, the "first shot" in the war between initiative activists and the courts was fired in *Armatta*. Since then, the escalation in tensions between courts and direct democracy has continued to increase.

The historical narrative, taken in the context of the Positive Theory of Institutions, offers some insight into why rates of judicial nullification have remained constant over a 30-year period. Chapter 4 introduced PTI theory, arguing that institutions react to one another bringing about an eventual equilibrium. Institutions send information cues about what is or is not acceptable, and in response, other institutions alter their behavior accordingly. However, the fact that rates of judicial invalidation of initiatives have been constant for 30 years, even though the aggregate number of nullifications has been on the increase, suggests that PTI fails to describe the institutional interaction of courts and direct democracy. This may not be so. Instead, it is likely that the competition between courts and initiative drafters has created a situation in which the equilibrium has indeed occurred, but the equilibrium occurs at very high rates of invalidation. As the courts and the initiative process mirror each other with reaction and counter-reaction, a relatively stable rate of invalidation has developed. It seems clear that initiative elites have engaged in professionalization, adaptation, and strategic improvements, while at the same time courts have taken an increasingly activist role in scrutinizing initiatives. The end result is that initiative elites have become more adept and savvy in drafting legislation, but these improvements have not resulted in an aggregate increase in their survival rates. This is because the environment in which these initiatives are being drafted has become more restrictive. As initiative drafters become better at doing what they do, courts become less willing to accommodate them. Analogously speaking, the relationship between initiative drafters and the courts is akin to an athlete who has spent years improving her skills, while at the same time the competition has become more difficult. She may be better at what she does, but that improvement is not reflected on the playing field because everyone else has become better too.

Furthermore, the research shows that we cannot assume that passing judicially sustainable initiatives is always the primary goal of initiative elites. Chapter 6 clearly highlights the fact that some experienced initiative actors expend their energies on other aspects of the initiative process. Some initiative drafters use their skills to send political messages, deplete the resources of other political groups, or simply to influence the state legislature. To continue the athletic analogy, just because one is not scoring more points does not necessarily mean they are not winning more games.

Seeing the relationship between initiative drafters and the courts as a historical process is enlightening. However, the relationship is also a competitive process. The initiative process is one of many institutions that interact with others in order to create policy. From one perspective, this is an accurate portrayal. Governors, legislatures, and courts all have the ability to affect the eventual implementation of direct democracy legislation. However, from an alternative perspective, the initiative process exists outside the traditional three branches of government that traditionally make up the American political system. The fact that the initiative process lies outside the traditional triumvirate is important.

None of the other three branches of government—the courts, the executive branch, and the legislature—need the initiative process to carry out their functions. This cannot be said in the traditional checks and balances system. The Positive Theory of Institutions, in its "balance of power" manifestation, suggests that political institutions respond to the cues of other institutions because it is necessary that they do so. Congress or legislatures must pay attention to the cues of the courts; otherwise their legislation will not be upheld. The courts must pay attention to the executive and legislative branches, or their jurisdictions can be eliminated, the courts can be packed, or in some cases, they can be removed from office. The same is true for the executive branch. Governors and presidents who ignore the cues of the legislature or the courts do so at their own peril. But can this be said about the initiative process? It's true that initiative elites must pay close attention to the information cues of the other three branches, but is there a need for reciprocity? The initiative process has no built-in, immediate veto over any action that the legislature, the executive, or the judicial branch carries out. As a result, the primary institutions have no need to develop relationships or compromises with initiative elites. Executives compromise with legislatures because it's necessary to enact legislation. But do executives need to compromise with an initiative elite—singularly or collectively? No. The same is true for all the traditional branches of government. The initiative process, lacking the ability to veto the actions of institutional actors, finds itself alone in a multi-institutional environment.

Of course, individual initiative elites can attempt to interfere with the process of government. Referenda can be held to overturn legislative acts. However, the process is extremely rare. Elites can try to politicize the courts. However, despite a few victories, this too has been a rare occurrence. And elites can pass legislation that seizes the agenda-setting power from governors. But these types of actions are markedly different than institutionally embedded powers, such as vetoes and judicial review, which are readily available to governors and courts. It is more likely that a legislature will amend its bill upon a veto threat, than it will upon the threat of a referendum from an initiative activist. In the case of the veto threat, other than the possibility the governor is bluffing, there can be no doubt that she has the power to carry out the threat. However, the threat of an initiative drafter to carry out a referendum is weak at best. There is a strong possibility he will not get the signatures or money he needs. And if he does, there is no guarantee the measure will pass. In essence, the threat is less credible.

Simply put, the environment described above is not one in which there will be an "evolution of cooperation." In order for cooperation to develop, all actors need the ability to "punish" the others. In a situation where only one actor has the ability to punish, we expect only one actor (the one without the ability to punish) to "learn." In some respects, this is what is happening with the initiative process. The courts can punish initiative elites. Governors, through their attorneys general, can punish initiative elites. And legislatures can punish initiative elites. Of course, they can also all punish each other. Being able to punish each other, the courts, legislatures, and governors have learned to "cooperate." However, being *relatively* free from punishment from initiative elites, little cooperation has developed. The lack of cooperation is manifested in high rate of initiative invalidation.

And finally, the initiative process must be seen as an internally adaptive process. As the "stepchild" institution, it is often punished by the more established institutions. Initiative elites must learn, and in turn adapt, to new environments and demands. However, adaptation is not always a positive event. Again, speaking analogously, it is just as likely that an inner city youth will adapt to his unfortunate surroundings by joining a violent gang, as it is for him to seek more education. The tale of initiative elites reacting to the courts tells two different stories. On one level we have seen some elites sincerely try to improve their initiative-writing capabilities—what might be called "defensive adaptation." They have hired lawyers to ensure the legality of the initiative. They have scaled back initiatives to ensure legality. Some have tried to mimic the internal peer review process of the legislature.

Concurrently, some initiative elites seek adaptation by attacking other institutions—what might be called "offensive adaptation." Chapter 7 highlights a variety of ways in which disgruntled initiative drafters sought to attack the independence of the courts. Chapter 6 highlights the many ways that the initiative process has degenerated into a process of depleting the resources of other interest groups, or passing divisive symbolic measures.

To truly understand the impact of the relationship between the courts and the initiative process, one must understand how initiative drafters will react to encroachments by other institutions. If elites adopt "defensive adaptation" as a way of avoiding nullification, we should expect to see a relationship develop that is similar to the relationship between the traditional branches of government— fewer nullifications and lower intensity in the conflicts between institutions. However, if elites elect to adopt "offensive adaptation" methods, we should expect to see a continuing increase in the intensity of the competition between initiative drafters and other institutions, especially the courts.

APPENDIX A

LEGAL REQUIREMENTS FOR INITIATIVES BY STATE

Signature, Geographic Distribution and Single-Subject Requirements for Initiative Amendments and Initiative Statutes[1]

State	SS Rule	Net Signature Requirement for Constitutional Amendments	Net Signature Requirement for Statutes	Geographic Distribution	Deadline for Signature Submission	Circulation Period
AK	Y	Not allowed by state constitution	10% of votes cast in last general election	At least 1 signature in 2/3 of Election Districts.	Prior to the convening of the legislature	1 year
AZ	Y	15% of votes cast for Governor	10% of votes cast for Governor	No geographical distribution	Four months prior to election	20 months
AR	N	10% of votes cast for Governor	8% of votes cast for Governor	5% in 15 of 75 counties	Four months prior to election	Unlimited
CA	Y	8% of votes cast for Governor	5% of votes cast for Governor	No geographical distribution	To be determined by state each year	150 days
CO	Y	5% of votes cast for SOS	5% of votes cast for SOS	No geographical distribution	Three months prior to election	6 months
FL	Y	8% of ballots cast in the last Presidential Election	Not allowed by state constitution	8% in 12 of 23 Congressional Districts	90 days prior to election	4 years
ID	N	Not allowed by state constitution	6% of registered voters	6% in each of the 22 counties	Four months prior to election	18 months
ME	N	Not allowed by state constitution	10% of votes cast for Governor	No geographical distribution	To be determined by state each year	1 year
MA	N	3% of votes cast for Governor	3½% of votes cast for Governor	No more than 25% from a single county	To be determined each year by state	64 days
MI	N	10% of votes cast for Governor	8% of votes cast for Governor	No geographical distribution	Constitutional amendment Statute	180 days
MS	N	12% of votes cast for Governor	Not allowed by state constitution	20% from each Congressional District	90 days prior to the convening of the legislature	1 year
MO	Y	8% of votes cast for Governor	5% of votes cast for Governor	5% in 6 of 9 Congressional Districts	Eight months prior to election	18 months
MT	Y	10% of votes cast for Governor	5% of votes cast for Governor	Statute: 5% in 34 of 50 Legislative Districts Amendment: 10% in 40 of 50 Legislative Districts	Second Friday of the fourth month prior to election	1 year
NE	Y	10% of registered	7% of registered	5% in 38 of 93	Four months	1 year

State	SS Rule	Net Signature Requirement for Constitutional Amendments	Net Signature Requirement for Statutes	Geographic Distribution	Deadline for Signature Submission	Circulation Period
		voters	voters	counties	prior to election	
NV	N	10% of registered voters	10% of votes cast in last general election	10% in 13 of 17 counties	Constitutional amendment Statute	11 months
ND	N	4% of population	2% of population	No geographical distribution	90 days prior to election	1 year
OH	Y	10% of votes cast for Governor	6% of votes cast for Governor	Statute: 1½% in 44 of 88 counties Amendment: 5% in 44 of 88 counties	Constitutional amendment Statute	Unlimited
OK	Y	15% of votes cast for Governor	8% of votes cast for Governor	No geographical distribution	Eight months prior to election	90 days
OR	Y	8% of votes cast for Governor	6% of votes cast for Governor	No geographical distribution	Four months prior to election	Unlimited
SD	N	10% of votes cast for Governor	5% of votes cast for Governor	No geographical distribution	Constitutional amendment Statute	1 year
UT	N	Not allowed by state constitution	Direct statute: 10% of votes cast for Governor In-direct statute: 10% of votes cast for Governor	10% in 20 of 29 counties	Direct statute In-direct statute†	Direct: Unlimited In-direct: Unlimited
WA	Y	Not allowed by state constitution	8% of votes cast for Governor	No geographical distribution	Direct: statute In-direct statute	Direct: 6 months In-direct: 10 months
WY	N	Not allowed by state constitution	15% of votes cast in last general election	15% of total votes cast in the last election from at least 2/3 of the counties	One day prior to the convening of the legislature	18 months

Ability of Legislatures to Amend Initiatives

State	Legislative Power
Alaska	Can repeal only after two years; can amend anytime. (Alaska Const. XI, §6)
Arizona	Can not repeal; but, can amend an initiative law if the amending legislation furthers the purposes of such measure and at least three-fourths of both houses, by a roll call vote, vote to amend the measure. (Const. Art. 4, pt. 1, §1 (6) Also, see Adams v. Bolin, 74 Ariz. 269, 247 P.2d 617 (1952.))
Arkansas	Can repeal or amend by a 2/3 vote of each house. (Const. Amend. No. 7)
California	Can not repeal or amend unless permitted by the initiative (Const. art. 2, §10(c))
Colorado	Can repeal and amend. (Zimmerman v. Herder, 122 Colo. 456, 233 P.2d 197 (1950))
Florida	Florida's initiative process only allows constitutional amendments.
Idaho	Can repeal (by court ruling, see Luker v. Curis, 64 Idaho 703, 136 P. 2d 978 (1943)) and amend (by common practice.)
Maine	Can both repeal and amend. (By common practice.)
Massachusetts	Can repeal and amend. (Mass. Const. amend. Art. 48, Gen. Prov. Pt. 6)
Michigan	Can repeal and amend by a ¾ vote of each house or as otherwise provided by the initiative (Mich. Const. art. 2, §9)
Mississippi	Mississippi's initiative process only allows constitutional amendments..
Missouri	Can both repeal and amend. (Halliburon v. Roach, 230 Mo. 408, 130 S.W. 689 (1910))
Montana	Can both repeal and amend. (By common practice.)
Nebraska	Can both repeal and amend. (By common practice.)
Nevada	Can only repeal or amend after three years of enactment. (Nevada Const. art. 19, §2)
North Dakota	Can repeal or amend by a 2/3 vote of each house for seven year after passage, majority vote thereafter. (N.Dak. Const. art. III, §8)
Ohio	Can both repeal and amend. (Singer v. Canledge, 129 Ohio St. 279, 195 N.E. 237 (1935))
Oklahoma	Can both repeal and amend. (Expane Haley, 202 Okla. 101, 210 P.2d 653 (1949))
Oregon	Can both repeal and amend. (Pierce v. Shisher, 119 Or. 141, 249 P. 358 (1926))
South Dakota	Can both repeal and amend. (Richards v. Whisman, 36 S.D. 260, 154 N.W. 707 (1915))
Utah	Can amend only at subsequent sessions. (Utah code Ann. §20-11-6).
Washington	Can repeal or amend by a 2/3 vote of each house during the first two years of enactment, majority vote thereafter. (Wash. Const. art. 11, §41)
Wyoming	Can not repeal for at least two years after enactment, but may amend at any time. (Wy. Const. Art. 3, §52(f))

Subject Matter Restrictions

State	Legislative Power
Alaska	Single subject only. No revenue measures, appropriations, acts affecting the judiciary, or any local or special legislation. Also, no laws affecting peace, health, or safety.
Arizona	Single subject only; legislative matters only.
Arkansas	Limited to legislative measures.
California	Single subject only.
Colorado	Single subject only.
Florida	Single subject only.
Idaho	No restrictions.
Maine	Legislative matters only. Must also only deal with structural and procedural subjects.
Massachusetts	Any expenditure in excess of appropriations is void 45 days after legislature convenes.
Michigan	No measures involving religion, the judiciary, local or special legislation, or specific appropriations.
Mississippi	Applicable to statutes which Legislature may enact.
Missouri	No modifications of bill of rights and no modifications of public employees' retirement system or labor-related items. Initiatives rejected by the voters cannot be placed on the ballot for two years after the election.
Montana	Single subject only; no appropriations without new revenue, and nothing that is prohibited by the constitution.
Nebraska	Single subject only; no appropriations, and no special or local legislation.
Nevada	Single subject only. Limited to matters which can be enacted by the legislature. The same subject can not appear on the ballot more than once in three years.
North Dakota	No appropriations or expenditures of money, unless the measure includes a sufficient tax not prohibited by Nevada's constitution.
Ohio	No emergency measures, or appropriations for support and maintenance of state departments and institutions.
Oklahoma	Single subject only. No measures involving property taxes. Legislative matters only.
Oregon	Single subject only. The same subject can not appear on the ballot more than once every three years. Legislative matters only.
South Dakota	Single subject only. Legislative matters only.
Utah	Except laws as necessary for the immediate preservation of public peace, health or safety support of state government and existing public institutions.
Washington	Legislative matters only.
Wyoming	Single subject only; limited to legislative matters.

1. All material in Appendix A was compiled by the Initiative and Referendum Institute at www.iandrinstitute.org. Accessed February, 24, 2003.

APPENDIX B

LEGAL CASES 1990 – 1998

Measure #	Date	State	Upheld or Over-turned	Moved the Target	No Future Guidance	No Prior Guidance	Well Established Precedent
115 Restricts CA from granting a criminal defendant more rights than the Fed. Govt.	1990	CA	Over turned	Shifted issue to concept of constitutional revision vs. constitutional amendment, a standard with almost no precedents and gives the court complete discretion. Even then court could not rely on the quantitative standard and had to rely on what they termed a "qualitative standard."[9]			
140 (state) Term Limits	1990	CA	Over turned	State court overturned state term limits on the grounds the ballot title did not give voters enough information, specifically, the title did not indicate term limits were lifetime limits. Fed court overturned this aspect of decision.			Based on a long line of Contract Clause cases, court prevented initiative from altering the retirement benefits of legislators
140 (fed) Term Limits	1990	CA	Upheld				Court notes *Thornton* did not declare term limits unconstitutional, only said states can't impose them on federal offices.
132 Restricts the use of gill nets	1990	CA	Upheld			First case to determine if there was a constitutional right to fish	
164 Term	1992	CA	Over turned			*Thornton v. US Term Limits*: Stevens relied	

---

[9] What makes this case more of a "moving target" case is the fact that Proposition 13, an incredibly long and complex measure which restructured the California tax system was upheld as an amendment and not a revision to the state constitution. See *Amador Valley Joint Union H.S. v. State Brd of Equalization*. 22 Cal.3d 208 (1978). After this case it was assumed by many initiative drafters they would have to do something quite radical to have their initiative invalidated as a revision. Therefore, it came as a surprise to the drafters of Proposition 115 that their requirement that the California Supreme Court follow the US Supreme Court precedent on criminal rights law was nullified as a revision to the constitution.

Limits							on an originalist approach to
184 "Three Strikes" law.	1994	CA	Upheld				Court rejects plaintiffs argument three-strikes law violates separation of powers. Court notes legislatures have always set criminal penalties.
187 Limits social services for illegal immigrant	1994	CA	Over turned				Court cites clear precedent of *Plyer v. Doe* to overturn initiative that prevented immigrant children from receiving education and health benefits.
208 Limits campaign contribu-tions	1996	CA	Over turned		Court only indicates that contributi on limits are too low.	No prior case established what limits were too low. Only *Buckley* establishes $1,000 is not too low.	
209 Bans aff. action in CA colleges	1996	CA	Upheld				Court relies on large body of civil right law to uphold non-discrimination statute.
213 Tort reform. Limits lawsuits by drunk or uninsured motorists	1996	CA	Upheld				The initiative was challenged on the very technical issue of "secondary retroactivity." But the courts upheld citing a long line of precedent.[10]
215 Medical use of marijuana	1996	CA	Upheld			First bill of its kind. No case law on medical marijuana	

---

[10] This case is somewhat of an "outlier" as it does not easily fit into any of the four categories I have developed. The basis of the challenge came due to the fact civil courts were backlogged. The initiative banned uninsured motorists from seeking non-economic damages in civil court, but only applied the law to people who were not already in the midst of litigation (to avoid *ex post facto* problems). However, some people had already been involved in accidents, but were waiting to get into court. The backlog meant they were subject to the new law even though their accident occurred before the passage of the initiative.

218 voters must approve new taxes	1996	CA	Upheld				Court relies on large body of law upholding legislature's right to cut taxes.
5 [11] Authorize Indian casinos	1998	CA	Over turned			In reference to "of the type operating in NV or NJ" the court notes "Section 19(e) contains no definition of this phrase."	The California Constitution states, "The Legislature has no power to authorize casinos of the type operating in Nevada and New Jersey"
24 Requires judges to draw all Congressional district lines	1998	CA	Over turned	After rejecting every Single Subject rule challenge but one for the previous 50 years, court changes course and re-adopts single subject standard.		Court states initiative clauses must be "reasonably germane" but sets no criteria for such a standard. [12]	
225 "scarlet letter" term limits bill	1998	CA	Over turned		No state case law on the issue. Relied on cases from other states. Found one federal case from 1920 dealing with a tangential issue.	Ruling states "scarlet letter" language is "impermissibly coercive". However, no guidelines as to what language would be acceptable.	
227 Bans bilingual education in the public schools	1998	CA	Upheld				*Lau v. Nichols* provided clear signals to the initiative drafters what they needed to do in order to ensure constitutionality of bilingual education measure.
5 Tax limitation	1990	OR	Upheld				Court relies on large body of law uphold legislature's

---

[11] This case too, does not fit easily into the developed classification scheme. On one level, the California Constitution is clear about banning casinos, but on another level, it is unclear as to how the law defines a casino. Proponents of Proposition 5 tried to argue that the games that are authorized are different that Nevada and New Jersey casino games. The court disagreed.

[12] The court declares initiatives must "disclose a reasonable and common sense relationship among their various components in furtherance of a common purpose." *Senate v Jones* 21, CAL 4th 1142 (1999).

							right to cut taxes.
3 Term Limits	1992	OR	Over turned	*Armatta* decision created a completely new standard of review based on completely new legal concept. Had to base decision on Indiana's Constitutional debates in 1851.			
6 Bans out of state campaign contribu-tions.	1994	OR	Over turned		Initiative arose because drafter was looking for novel way to limit campaign donations. Court had never ruled on the issue of out-of-district donations. In ruling, court simply notes, "measure does not survive scrutiny under First Amendme nt."	Court admits previous rulings "did not define actual public support." And "the court did not concern itself with a distinction between in-district and out-of district [funding]."	
8 Alters the way in which PERS is financed	1994	OR	Over turned	Novel interpretation of the contract clause. Overturns *Hughes v State of Oregon* (1992) "Opinion only does so by ignoring the cardinal principle that this court long ago created to assure that legislative enactments would be deemed contracts only in those circumstances in which the legislature intended."			
9 Limits campaign contribu-Tions	1994	OR	Over turned	Court first notes that Oregon is not bound by the case of *Buckley v Valeo*, the most well recognized campaign finance ruling. Court then concludes no contribution limits are acceptable under the Oregon Constitution.			
11 Mandatory criminal	1994	OR	Upheld				Court notes Oregon Constitution has always left sentencing

sentences								discretion to legislature (except cruel and unusual punishment).
16 Dr.-assisted suicide	1994	OR	Upheld				First bill of its kind in US. No case law on doctor assisted suicide.	
40 Alters criminal justice system	1996	OR	Over turned	*Armatta* decision created a completely new standard of review based on completely new legal concept. Had to base decision on Indiana's Constitutional debates in 1851.				
44 Increases cigarette tax	1996	OR	Upheld					Court upholds legislature's right to tax.
58 Open adoption law. Allows access to birth certificat es	1998	OR	Upheld					State has clear contract clause case history to deny that adoption records are a binding contract between birth mother and state
60 Requires mail in voting system	1998	OR	Upheld				First case to deal with mail in elections. Court adopts an originalist approach researching the intent of 1844 legislators that required voting on a single day. No direct precedent to follow, only cases about absentee voting.	
62 Limits campaign contribu-tions and requires disclosure	1998	OR	Overt urned	*Armatta* decision created a completely new standard of review based on completely new legal concept. Had to base decision on Indiana's Constitutional debates in 1851.				

134 Requires unions get permission from members before using dues for political purposes	1992	WA	Partially overturned				Initiative held to violate Federal Contracts Clause. Large body of case law to follow.
573 Term Limits	1992	WA	Over turned			Term limits case had to rely on Federalist Papers, and one tangential case *Powell v McCormack*	
593 Increases mandatory sentence for some crimes	1993	WA	Upheld				Court upholds legislature's long held rights to enact criminal punishment statutes.
695 Requires public approval of all taxes	1999	WA	Over turned	Like the *Armatta* decision, created a completely new standard of review. First WA initiative nullified due to Single Subject restrictions.			
722 Requires public approval of all taxes	1999	WA	Over turned	Like the *Armatta* decision, created a completely new standard of review. Second WA initiative nullified on Single Subject restriction. Bill was drafted before I-695 ruling was announced.			
5 Term limits	1990	CO	Over turned			*Thornton v. US Term Limits*: Stevens relied on an originalist approach to the case.	
2 Prohibits laws protecting gays	1992	CO	Over turned			In order overturn measure banning specific protections for gays, court relied on reapportionment cases.	

17 Term limits	1994	CO	Over turned			*Thornton v. US Term Limits*: Stevens relied on an originalist approach to the case.	
12 "Scarlet letter" term limit bill	1996	CO	Over turned		Nullified "scarlet letter" bill because language was "pejorative." Subsequent drafters unsure how to interpret for future attempts to regulate incumbency.	Only existing term limit law is *Thornton*. Case only states that States cannot impose term limits.	
15 "Scarlet letter" campaign finance limitation. Must report on literature that group did not accept voluntary limits.	1996	CO	Over turned		Part of the initiative required individuals who made "independent expenditures" of over $1,0000 to publicly disclose the action within 24hrs. Court said 24hs was short. However, court noted, "We cannot substitute our judgment as to an appropriate time frame."	Because this is the first bill to impose a time limit, no previous case law determines what time limit is acceptable.	Court also rejected initiatives attempt to ban "anonymous speech" and the court had ample precedent to follow on this issue.
16 Changes the way the State's Land Trust is run.	1996	CO	Upheld			First case to deal with 1875 law which allowed Colorado to enter the Union	
12 Parental notifica-tion prior to a minor's abortion.	1998	CO	Over turned				Court followed precedent of *Roe v Wade* and *Casey v. Planned Parenthood* to strike overly restrictive abortion measure.
18 Voluntary term limits	1998	CO	Upheld				

BIBLIOGRAPHY

Confidential Interview # 1. Personal Interview. 8 Jan. 2002.

Confidential Interview # 4. Personal Interview. 19 Jan. 2002.

Confidential Interview # 9. Personal Interview. 22 Jan. 2001.

Confidential Interview # 10. Personal Interview. 8 Feb. 2002.

Confidential Interview # 11. Personal Interview. 4 March. 2002.

Confidential Interview # 12. Personal Interview. 27 Oct. 2001.

Confidential Interview # 14. Personal Interview. 8 Jan. 2002.

Confidential Interview # 16. Personal Interview. 9 Jan. 2002.

Confidential Interview # 17. Personal Interview. 12 Dec. 2001.

Confidential Interview # 18. Personal Interview. 20 Nov. 2001.

Confidential Interview # 19. Personal Interview. 23 Nov. 2001

Confidential Interview # 20. Personal Interview. 10 Nov. 2001.

Confidential Interview # 21. Personal Interview. 5 Feb. 2002

Confidential Interview # 22. Personal Interview. 6 Feb. 2002.

Confidential Interview # 23. Personal Interview. 20 Feb. 2002.

Confidential Interview # 25. Personal Interview. 12 Jan. 2002.

Confidential Interview # 30. Personal Interview. 10 Jan. 2002.

Confidential Interview # 31. Personal Interview. 10 Jan. 2002.

Confidential Interview # 40. Personal Interview. 15 Nov. 2001.

Confidential Interview # 41. Personal Interview. 4 Jan. 2002.

Confidential Interview # 42. Personal Interview. 12 Jan. 2002.

Confidential Interview # 43. Personal Interview. 22 Feb. 2002.

Confidential Interview # 44. Personal Interview. 15 Feb. 2002.

Confidential Interview # 48. Personal Interview. 1 Feb. 2002.

Confidential Interview # 51. Personal Interview. 24 Jan. 2002.

Confidential Interview # 52. Personal Interview. 25 Jan. 2002.

Confidential Interview # 53. Personal Interview. 9 Apr. 2002.

Confidential Interview # 54. Personal Interview. 18 Feb. 2002.

Confidential Interview # 60. Personal Interview. 11 Jan. 2002.

Confidential Interview # 61. Personal Interview. 20 Feb. 2002.

Confidential Interview # 70. Personal Interview. 7 Mar. 2002.

Confidential Interview # 80. Personal Interview. 22 Jan. 2002.

Confidential Interview # 81. Personal Interview. 22 Mar. 2002

Confidential Interview # 82. Personal Interview. 25 Oct. 2001.

Confidential Interview # 83. Personal Interview. 29 Jan. 2002.

Confidential Interview # 84. Personal Interview. 3 Apr. 2002.

Confidential Interview # 85. Personal Interview. 11 Apr. 2002.

Confidential Interview # 87. Personal Interview. 11 Feb. 2002.

Confidential Interview # 88. Personal Interview. 8 Dec. 2001.

Confidential Interview # 91. Personal Interview. 17 Apr. 2002.

Confidential Interview # 92. Personal Interview. 3 Apr. 2002.

Confidential Interview # 93. Personal Interview. 17 Apr. 2002.

Confidential Interview # 97. Personal Interview. 11 Apr. 2002.

Confidential Interview # 98. Personal Interview. 18 May. 2002.

Confidential Interview # 101. Personal Interview. 23 July. 2002.

Arrow, D. (1992). "Representative Government and Popular Distrust: The Obstruction/Facilitation Conundrum Regarding Amendment by Initiative." *Oklahoma City Law Review* 17(1): 3-88.

Axelrod, R. (1980). *The Evolution of Cooperation*. New York, Basic Books.

Barber, J. (1972). *The Presidential Character*. New Jersey: Prentice Hall.

Baker, G. (1978). *Judicial Review of Statewide Initiatives in California*. American Political Science Association, New York.

Barkan, S. (1979). "Strategic, Tactical and Organizational Dilemmas of the Protest Movement Against Nuclear Power" *Social Problems* (vol. 27) no. 1. pp. 19-35.

Baum, L. (1987). "Explaining the Vote in Judicial Elections: The 1984 Ohio Supreme Court Elections" 40 *Western Political Quarterly* 361-371.

Bonneau, C and M. Hall. (2003). "Predicting Challengers in State Supreme Court Elections: Context and the Politics of Institutional Design," 56 *Political Research Quarterly* 337-349.

Bell, D. (1976). *The Cultural Contradictions of Capitalism*. New York, Basic Books.

Bell, D. (1978). "The Referendum: Democracy's Barrier to Racial Equality." *Washington Law Review* 54(1).

Bowler, S., T. Donovan, et al. (1998). *Citizens as Legislators*. Columbus, Ohio State University Press.

Bowler, S. and T. Donovan (2000). *Demanding Choices: Opinion, Voting, and Direct Democracy*. Ann Arbor, University of Michigan Press.

Brace, P. and M. Hall. (1995). "Studying Courts Comparatively: The View from the American States" 48 *Political Research Quarterly* 5-29.

Brace, P. and L. Langer (2002). The Preemptive Power of Sate Supreme Courts: Enactment of Abortion and Death Penalty Laws in the American States. Working Paper, Rice University.

Brigham, J. (1999). The Constitution of the Supreme Court. *The Supreme Court in American Politics*. Gillman and Clayton. Lawrence, University Press of Kansas.

Broader, D. (2000). *Democracy Derailed: Initiative Campaigns and the Power of Money*. New York, Harcourt.

California Committee on Campaign Financing. (1992). Democracy by Initiative. San Francisco, Center for Responsive Government.

Calvert, R. (1987). *Coordination and Power: The Foundation of Leadership among Rational Legislators*. American Political Science Association, Chicago, Ill.

Campbell, A. (2000). *Unintended Consequences of the Single Subject Rule for Ballot Initiatives: The Judiciary's Influence Over a Legislative Power*. Western Political Science Association, San Jose, California.

Castells, M. (1997). *The Power of Identity*. Massachusetts: Blackwell Publishers.

Charlow, R. (1994). "Judicial Review, Equal Protection and the Problem with Plebiscites." *Cornell Law Review* 79: 527-570.

Chemerinsky, E. (1994). "Cases under the Guarantee Clause Should Be Justicable." *University of Colorado Law Review* **65**(1): 849-944.

Clayton, C. and H. Gillman (1999). *Supreme Court Decision-Making: New Institutionalist Approaches.* Chicago, University of Chicago Press.

Collins, R. and D. Osterle (1995). "Governing by Initiative: Procedures That Do and Don't Work." *University of Colorado Law Review* 66(2): 47-93.

Cronin, T. (1988). *Direct Democracy.* Cambridge, Massachusetts, Harvard University Press.

Dahl, R. (1956). *A Preface To Democratic Theory.* Chicago, University of Chicago Press.

Davidson, R. and W. Oleszek (1977). *Congress Against Itself.* Toronto, Indiana University Press.

Donovan, T and S Bowler. (1998). "Direct Democracy and Minority Rights: An Extension." *American Journal of Political Science* 42, No. 3. pp. 1020-1024.

Dority, B. (1994). "Majority Knows Best." *The Humanist* 54(5): 34-37.

Downey, Gary. (1985). "Ideology and the Clamshell Identity: Organizational Dilemmas in the Anti-Nuclear Power Movement" *Social Problems* (vol. 33) no. 5. pp.357-372.

Dubois, P. (1986). "Penny for Your Thoughts? Campaign Spending in California Trial Court Elections, 1976-1982" 39 *Western Political Quarterly* 265-284.

Ducat, C. (2000). *Constitutional Interpretation: Powers of Government Vol 1.* Stamford, Thomas Learning Center.

DuVivier, K. K. (1999). Ballot Box Battles with the Counter Initiative, Initiative and Referendum Institute. 2001.

Ellis, R. (1999). *The Myth of the Golden Age of the Initiative and Referendum.* Pacific Northwest Political Science Association Annual Conference, Eugene, Oregon.

Ellis, R. (2002). *Democratic Delusions: The Initiative Process in America.* Lawrence, University of Kansas Press.

Emmert, C. (1988). "Judicial Review in State Supreme Courts: Opportunity and Activism." Midwest Political Science Association Meeting in Chicago.

Epp, C. (1998). *The Rights Revolution.* Chicago, University of Chicago Press.

Epstein, L, and J. Knight. (1998). *The Choices Justices Make.* Washington: CQ Press.

Eule, J. (1990). "Judicial Review of Direct Democracy." *Yale Law Journal* **99**(1): 1503-1571.

Eule, J. (1994). "Crocodiles in the Bathtub: State Courts, Voter Initiatives and the Threat of Electoral Reprisal." *University of Colorado Law Review* 65: 733-741.

Evera, S. (1990). *Guide to Methodology for Students of Political Science.* Cambridge, Massachusetts Institute of Technology.

Faigman, C. (1996). ""And to the Republic for Which It Stands": Guaranteeing a Republican Form of Government." *Hastings Constitutional Law Quarterly* 23(1): 1057-1071.

Farah, M. and A. Karls (1999). *World History: The Human Experience.* New York, McGraw-Hill.

Farge, D. (1995). Microcosm of the Movement: Term Limits in the US, USA Term Limits. 2002.

Feeney, P. (1998). *Lawmaking by Initiative: Issues, Options and Comparisons.* New York, Agathon Press.

Fenno, R. (1978). *Home Style: House Members in their Districts.* Boston, Brown, Little and Company.

Fiorina, M. (1977). *Congress: Keystone of the Washington Establishment.* New Haven, Yale University Press.

Ferejohn, J. and C. Shipman. (1990). "Congressional influence on Bureaucracy." *Journal of Law Economics and Organization* 6: 1-20.

Frey, J. (1989). *Survey Research By Telephone*. Newbery Park, Ill, Sage Publications.

Frickey, P. (1997). "Interpretation on the Borderline: Constitution, Cannon, Direct Democracy." *New York University Journal of Legislation and Public Policy* **1**(1): 105-136.

Galanter, M. (1974). "Why the Haves Come Out Ahead." *Law and Society Review* 8: 95-154.

Galanter, M. (1983). The Radiating Effects of Courts. *Empirical Theories of Courts*. Lynn. Mather. New York, Longman.

Gamson, W (1975, 1990). *The Strategy of Social Protest*. Homewood, Ill: The Dorsey Press.

Garrett, E. and E. Gerber (2001). Money in the Initiative and Referendum Process: Evidence of Its Effects and Prospects for Reform. *The Battle Over Citizen Lawmaking*. D. Waters. Durham, Carolina Academic Press.

Gely, R. and R. Spiller. (1990). "A Rational Choice Theory of Supreme Court with Applications to the *State Farm* and *Grove City* Cases." *Journal of Law Economics and Organization*. 6:263-300.

Gerber, Elisabeth. (1996). "Legislative Response to the Threat of the Popular Initiative." *American Journal of Political Science*. 40(1): 99-128.

Gerber, E. (1998). Pressuring Legislatures Through the Use of Initiatives: Two Forms of Indirect Influence. *Citizens as Legislators*. S. Patterson. Columbus, Ohio State University Press.

Gerber, E. (1999). *The Populist Paradox: Interest Group Influence and the Promise of Direct Legislation*. Princeton, NJ: Princeton University.

Gerlach, L. (1999). "The Structure of Social Movements: Environmental Activism and Its Opponents" in *Waves of Protest* edited by Jo Freeman and Victoria Johnson. New York: Rowman & Littlefield Publishers.

Green, D. and I. Shapiro (1994). *Pathologies of Rational Choice Theory*. New Haven, Yale University Press.

Haines, Herbert. (1988). *Black radicals and the civil rights mainstream 1954-1970*. Knoxville: University of Tennessee Press

Halcli, Abigail. (1999). "AIDS, Anger, and Activism: ACT UP As a Social Movement Organization" in *Waves of Protest* edited by Jo Freeman and Victoria Johnson. New York: Rowman & Littlefield Publishers.

Hall, M. (1987). "Constituent Influences in State Supreme Courts: Conceptual Notes and a Case Study." *The Journal of Politics* 49(1): 1117-1124.

Hall, M. (1992). "Electoral Politics and Strategic Voting in State Supreme Courts." *The Journal of Politics* 54(2): 427-446.

Hall, M. (2001). "State Supreme Courts in American Democracy: Probing the Myths of Judicial Reform." *American Political Science Review* 95(2): 315-329.

Hall, M. and P. Brace (1988). "Order in the Courts." *Western Political Quarterly* 73(3): 391-405.

Hibbing, J. (1991). *Congressional Careers: Contours of Life in the US House of Representatives*. Chapel Hill, University of North Carolina Press.

Hirschman, A. (1970). *Exit, Voice and Loyalty*. Cambridge, Harvard University Press.

Holmstrom, B. (1979). "Moral Hazard and Observability." *The Bell Journal of Economics* 4: 74-91.

Initiative and Referendum Institute. (2001). I & R Update: Legal News. 2001.

Initiative and Referendum Institute. (2000). California Survey

Initiative and Referendum Institute. (1999). Washington Opinion Survey.

Jaros, B. and D. Canon. (1971). "Dissent on State Supreme Courts: The Differential Significance of Characteristics of Judges," *Midwest Journal of Political Science*, 15: 322-346.

Jenkins, C. (1983). "Resource Mobilization Theory and the Study of Social Movements." *Annual Review of Sociology* 9. pp. 527-53.

Jones, J. (2000). Public Willing to Accept Supreme Court as Final Arbiter of Election Dispute, Gallop Organization. 2001.

King, G., R. Keohane, et al. (1994). *Designing Social Inquiry*. Princeton, Princeton University Press.

Knight, J. (1992). *Institutions and Social Conflict.* Cambridge, Cambridge University Press.

Krehbiel, K. (1991). *Information and Legislative Organization.* Ann Arbor, University of Michigan Press.

Landes, W. and R. Posner (1975). "The Independent Judiciary in an Interest Group Perspective." *The Journal of Law and Economics* 18(3): 875-901.

Lascher, E., M. Hagen and S. Rochlin. (1996). "Gun Behind the Door? Ballot Initiatives, State Policies and Public Opinion." *The Journal of Politics* 58, No. 3. pp. 760-775.

Lee, R. (1995). "Pre-Election Initiative Review in Florida." *The Florida Bar Journal*(March): 14-20.

Linde, H. (1989). "When Is Initiative Lawmaking Not "Republican Government?"." *Hastings Constitutional Law Quarterly* 17(Fall): 159-173.

Linde, H. (1993). "When Initiative Lawmaking Is Not Republican Government: The Campaign Against Homosexuality." *Oregon Law Review* 72(1): 19-45.

Lorvich, N. and C. Sheldon. (1984). "Voters in Judicial Elections: An Attentive Public or An Uninformed Electorate" 9 *Judicial Systems Journal* 923-39.

Lowenstein, D. (2001). "Initiatives and the New Single Subject Rule." *Election Law Journal* 1(1): 31-44.

Luce, D. and H. Raiffa (1957). *Games and Decisions.* New York, Dover Publications.

Luker, K. (1984). *Abortion and the Politics of Motherhood.* Los Angeles, University of California Press.

Lupia, A., E. Gerber, et al. (2001). *Stealing the Initiative: How State Governments Respond to Direct Democracy.* New Jersey, Prentice-Hall.

Madison, J., A. Hamilton, et al. (1983). *The Federalist Papers.* New York, Bantam Books.

Magleby, D. (1984). *Direct Legislation.* Baltimore, Johns Hopkins University Press.

Maltzman, F., J. Spriggs, et al. (1999). Strategy and Judicial Choice: New Institutionalist Approaches to Supreme Court Decision-Making. *Supreme Court Decision-Making*. H. Gillman and C. Clayton. Chicago, University of Chicago Press.

Mansbridge, J. (1986). *Why We Lost the ERA*. Chicago, University of Chicago Press.

March, J. and J. Olsen (1984). "The New Institutionalism: Organizational Factors in Political Life." *American Political Science Review* 78(734-748). le University Press.

Marks, B. (1989) "A Model of Judicial Influence on Congressional Policymaking: Grove City College v. Bell" Ph.D. diss, Washington University.

Matsusaka, J. (1995). "Fiscal Effects of the Voter Initiative: Evidence from the Last 30 Years." *The Journal of Political Economy* 103, No. 3. pp. 587-623.

Mayhew, D. (1974). *Congress: The Electoral Connection*. New Haven: Yale University Press.

McAdam, D., J. McCarthy, and M. Zald. (1996). *Comparative Perspectives on Social Movements*. Cambridge: Cambridge University Press.

McCann, M. (1999). How the Supreme Court Matters in American Politics: New Institutionalist Perspectives. *The Supreme Court in American Politics*. H. Gillman and C. Clayton. Lawrence, University Press of Kansas.

McCuan, D., S. Bowler, et al. (1998). California's Political Warriors: Campaign Professionals and the Initiative Process. *Citizens as Legislators*. S. Bowler, T. Donovan and C. Tolbert. Columbus, Ohio State University Press.

McCubbins, R. and M. McCubbins. (1991). *The Logic of Delegation*. Chicago, University of Chicago Press.

McKenzie, R. (1984). *Constitutional Economics*. Toronto, Lexington Books.

McKenzie, R. and G. Tullock (1981). *The New World of Economics*. Illinois, Richard Irwin, Inc.

Merton, R. (1954). *The Focused Interview: A Manual of Problems and Procedures*. New York, The Free Press.

Michels, R. (1915). *Political Parties: A Sociological Study of the Oligarchical Tendencies of Modern Democracy*. New York, Hearst International Library.

Miller, K. (1999). *The Role of Courts in the Initiative Process: A Search for Standards*. American Political Science Association, Atlanta, Georgia.

Miller, K. (2001). "Courts as Watchdogs of the Washington State Initiative Process." *Seattle University Law Review* 24(4): 1053-1085.

Miller, K. (2003). "The Courts and the Initiative Process" in, *Initiative and Referendum Almanac* edited by Dane Waters. Durham: Carolina Academic Press.

Mirrlees, J. (1976). "The Optimal Structure of Incentives and Authority within an Organization." *The Bell Journal of Economics* 7: 105-131.

Mitchell, W. and R. Simmons (1994). *Beyond Politics*. Boulder, The Independent Institute.

Mueller, D. (1996). *Public Choice II*. New York, Oxford University Press.

Nagel, J. (1997). "Direct Democracy and Hastily Enacted Statues." *Legislation and Public Policy* 1: 163-181.

Natelson, R. (1999). Are Initiatives and Referenda Contrary to the Constitution's "Republican Form of Government"?, Independence Institute: 1-14.

Neumann, J. and O. Morgenstern (1944). *Theory of Games and Economic Behavior*. Princeton, Princeton University Press.

North, D. (1981). *Structure and Change in Economic History*. New York, Norton & Co.

O'Brien, D. (2003). *Storm Center: The Supreme Court in American Politics*. New York: W.W. Norton & Co.

Olson, M. (1965). *The Logic of Collective Action*. Cambridge, Harvard University Press.

Orbell, J. and T. Uno (1972). "A Theory of Neighborhood Problem Solving: Political Action vs. Residential Mobility." *American Political Science Review* 66: 471-89.

Ostrom, E. (1994). *Rules, Games and Common Pool Resources*. Ann Arbor, University of Michigan Press.

Patterson, D. (1998). "Consultants and Direct Democracy." *PS: Political Science and Politics* 31(2): 160-170.

Peltason, J. W. (1961). *Fifty-Eight Lonely Men: Southern Federal Judges and School Desegregation.* New York, Hardcourt, Brace & World Inc.

Piantanida, M. and N. Garman (1992). *The Qualitative Dissertation.* Thousand Oaks, Corwin Press, Inc.

Piott, Steven (2003). Giving Voters a Voice: The Origins of the Initiative and Referendum in America. Columbia: University of Missouri Press.

Pizzorno, A. (1978). "Political Science and Collective Identity in Industrial Conflict." In, *The Resurgence of Class Conflict in Europe Since 1968,* ed. C. Crouch and A. Pizzorno. New York: Holmes and Meier.

Poster, W (1995). "The Challenges and Promises of Class and Racial Diversity in the Women's Movement: S Study of Two Organizations." *Gender and Society* 9 no. 6. pp. 659-679.

Price, C. (1997). "Shadow Government." *California Journal* 28(10): 32-38.

Pritchett, H. (1961). *Congress versus the Supreme Court, 1957-60.* Minneapolis, University of Minnesota Press.

Qvortrup, M. (2001). Regulation of Direct Democracy Outside the USA. *The Battle Over Citizen Lawmaking.* D. Waters. Durham, Carolina Academic Press.

Radcliffe, S. (1994). "Pre-Election Judicial Review of Initiative Petitions: An Unreasonable limitation on Political Speech." *Tulsa Law Review* 30(2): 425-445.

Rehnquist, W. (1999). *Grand Inquests: The Historic Impeachments of Justice Samuel Chase and President Andrew Johnson.* New York: Morrow,William & Co.

Richardson, R. and K. Vines. (1970). *The Politics of Federal Courts: Lower Courts in the United States.* Boston: Little, Brown, and Company.

Riker, W. (1980). "Implications from the Disequilibrium of Majority Rule for the Study of Institutions." *The American Political Science Review, 74*(1), 432-445.

Roche, J and S. Sachs. (1969). "The bureaucrat and the enthusiast: An exploration of the leadership of social movements" in *Studies in Social Movements*, edited by Barry McLaughlin. New York: The Free Press.

Rogers, J. (2001). "Information and Judicial Review: A Signaling Game of Legislative-Judicial Interaction." *American Journal of Political Science*, Vol. 45, No. 1, pp. 84-99.

Rohde, D. and H. Spaeth (1976). *Supreme Court Decision Making*. San Francisco, W.H. Freeman.

Rosenburg, G. (1991). *The Hollow Hope*. Chicago, The University of Chicago Press.

Schattschneider, E. E. (1960). *The Semisovereign People*. Illinois: The Dryden Press.

Schelling, T. (1960). *The Strategy of Conflict*. Cambridge, Harvard University Press.

Segal, J. (1997). "Separation of Powers Games in Positive Theory of Law and Courts." *American Political Science Review* 91: 28-44.

Segal, J. and H. Spaeth (1993). *The Supreme Court and the Attitudinal Model*. New York, Cambridge University Press.

Segal, J. and H. Spaeth (1996). "The Influence of Stare Decisis on the Votes of US Supreme Court Justices." *American Journal of Political Science* 40: 971-1003.

Shepsle, K. and B. Weingast (1995). *Positive Theories of Congressional Institutions*. Ann Arbor, University of Michigan Press.

Shipan, J. (1990). "Congressional Influence on Bureaucracy." *Journal of Law Economics and Organization* **6**: 1-20.

Silak, C. (1996). "The People Act, The Courts React: A Proposed Model for Interpreting Initiatives in Idaho." *Idaho Law Review* **33**(1): 19-63.

Skocpol, T. (1982). "Bringing the State Back In." *Items*(June).

Skowronek, S. (1982). *Building a New American State*. New York, Cambridge University Press.

Smith, D. (2001). *Ballot Initiatives and the Democratic Citizen*. Western Political Science Association, Las Vegas, NV.

Snow, D. and R. Benford. (1988). "Ideology, Frame Resonance, and Participant Mobilization." *International Social Movement Research* 1. pp. 197-217.

Snow, D and R. Benford. (1992). "Master Frames and Cycles of Protest." In, *Frontiers in Social Movements*, ed. Aldon Morris and Carol Mueller. New Haven: Yale University Press.

Southwell, P. and P. Paaso (2001). "The Relationship between Voter Turnout and Ballot Measures," *Journal of Political and Military Sociology*, Vol. 29, No. 2, pp. 275-281.

Spiller, R. (1990). "A Rational Choice Theory of Supreme Court with Applications to the State Farm and Grove City Cases." *Journal of Law Economics and Organization* 6: 263-300.

Staggenborg, S. (1999). "The Consequences of Professionalization and Formalization in the Pro-Choice Movement" in *Waves of Protest* edited by Jo Freeman and Victoria Johnson. New York: Rowman & Littlefield Publishers.

Stern, C and B. Stern. (1998). Judicial Review of Ballot Initiatives: The Changing Role of State and Federal Courts, Initiative and Referendum Institute. 1999.

Stien, E. (1993). "The California Constitution and the Counter-Initiative Quagmire." *Hastings Constitutional Law Quarterly* 21(143): 160-187.

Taylor, V. and N. Whittier. (1992). "Collective Identity in Social Movement Communities: Lesbian Feminist Mobilization.' In *Frontiers in Social Movements*, ed. Aldon Morris and Carol Mueller. New Haven: Yale University Press.

Teixeira, R. (1992). *The Disappearing American Voter*. Washington D.C., The Brookings Institute.

The Elway Poll. (2000). "Support for the Initiative Process Stronger than Ever." Seattle, Elway Research.

The Field Institute. (1999). Legislation by Initiative vs. Through Elected Representatives. San Francisco, The Field Institute.

Tolbert, C. (2001). Public Policy and Direct Democracy in the Twentieth Century. *The Battle Over Citizen Lawmaking*. M. D. Waters. Durham, Carolina Academic Press.

Tolbert, C., D. Lowenstein, et al. (1998). Election Law and Rules for Using Initiatives. *Citizens as Legislators*. Columbus, Ohio State University Press.

Tushnet, M. (1996). "Fear of Voting: Differential Standards of Judicial Review of Direct Legislation." *Annual Survey of American Law*: 373-392.

Uelmen, G. (1977). "Crocodiles in the Bathtub: The Independence of State Supreme Courts in an Era of Judicial Politicalization." *Notre Dame Law Review* **72**: 1133-1153.

Vitiello, M. and A. Glendon (1998). "Article III Judges and the Initiative Process: Are Article III Judges Hopelessly Elitist?" *Loyola of Los Angeles Law Review* 31: 1275-1303.

Voss, K. (1996). "The collapse of a social movement: The interplay of mobilizing structures, framing, and political opportunities in the Knights of Labor" in *Comparative Perspectives on Social Movements* edited by McAdam, Doug, John McCarthy, and Mayer Zald. Cambridge: Cambridge University Press.

Warwick, D and C.P. Lininger (1975). *The Sample Survey: Theory and Practice*, New York: McGraw-Hill.

Waters, M. D. (1998). A Century Later--The Experiment with Citizen-Initiated Legislation Continues. *America at the Polls*. New York.

Waters, M. D. (2001). *The Battle Over Citizen Lawmaking*. Durham, Carolina Academic Press.

Weingast, B. (1979). "A Rational Choice Perspective on Congressional Norms." *American Journal of Political Science* 23: 245-62.

Whittier, N. (1997). "Political Generations, Micro-Cohorts, and the Transformation of Social Movements." *American Sociological Review* 62, No. 5. pp. 760-778.

Whittman, D. (1995). *The Myth of Democratic Failure*. Chicago, The University of Chicago Press.

Wilcox, C., T. Jelen, and R. Gunn. (1997). "Religious Coalitions in the New Christian Right." *Social Science Quarterly* 77, no. 3. pp. 543-58.

Wright, R. (1995). Hyperdemocracy. *Time*. 145: 15-21.

Zisk, B. (1987). *Money, Media, and the Grass Roots: State Ballot Issues and the Electoral Process*. New York, Sage Publishers.

Zorn, C. (1995). *Congress and the Supreme Court: Reevaluating the Interest group Perspective.* Midwest Political Science Association, Chicago, Ill.

INDEX